ROUTLEDGE LIBR
HIGHER ED

CW01511692

Volume 21

KEY PROFESSION

KEY PROFESSION
The History of the Association of University Teachers

HAROLD PERKIN

Routledge
Taylor & Francis Group

LONDON AND NEW YORK

First published in 1969 by Routledge & Kegan Paul Ltd

This edition first published in 2019
by Routledge
2 Park Square, Milton Park, Abingdon, Oxon OX14 4RN

and by Routledge
52 Vanderbilt Avenue, New York, NY 10017

Routledge is an imprint of the Taylor & Francis Group, an informa business

© 1969 Harold Perkins

All rights reserved. No part of this book may be reprinted or reproduced or utilised in any form or by any electronic, mechanical, or other means, now known or hereafter invented, including photocopying and recording, or in any information storage or retrieval system, without permission in writing from the publishers.

Trademark notice: Product or corporate names may be trademarks or registered trademarks, and are used only for identification and explanation without intent to infringe.

British Library Cataloguing in Publication Data
A catalogue record for this book is available from the British Library

ISBN: 978-1-138-32388-9 (Set)
ISBN: 978-0-429-43625-3 (Set) (ebk)
ISBN: 978-1-138-33584-4 (Volume 21) (hbk)
ISBN: 978-1-138-33588-2 (Volume 21) (pbk)
ISBN: 978-0-429-44348-0 (Volume 21) (ebk)

Publisher's Note
The publisher has gone to great lengths to ensure the quality of this reprint but points out that some imperfections in the original copies may be apparent.

Disclaimer
The publisher has made every effort to trace copyright holders and would welcome correspondence from those they have been unable to trace.

Key Profession

The History of the Association of University Teachers

Harold Perkin

Professor of Social History
University of Lancaster

Perkin, H. (20/9/1969) 2019
edition

LONDON
ROUTLEDGE & KEGAN PAUL

First published 1969
by Routledge & Kegan Paul Ltd
Broadway House, 68–74 Carter Lane
London, E.C.4
Printed in Great Britain
by Ebenezer Baylis and Son Ltd.,
The Trinity Press, Worcester, and London
© *Harold Perkins* 1969
No part of this book may be reproduced
in any form without permission from
the publisher, except for the quotation
of brief passages in criticism
RKP SBN 7100 6501 9

To the Memory of

ROBERT DOUGLAS LAURIE

Founder of the A.U.T.,
First President 1919–20, and
Honorary General Secretary, 1920–53,
whose creative ability,
dedication, modesty and charm
shine through the records

Contents

[It comes as no surprise that Harold Perkin in writing on the history of the AUT in 1969 draws on the elitist part of the work of Terry Davies, Dr Kenneth Urwin !](handwritten annotation)

Acknowledgment

The author wishes to thank the Officers and Executive Committee
of the Association of University Teachers for access to their
archives, and for paying part of the expenses of typing the manu-
script and the postage of the sample survey of the profession.
He also wishes to make clear that the opinions expressed in the
book are his own, and not necessarily those of the Association
of University Teachers.

Borwicks,   HAROLD PERKIN
Caton,   *January 1969*
Lancaster

[well, if so, God help these not served by white supremacy.](handwritten annotation)

Background on elite
part university.

Chapter 1

Harold Perkin (1969) in his book

The Demise and Resurrection of a Profession

University teaching is the key profession of the twentieth century. In a world increasingly dominated by the professional expert, on whose competence, reliability and integrity not merely the functioning of our complex industrial society but the very survival of civilization, if not of the human race itself, has come to depend, university teachers have become the educators and selectors of the other professions. Under whatever name we try to describe modern society in the 'developed' countries of East and West – 'managerialism', 'meritocracy', 'capitalism tempered by competitive education', 'socialism modified by bureaucracy', or, as I should prefer to call it *tout court*, 'professional society' – the defining characteristic which distinguishes it from the 'undeveloped' world is the organized application of trained intelligence. Not only are university teachers themselves the embodiment, which is not to say the monopolists, of trained intelligence and the competitive education on which it rests, but they are, in the words of one of the rare sociological studies of this most public and yet least studied of professions, 'the custodians of the selection process'.[1]

Nor is their influence confined to those they themselves personally educate, intra-murally or through extra-mural classes. Through the graduates they produce for service in the schools, colleges, central and local government, hospitals, law courts, and all the other institutions of modern society,

pretty well every person in the country is moulded, directly or indirectly, by university training.[2]

1 A. H. Halsey and Martin Trow, 'A Study of the British University Teachers' (unpublished interim report, 1967, kindly lent to me by Dr. Halsey), chap. ii, p. 35.
2 Kenneth Urwin, 'Presidential Address', *Universities Review*, 1959, XXXII. 3.

1

Cooley Ji

The Demise and Resurrection of a Profession

And through the direct application of trained intelligence in what is, too narrowly, called research they not only conserve by reappraising and in a real sense recreating for their own generation the inherited knowledge and the high culture which distinguish civilization from barbarism, but consolidate and extend that knowledge and culture by new discovery and fresh synthesis. Indeed, it is not too much to say that, in this century and for the future, the universities are the growth points of new knowledge, the leading shoots of intellectual culture, and the institutionalization of innovation in the arts, in pure science and even, to an increasing extent, in the technologies, both science-based and social.

It has not always been so. The rise of the university teacher to this key role in the reproduction of society and in its mastery of the physical and social environment is a comparatively recent phenomenon. Until little more than a hundred years ago the universities of England, if not of Scotland, were peripheral institutions, chiefly finishing schools for young gentlemen of the landed aristocracy and gentry, and, since the private tutor and the grand tour provided a superior and more relevant education, they were not essential even for them. If eighteenth-century Oxford and Cambridge were concerned at all with professional education, it was with the education of the clergy, and only the Anglican clergy, and was not even for them obligatory. Other professions were in theory catered for, notably the law and medicine, and in the latter case incorporation as an M.A. of one of the two ancient universities was a prerequisite for the diploma of the Royal College of Physicians;[1] but in practice the universities were irrelevant to professional training. The physicians were a small minority of medical practitioners, and many of them licentiates, educated in Scotland or abroad, or incorporated at Oxford or Cambridge after a nominal residence and payment of a fee. The surgeons and apothecaries who were the bulk of the medical profession were trained chiefly by apprenticeship to existing practitioners, as indeed were the vast majority of other professional men, barristers, attorneys and solicitors, surveyors, architects, and so on, whose training was in no way distinguished by contemporaries from that of any other occupation, from a

1 Under an Act of 1676 – cf. Charles Newman, *The Evolution of Medical Education in the 19th Century* (Oxford, 1957), p. 7.

2

banker, merchant or insurance underwriter to a tailor, potter or pin-maker.[1]

Before the reforms of the early nineteenth century, in fact, it is doubtful whether there was a university teaching profession in any meaningful sense, at least in England. At Oxford and Cambridge the dons – strictly, the fellows of the colleges – were not, except occasionally and by accident, permanent members of a profession with a recognizable function and an articulated career structure. They were privileged but for the most part temporary members of a corporate, self-perpetuating, property-owning society, enjoying their 'dividends' in return for the moral rather than intellectual supervision of a small number of mostly wealthy young men only slightly younger than themselves. With few exceptions they were all in holy orders, and since, short of becoming master of the college, they could not marry without resigning their fellowships, most of them, like Parson Woodforde the diarist, sometime fellow of New College, Oxford, were filling in time while they waited their turn for presentation to a college living in the Church.[2] Only the confirmed and unambitious bachelor, the dedicated scholar, or the university politician with his eye on the mastership, had any notion of remaining in the university for life. Whether he did so or not, the fellow's duties were light to the point of transparency, and almost completely voluntary. He could devote himself to learning, which still meant, in spite of the Renaissance and the Scientific Revolution, chiefly the reading and exegesis of Aristotle and the fathers of the early Christian Church, but he was under no obligation to do so. If he were additionally a tutor at Oxford or a supervisor at Cambridge, he was paid to keep an eye on a small group of undergraduates, to talk to them occasionally and suggest what they might read, and, if the student wished to work, to listen now and then to a paper, an essay or a Greek or Latin composition in prose or verse. If he became a professor, he might lecture if he wished, but with a few exceptions like Sir William Blackstone the professors did not wish, and there was no one who had the power and wished to make them do so. Except for the strings of

---

1 Cf. R. Campbell, *The London Tradesman* (1747), *passim.*
2 James Woodforde, *The Diary of a Country Parson, 1758–1802* (World's Classics, 1949); Woodforde was presented to a New College living in 1774, but remained a bachelor.

questions and answers repeated parrot-fashion into which the virile and exacting medieval disputation had degenerated, there were no examinations, until Cambridge instituted the (purely voluntary) Mathematical Tripos in 1747 and Oxford the (equally voluntary) Public Examination Statute of 1800.[1]

As for research in anything like the modern sense, that was not the university's function. As late as the 1850's Newman, though representing the conservative side of the debate on university reform, could still claim (with etymological inaccuracy) that a university was 'a place of *teaching* universal *knowledge*' and that research was the preserve of scientific academies like the Royal Society and the Antiquarian Society and of self-dedicated individuals like Bacon and Cavendish:

> To discover and to teach are distinct functions; they are also distinct gifts, and are not commonly found in the same person. He, too, who spends his day in dispensing his existing knowledge to all corners is unlikely to have either leisure or energy to acquire new. . . . The great discoveries in chemistry and electricity were not made in universities. Observatories are more frequently out of universities than in them, and even when within their bounds need have no moral connexion with them. Porson had no classes; Elmsley lived a good part of his life in the country. I do not say that there are no great examples the other way . . .; still I think it must be allowed on the whole that, while teaching involves external engagements, the natural home for experiment and speculation is retirement.[2]

No doubt by then Newman was out of touch with what universities were becoming – and there is little wonder that he failed as Rector of the new Catholic University of Ireland – but he was right about the preceding two centuries or more. If the universities, through the persons of Grocyn, Colet and Erasmus and through Cranmer, Latimer and Ridley, had played a part in the Renaissance and the Reformation, they had had little to do with the Scientific and still less with the Industrial Revolution. Trinity College, Cambridge, had offered house-room to Newton, though even he, it is said, had worked out his main discoveries before he returned as a fellow.[3] Glasgow University had lent

1 Cf. Albert Mansbridge, *The Older Universities of Oxford and Cambridge* (1923), esp. chap. vi.
2 J. H. Newman, *The Idea of a University* (1873, Image books ed., 1959), pp. 7, 10–11.
3 Mansbridge, *op. cit.*, p. 79.

working space to James Watt to save him from the restrictive regulations of the City Corporation.[1] Apart from him, almost the only inventor connected with a university was the Rev. Edmund Cartwright, sometime fellow of Magdalen College, Oxford, and inventor of the power loom, a wool-combing machine, a precursor of the bicycle and even a form of internal combustion engine; but he resigned his fellowship to marry an heiress long before he turned his mind to mechanical invention.[2] Scientific and technological research had been left to rich individuals like Henry Cavendish and the Earl of Dundonald or to working craftsmen like James Hargreaves of the spinning jenny and Samuel Crompton of the mule. Indeed, the universities' indifference to research had led to the foundation of a whole series of research institutions – Newman's academies – from the Royal Society, which through Sir Robert Boyle's air-pump experiments and Thomas Savery's steam pump provided a direct link with Newcomen's steam engine, through the Society of Arts, which offered prizes for every kind of invention from the measurement of longitude to the spinning of textiles, down to the Royal Institution, which employed and fostered the experiments of Humphrey Davy and Michael Faraday. The very existence of these institutions was proof that the universities did not consider scientific research their business.

It is often claimed that the four Scottish universities, with their powerful professoriates and medical schools, were an exception to the neglect of teaching and research which characterized their English counter-parts, and to some extent they were. The powerful eighteenth-century Scottish historical school of philosophy which embraced such European-renowned figures as Adam Ferguson, Francis Hutcheson, Dugald Stewart, Adam Smith and John Millar, and which was the original fountain of classical economics, utilitarian philosophy and, some would claim, of modern sociology, was in marked contrast to the bumbling Aristotelianism of Oxford and Cambridge; while Scottish medical education, reorganized on Dutch lines in the early eighteenth century by the first Professor Monro, left that in England standing.[3]

1 Samuel Smiles, *Lives of the Engineers* (1866 ed.), IV. 105–6.
2 *Dictionary of National Biography*, IX. 221f.
3 Cf. R. L. Meek, 'The Scottish Contribution to Markist Sociology', in John Saville, ed., *Democracy and the Labour Movement* (1954); C. Newman, *op cit.*, pp. 12–13.

5

And certainly the Scottish universities preserved enough of the medieval and Continental tradition of the academic profession to be the main channel of its revival in the nineteenth century. Yet their flourishing state can be exaggerated and misunderstood, since their principal function was to provide the secondary education which in England was provided by the grammar and public schools. As *Blackwood's Edinburgh Magazine* said of the largest of them in 1823,

> The University of Glasgow is composed of two things; first, a school where boys from twelve years of age up to sixteen or seventeen, are instructed in the elements of Classical learning – for they do not know even the *alphabet* of the Greek tongue when they are matriculated – and also, in the first elements of Mathematics, Logic, Ethics, etc.; and secondly, of an institution in which lectures are delivered on Medicine, Law, and Theology for the benefit of those of rather riper years. . . . The boys who attend the school wear red frieze gowns – and miserable filthy little urchins the far greater part of them are. To dream of comparing them with the boys of Eton, or Westminster, or Winchester, or Harrow, either in regard to appearance, or manners, or what is of higher importance than all, in regard to SCHOLARSHIP, would be about as absurd, as it would be to compare a Spouting Club in Cheapside with the British House of Commons.[1]

No doubt the admirable Scottish parochial schools and cheap university education provided poor boys of talent like James Mill and Thomas Carlyle with a ladder to fame and modest fortune, but the second step was not quite so high as it has been made out to be; while, as the careers of Richard Porson the great classicist, John Shakespear the orientalist, or even Stephen Duck 'the thresher-poet' show, a ladder for the intelligent poor was not wholly absent in England.[2] It led less often to the university because the university was less obviously the field for exercising or rewarding talent or for training for a useful career.

It would be easy but irrelevant to blame the sloth and indolence of eighteenth-century Oxford and Cambridge. Society gets the universities it wants and deserves, and the two English universities were the creatures and expressions of an older, pre-industrial,

1 'Vindiciae Gaelicae', *Blackwood's Edinburgh Magazine*, 1823, XIII. 94.
2 *Dictionary of National Biography*, XVI. 89f., XLVI. 154f., LI. 345f.; R. G. Furnivall, 'Stephen Duck, the Wiltshire Phenomenon, 1705–56', *Cambridge Journal*, 1953, VI. 8f.

aristocratic society which is difficult for us, reared in a modern, post-industrial, meritocratic one, to understand. It was a hierarchical society based on property and patronage, in which men found their place according to their wealth, preferably unearned and therefore leisured wealth, or that of their friends, relations and patrons.[1] The ideal citizen of that society was the leisured country gentleman, with time and resources to devote to any activity which he valued, from sport, drinking or wenching to agriculture, literature or even science and invention; while the next-best thing to be was a client of such a patron, a Newcomen, Coleridge or Faraday, with the talent to make better use than he himself of his resources. Leisured patrons and their clients then supplied most of the cultural and scientific activity now catered for by universities, while the universities had a different function, to provide, along with the public schools and private tutors which in turn were supplied from the universities, a common cultural background for the leisured ruling class and for their chief lieutenants in the moral control of society, the Anglican clergy.

If the wealth, leisure and political power of the ruling aristocracy and the status and influence of the clergy were based on the ownership, inherited or acquired, individual or quasi-corporate, of land, so indeed were the power, wealth and autonomy of the universities and of the colleges which composed them. They were property-owning corporations, with the same 'right over their own wealth, to use it or abuse it',[2] as individual landowners. And if the individual dons were not the heirs but the appointed incumbents of official property, so were the bishops, deans, the parsons with their 'freeholds', and all the great officers of state. In that property-conscious society even office was defined by Blackstone, the undisputed authority, in proprietorial terms, as 'a *right* to exercise a public or private employment and to take the fees and emoluments thereunto belonging.'[3] In short, university dons were leisured gentlemen by appointment rather than inheritance, and, saving the rule of celibacy, were as free to do what they pleased with their time and

---

1 For a fuller account of 'the old society' before the Industrial Revolution see Harold Perkin, *The Origins of Modern English Society, 1780–1880* (1969), chap. ii.
2 W. Vincent, *Sermons* (ed. R. Nares, 1817), I. 281f.
3 Quoted by Emmeline W. Cohen, *Growth of the British Civil Service, 1780–1939* (1941), p. 21n. (my italics).

resources, to teach or not to teach, to work or not to work, as the rest of the leisured but not necessarily idle class.

This view of the university don's role and function, so strange – and enviable – to a modern university teacher's eyes, was peculiarly that society, and could not survive its demise in the new industrial world of the nineteenth century. Nor for that matter was it older than the society, but had grown up with it as it emerged from the still older society of medieval England, when property was still contingent rather than absolute, a responsibility rather than an unfettered privilege, and office was a charge and a burden rather than an endowment. The story of that transition, in which the English landlords beat the peasants, the Church and the Crown to turn lordship into ownership and the institutions of Church and State into instruments of their power, is told elsewhere.[1]

The universities were only one, and not the most significant, of those instruments, but they illustrate the change as well as any. The two English universities had grown up in the twelfth and thirteenth centuries to meet the needs not of the State or the ruling class but of the Church and society. The Church needed trained, literate clerks, at least for its higher positions, society was developing the need for lawyers and medical men, and, perhaps most pertinent of all, 'poor scholars' from every level of society were crowding to the new, spontaneous centres of speculative thought and learning which, under the name *studium generale*, grew up around the cathedrals, of, most notably, Bologna and Paris. Paris under the influence of the dialectical scholasticism founded by Peter Abelard became famous for theology and philosophy, Bologna under a still older tradition for Roman Law. Both acquired the name of *universitas*, which had nothing to do with 'universal learning' but was merely one of the many medieval words for a would-be-permanent group or society of men organized for a common purpose, and cognate with the gilds of merchants and craftsmen which emerged at much the same time in most of the towns of Europe. Indeed, the parallel is still closer and embraces the stages and some of the nomenclature of membership. The students, scholars or undergraduates were the apprentices or tyros of the gild of learning, the bachelors of arts the bachelors, journeymen or yeomen (cf. the bachelors' or

1 See Perkin, *op. cit.*, pp. 52–5, 64–7.

yeomen gilds attached to some of the crafts), and the masters of arts the masters, those qualified to set up on their own as teachers of others. There was an important difference in organization between the two: while Paris, like most of the gilds, was controlled by the masters, Bologna was controlled by the students, who employed, paid and could dismiss the professors.

Although the influence of Bologna can be traced in an educated form in the professoriate and the elective rectorship of the Scottish universities, the English ones followed the pattern of Paris, of which in fact they were offshoots, in the troubled times of the late twelfth and the early thirteenth century when the English kings' relations with the Papacy and the kings of France made it prudent for English scholars to remain in England, first, after the expulsion of English scholars from France in 1167, at Oxford and then, when internal quarrels caused some of them to migrate once more, at Cambridge. At first, in the tradition of the medieval schools, there were no colleges, but simply groups of students in cheap lodgings or later in halls under a master, and gathering where they could to listen to the acknowledged *magisters* expound the seven liberal arts. As time went on the course of studies became formalized, successful disputations (examinations in the form of debates with fellow students) in the *trivium* – the first three liberal arts of grammar, logic and rhetoric – conferring the 'degree' or status of bachelor, or journeyman-teacher, and in the *quadrivium* – the other four, arithmetic, geometry, astronomy and music – that of master of arts, the full licence to teach. In fact, the newly qualified masters were compelled to teach for at least a year, and as regent (that is, teaching) masters of less than three years' standing were in charge of the education of the unqualified scholars and bachelors. After this spell of repaying their debt to learning by teaching, they were free to continue their studies in the postgraduate faculties of theology, law and medicine, to become in six to twelve more years doctors of their subjects.[2]

It will be seen that the medieval university was thus concerned entirely with professional education. The students, undergraduate and postgraduate, were in process of acquiring, first, a

---

1 Cf. Hastings Rashdall, *Universities of Europe in the Middle Ages* (1936 ed.), esp. I, chaps. iv and v.
2 Cf. Mansbridge, *op. cit.*, pp. 13–14.

licence to teach and, second, a licence to practise law, medicine or theology. In a society divided mainly into feudal lords, peasants and a few merchants and craftsmen, the value of the learned (i.e. literate) professions to Church and State was well recognized: they were the only source of trained intelligence and intellectual labour for every purpose from the curing of wealthy bodies and the saving of complicated souls to the documentary preservation of great estates and the civil administration of Church and realm. King John conferred special privileges on Oxford in 1214, and Henry III on Cambridge in 1231. The latter in 1229 attempted to seduce the whole school of Paris to settle in England – 'We will assign to you whatever cities, boros and towns you may choose, and in liberty and tranquillity. We will do all such things becoming to give you pleasure as shall suffice you and be pleasing to God' – and two years later, in one of the first recorded attempts to stop the brain-drain, ordered the grasping lodging-house keepers of Cambridge not to drive away the university by exorbitant rents:

It is well known to you that a multitude of scholars flow together to our City of Cambridge for the sake of study from various places at home and abroad; which We hold right pleasing and acceptable for that from thence no small profit comes to our kingdom, and honour to Ourself; and above all you, amongst whom the students have their daily life, should rejoice and be glad. But We have heard that in letting your lodgings you are so heavy and burdensome to the scholars dwelling amongst you, that unless you behave yourselves more measurably and modestly towards them in this matter of your exactions they must leave our city, and having abandoned the University, depart from our land, which We in no respect desire.[1]

The Pope recognized Oxford as a *studium generale* in 1296, and Cambridge in 1318, and at various times granted them legal privileges beyond those of any other corporation in Church or State. Henry VIII refused to extend the dissolution of the monasteries to the colleges:

I tell you, sir, that I judge no land in England better bestowed than that which is given to our Universities, for by their maintenance our realm shall be well-governed when we be dead and rotten.[2]

1 *Ibid.*, pp. 9 and 10n.
2 *Ibid.*, p. 50.

The Demise and Resurrection of a Profession

In Queen Elizabeth's day John Lyly still emphasized their professional character:

the learning of them neyther lyeth in the free stones of the one, nor the fine streates of the other, for out of them both do dayly proceede men of great wisedome, to rule in the common wealth, of learning to instruct the common people, of all singular kinde of professions to do good to all.[1]

By 1580, however, the transition from training centres for the learned professions to finishing schools for young gentlemen was already well under way. Even in the thirteenth century the sons of feudal lords, seeking intellectual excitement rather than the military pursuits of chivalry, the tournament and the crusade, had mingled with the poor scholars at the universities:

> Gentlemen's sons while young they be
> Are sent to France to get a degree.

The colleges which from the fourteenth century had gradually taken over from the halls and regent masters the accommodation and most of the teaching of the undergraduates, though normally confined by poverty clauses in their statutes to poor scholars, began to admit 'gentleman commoners' as paying, and ultimately privileged, guests.[2] By the late fifteenth century newly-founded colleges such as Magdalen, Oxford (1482), provided in their statutes for *commensales*, 'the sons of noble and worthy persons, friends of the College,' and with St. John's and Corpus Christi, Oxford, in 1516 and Trinity, Cambridge, in 1546 provision for gentleman commoners or pensioners became the rule.[3] With the Reformation and the Tudor secularization of society and politics came a veritable invasion by the landed classes, seeking the intellectual equipment and the social cachet of the educated man of affairs, the new, administratively competent courtier and non-clerical statesman. 'Beginning some time in the reign of Henry VIII, the sons of the titled nobility swarm into those citadels of clerkly learning, the English universities.'[4] Bishop Latimer complained in a famous sermon in 1549 that 'there be

1 John Lyly, *Euphues* (1580), part II.
2 Mansbridge, *op. cit.*, p. 9.
3 Kenneth Charlton, *Education in Renaissance England* (1965), p. 133.
4 J. H. Hexter, 'The Education of the Aristocracy in the Renaissance', *Journal of Modern History*, 1950, XXII. 4.

none but great men's sons in Colleges and their fathers look not to have them preachers'.[1] By the end of the century the numbers of undergraduates had risen to over 2,000, by 1620 to 3,000 – more than at any other period before the twentieth century – while at Oxford gentlemen's sons outnumbered plebeians (*filii plebei*) by six to five.[2] In the 1593 Parliament over half the M.P.s had been to the university or the Inns of Court or both.[3]

It was not merely that the landed class had taken over the universities for their own purposes, the education of Renaissance gentlemen and the training of secular politicians. They had also distorted their whole pattern of pedagogy. The new and increasingly predominant type of undergraduate showed little or no interest in the traditional exercises and disputations of the scholar. Indeed, 'the vast majority of gentleman-commoners and pensioners stayed only for a year or two,' and only a small minority took even the bachelor's degree.[4] Their failure to attend lectures and exercises encouraged their teachers, who were now almost automatically of inferior social status to most of their pupils, in that neglect of teaching to which they were traditionally prone. The statutory lecturing of the regent masters and their supervision of students' disputations and orations fell away. Attempts were made to revive them, and to compel the attendance of students, who stubbornly insisted, as at Oxford in 1599, on their right to pay the fine instead. In their place two other institutions arose, both ultimately of prime importance to the academic profession: endowed professorships, readerships and lectureships like the Lady Margaret Divinity Lectureships (1497) permanently endowed only in 1502, and Henry VIII's Regius Chairs of Divinity, Greek, Hebrew, Civil Law, and Physic (1540); and college lecturers and tutors appointed under the statutes of the newer colleges and the revised statutes of old ones. But the habit of non-lecturing infected the new professors and readers within a generation or two of their foundation. Archbishop Parker told the Queen in 1570 that 'in your university of Cambridge not two in the whole are able or willing to read the Lady Margaret Lecture', and Archbishop Whitgift in 1602 similarly

1 Hugh Latimer, *Sermons* (Parker Society ed., Cambridge, 1845), p. 179.
2 Charlton, *op. cit.*, p. 136.
3 J. E. Neale, *The Elizabethan House of Commons* (1949), p. 303.
4 Charlton, *op. cit.*, p. 138.

complained that 'of those who should read four times a week some read not four times a year'. At Oxford in 1576 fines were laid down for failure to lecture but, witness the frequent repetitions of the order, without success. As for the college tutors, although there were some assiduous ones like Robert Norgate of Corpus Christi College and John Preston of Queen's, Cambridge, they do not seem to have been able to make much impression on their wealthier students.[1] As William Harrison put it in 1577, the colleges

were erected by their founders at the first only for poor men's sons, whose parents were not able to bring them up to learning; but now they have the least benefit of them, by reason the rich do so encroach upon them . . . being placed, most of them [the richer sort] study little other than histories, tables, dice and trifles. . . . Besides this, being for the most part either gentlemen or rich men's sons they oft bring the university into much slander. For standing upon their reputation and liberty, they ruffle and roist it out, exceeding in apparel and banting riotous company (which draweth them from their books into another trade), and for excuse, when they are charged with breach of all good order, think it sufficient to say that they be gentlemen, which grieveth many not a little.[2]

A decree of 1578 for 'the restoring of the ancient modesty of students, scholars and all others that shall be accounted the same' summed up the change that had taken place in an institution once dedicated to the training of poor scholars for the professions, which,

especially by suffering of sundry young men, being the children of gentlemen of wealth at their coming to the same university, contrary to the ancient and comely usage . . . shall become rather a storehouse or a staple of prodigal, wasteful, riotous, unlearned and insufficient persons to serve or rather to unserve the necessity of the realm both in the church and civil policy.[3]

The last stage in the decline of the ancient universities as centres of learning and professional education came with the final triumph of the landed class over the Crown at the Civil War and Revolution of the seventeenth century. Like other perpetual

1 *Ibid.*, pp. 140–3, 148.
2 William Harrison, *Description of England* (1577, ed. L. Withington, 1876), pp. 252–3.
3 Charlton, *op. cit.*, p. 140.

corporations the universities and colleges took their stand, initially in self-defence against royal intervention (including the catholicizing intervention of James II), on the inviolability of their charters and statutes. Many of them, like Magdalen College, Oxford, which had suffered – temporarily – for its opposition to James II, required their fellows to take an oath on election 'not to seek for or to accept any change in the Founder's Statutes'.[1] Like other corporations, of cities, boroughs, gilds and companies, too, this had the effect of turning them into self-perpetuating oligarchies, answerable to no one but themselves. The result was that torpor, indolence and complacency which characterized not merely the universities but most established and privileged institutions in eighteenth-century England. Great scholars like Bentley and Porson continued to work, though they enjoyed their lucrative rights and neglected their teaching like the rest, while there were still tutors who took the pastoral care of undergraduates seriously. But for the most part they resembled 'the monks of Magdalen' amongst whom Edward Gibbon spent 'the fourteen months the most idle and unprofitable of my whole life': 'decent easy men, who supinely enjoyed the gifts of the founder.'[2] Under their regime even the numbers of undergraduates, which had risen to as much as 3,000 in each of them under the early Stuarts, shrank, as the private tutor and the grand tour of Europe replaced the non-learning and debauchery of the universities as the ideal education for a gentleman, by 1775 to 759 at Oxford and 396 at Cambridge.[3] The declension of the profession into a privileged caste of self-perpetuating property-holders was complete.

The rise of a modern profession of university teaching in the nineteenth century, though a revolution in itself, was therefore a revival rather than a new departure, a rebirth rather than a genesis, a resurrection rather than a new creation. It took two forms, both of which left their mark on the profession in the shape of two distinct ideals which are still struggling for ascendancy. On the one side there was the creation of alternatives to Oxford and Cambridge in London and the great and growing provincial cities, which borrowed from Scotland and the Continent, where

1 H. A. Wilson, *Magdalen College* p. 252.
2 Edward Gibbon, *Autobiography* (World's Classics, 1907), pp. 36, 40.
3 Mansbridge, *op. cit.*, p. xxn.

it had been kept alive, the professional principle of a powerful lecturing and researching professoriate. On the other, there was the reform, partly self-generated, partly imposed from without, of Oxford and Cambridge themselves, which revived another and no less professional principle, that of the working college tutor, which goes back beyond the college system to the regent masters of the earliest days, whose 'catechetical lectures' were really tutorials and who were solely responsible for the pastoral care of the undergraduates. Both forms appealed to the professionalism of university teaching, the professorial to the principle of expertise and, ultimately, of a hierarchy of experts, which characterizes all modern professions; the tutorial to the principle of fiduciary service to the client (in this case the student and, perhaps, his family and the community) – which, indeed, is not absent from the profesorial tradition – and, more challenging to the latter, the principle of equality not so much of expertise as of voice and status amongst qualified practitioners. Both were to operate, of course, in both types of university, the ancient collegiate where the professorial tradition – and, more challenging to the latter, intensive form, and the provincial or civic (including London, which in university matters was not initially metropolitan) where the tutorial tradition, in so far as it failed to inhere in the equality of the professors who at first comprised the whole teaching staff, crept in by the back door in the demand of their ill-paid and underprivileged assistants for a living wage and a share in the running of their universities which was to play so large a part in the origins of the Association of University Teachers. That the two principles were not totally incompatible is shown by the very foundation of the A.U.T. as a professional association embracing both professors and non-professorial tutors and lecturers, and (eventually) both Oxbridge and Redbrick. But that they make uneasy bedfellows is shown by the overwhelming support for the A.U.T. in non-collegiate universities where, paradoxically, the power of the professoriate both fosters its professionalism and provokes a demand for its egalitarianism, in contrast with its weakness in collegiate universities where, equally paradoxically, the strength of the gild principle of the equality of the qualified masters makes the A.U.T. seem less relevant.

To the mutually fertilizing contributions of these two professional traditions to the origins and development of the A.U.T. we shall return. Meanwhile, the revival of university teaching as a profession in the nineteenth century was not an isolated phenomenon, but one aspect of the general growth of professional expertise and the application of trained intelligence which accompanied as both cause and effect the Industrial Revolution. That Revolution was more than a transformation of industry. It was a revolution in human productivity which increased by a multiple, rather than a fraction, both the number of human beings who could be carried on a given area of land and their living standard or consumption per head of goods and services. It implied as its instrument a revolution in social organization, not merely in the creation of factories, mines, banks, commodity and stock exchanges, and other large-scale economic institutions, but in the increased scale and complexity of towns, local and central government, hospitals, churches, schools and, indeed, universities.[1] To provide the expert services for this new and more complex society there emerged a vast range of new or reorganized professions with their own professional institutions, beginning with the Institution of Civil Engineers, 1818, and the Law Society, 1825.[2] This development began, as in the decay of professional training there it had to, outside the universities, and what training was provided had to be supplied by the traditional means of individual pupillage or, as in the case of the Law Society from 1836 or the Pharmaceutical Society from 1842, by lectures and examinations offered by the professional bodies themselves.[3] But since professional bodies have other functions than training, are always short of funds, and can at best only deal with the committed student who already possesses the necessary general education, there arose a public demand for institutions of higher education to prepare either specifically, as in the case of the provincial medical schools, or more generally, as in the case of the Dissenting academies and their successors the provincial scientific and commercial colleges of the early Victorian age, for the professions and business.

The effect upon the universities of this proliferation of professions and the demand for trained intelligence was twofold. It

1 See Perkin, *op. cit.*, esp. chaps. i and iv.
2 Cf. Geoffrey Millerson, *The Qualifying Professions* (1964), esp. pp. 120–9 and Appendix II, pp. 246f.
3 *Ibid.*, pp. 121–3, 133–4.

led directly, through the founding of local colleges, to the creation of new universities in most of the great cities; and it led indirectly, through the pressure of public opinion acting both immediately on the dons themselves and via Parliament, to the reform of the old ones. There had of course been many previous attempts to found new universities, beginning with the migrations to Northampton and Stamford in the thirteenth century,[1] but they had all foundered on the opposition of Oxford and Cambridge, backed by ecclesiastical or royal *fiat*. The difference in the nineteenth century was that there arose powerful new classes, the industrial and professional middle classes, who refused to accept the *fiat* of Church and State, and indeed considered Oxford and Cambridge as mere bastions of aristocratic corruption, to be outflanked and/or reformed along with every other organ of aristocratic rule.

For Thomas Campbell, Henry Brougham and the group of middle-class Dissenters, Catholics, Jews and Benthamites who founded London University with the blessing of the Whigs in 1828, the opposition of Oxford, Cambridge, the Church of England and the Tory Government in the person of the Home Secretary, Sir Robert Peel, was simply proof of the political and moral necessity of the institution. As Brougham described the original bill of incorporation to the Radical Sir Francis Burdett in 1825,

> It is an event of the greatest moment in my view which will do more to crush bigotry and intolerance than all the Bills either of us will ever see carried, at least until a Reform happens. Accordingly the monasteries [Oxford and Cambridge] are loud in their howlings, but it all won't do.[2]

They went ahead, despite Parliamentary rejection of the bill, with the 'Godless college in Gower Street', appointed a group of professors on the Scottish model (half of them Scots), and within five years enrolled over 500 students, living mainly at home and paying a fraction of the fees charged at Oxford and Cambridge. The education offered was consciously geared to the needs of the professions. Chairs were established in medicine, jurisprudence, political economy, chemistry, natural philosophy (physics), as

---

1 Mansbridge, *op. cit.*, p. 31; W. H. G. Armytage, *Civic Universities* (1955), chap. ii.
2 M. W. Patterson, *Sir Francis Burdett and his Times* (1931), II. 554–5.

well as in modern languages, logic and the philosophy of the human mind, and planned in engineering (not filled till 1841), mineralogy, design and education – almost every subject, in fact, except theology. The medical school proved to be the lynch-pin of the enterprise, attracting three-quarters of all the students in 1834. James Bryce, later lecturer in law at Owens' College, Manchester, and Professor of Civil Law at Oxford, began the training of teachers there in 1836. Efforts were made to meet the needs of 'the gentlemen who hold places in the offices of Govern-ment' and in the City by evening courses in law, modern langu-ages and political economy.[1]

The Church of England and Wellington's Government, unable to prevent so useful a development, decided to compete with it by founding the rival King's College, which opened its doors in 1831 with even lower fees, equally professional courses, including by 1840 medicine, engineering, and architecture, and a professoriate which included research scientists of the stature of J. F. Daniell, inventor of the hygrometer and the constant battery, Sir Charles Wheatstone, pioneer of the electric telegraph, and Sir Charles Lyell, whose geological theories, ironically, did more to undermine traditional fundamentalist religion than any-thing emanating from the rival 'Godless college'. Here too medical students numbered in 1834 more than half the total. In 1836, in the new age inaugurated by the Reform Act, the two rivals came together under the newly-chartered examining University of London, the first officially recognized university to be founded in Britain since Edinburgh in 1582, and the first of the dozen or so civic universities and university colleges founded in the nineteenth century.[2] Not the least of its services to the rest was its capacity, under a later Charter of 1858, to grant external degrees and to affiliate other colleges to itself for that purpose, thus enabling new university colleges to spring up with the minimum of formality.

Nearly all the rest were founded by middle-class philan-thropists in the great provincial cities for specifically local middle-class education for business and the professions. The

1 Armytage, *op. cit.*, pp. 173–4; F. G. Brook, 'The Early Years of London University', *Universities Review*, 1960, XXXIII. 8f.
2 Armytage, *op. cit.*, p. 174; Brook, *loc. cit.*; strictly, a University of Durham had been granted letters patent by Cromwell in 1657, but these became null and void at the Restoration.

chief exception was the University of Durham, founded in 1832 by the Bishop, Dean and Chapter to ward off the anti-clerical attack expected after the Reform Act, and even there the first courses included chemistry, mineralogy and engineering.[1] The rest were chiefly amalgamations of medical, technical and commercial colleges founded from the 1830's onwards. Manchester, first constituent of the Victoria University (1880), was an amalgamation of Owens' College (1851), the Extension College of the 1870's, and the Royal School of Medicine, originally founded in the 1830's.[2] Liverpool and Leeds, the other two constituents admitted in 1884 and 1887, grew out of demands for commercial and for medical, mining and textile education, in the latter case by amalgamation of the School of Medicine (1831) and the Yorkshire College of Science (1874). Birmingham, incorporated as a university college in 1898 and a university in 1900, similarly grew out of the Medical School (1841), Mason Science College (1880) and the Training College (1894). Newcastle, a constituent college of Durham University until 1963, was an amalgamation (1908) of the School of Medicine and Surgery (1834) and the College of Physical Science (1871). Bristol University College (1876) incorporated in 1893 the Medical School founded in 1833, before receiving its charter as a full university in 1909. Sheffield University (1905) was established as a university college in 1897 by the amalgamation of the Medical School (1828), the Firth College of arts and science (1879) and the Technical School (1886). Nottingham University College (1881) traces its origin to the adult school founded in 1798, the Mechanics Institute, the People's College, and the beginnings of the Cambridge extension lectures in 1873. Reading and Exeter University Colleges (1892 and 1893) also grew out of the adult education movement as extension colleges, while Southampton (1902) developed out of the Hartley Institution, a similar body founded in 1862. The federal University of Wales (1893) was an amalgamation of colleges founded at Aberystwyth (1873), Cardiff (1883) and Bangor (1884). Finally, of all the nineteenth-century civic university colleges in the present United Kingdom, the only one apart from Durham which did not owe its origin to

1 Armytage, *op. cit.*, pp. 175–6.
2 H. B. Charlton, *Portrait of a University* (Manchester 1951); Armytage, *op. cit.*, pp. 224–5.

local pride and the middle-class demand for vocational education was Belfast, one of the Queen's Colleges founded by the Government, and amalgamated with Cork and Galway as the Queen's University of Ireland in 1850, as a concession to win over the Irish, and separated from the other two in 1908.[1]

This proliferation of new civic universities, revolutionary as it was both in catering for the new and growing professions and in creating a professional professoriate, in no way derogated from the primacy of Oxford and Cambridge, which indeed, with the help of the Scottish and some Continental universities, supplied them with most of their professors. The dons, too, remained in 1900 at least as numerous as the teaching staffs of all the rest of the English universities put together.[2] The professionalization of university teaching, therefore, turned even more on the reform of Oxford and Cambridge, which accompanied and, indeed, to a large extent preceded the founding of the civic universities. Conscientious teachers and scholars, though rarely both in the same persons, had not been entirely absent from the eighteenth-century universities, and in spite of the 'inert, almost moribund professoriate' of 1800[3] there survived into the nineteenth century tough minds and tender consciences not immune to the attractions of learning and the demands of society. The awakening when it came was initially self-induced, though it took much external pressure and several Royal Commissions to make it universal. There were stirrings even in the eighteenth century: Cambridge, as we have seen, instituted examinations in 1747 and Oxford in 1800. The bludgeonings of the *Edinburgh Reviewers*, Francis Jeffrey, Sydney Smith and Professor John Playfair, in 1808 and their successor Sir William Hamilton in the 1830's, and the campaign of James Heywood, the Manchester Unitarian banker, for reform in the 1840's,[4] although hotly repudiated by the majority of dons, were not without effect within the universi-

1 The above facts concerning the foundation of the civic universities and university colleges are derived mainly from Armytage, *op. cit.*, and his article in the *Commonwealth Universities Yearbook*.
2 Oxford resident M.A.s in 1900 numbered 471, and those in Cambridge a similar figure, out of less than 2,000 university teachers in Britain, of whom some 400 were in Scottish universities – Halsey and Trow, *op. cit.*, chap. ii, pp. 7, 12.
3 Mansbridge, *op. cit.*, p. 150.
4 Brian Simon, *Studies in the History of Education, 1780–1870* (1960), pp. 84–94, 290.

ties, where a generation of reformers as energetic and pugnacious as Thomas Arnold, Mark Pattison and Benjamin Jowett at Oxford and Adam Sedgwick and Baden Powell at Cambridge took up the struggle. By 1850, when the first Royal Commission was appointed, Mark Pattison saw the battle as already won:

If any Oxford man had gone to sleep in 1840 and had wakened up in 1850 he would have found himself in a totally new world. . . . The dead majorities of heads and seniors which had sat like lead on the energies of young tutors had melted away. Theology was totally banished from the Common Room and even from private conversation. Very free opinions on all subjects were rife, there was a prevailing dissatisfaction with our boasted tutorial system. A restless fever of change had spread through the Colleges – the wonder-working phrase 'University Reform' had been uttered and that in the House of Commons. The sound seemed to breathe new life into us. We against reform! Why it was the very thing we had been so long sighing for; we were ready to reform a great deal – everything – only show us how to set about it and give us the necessary powers.[1]

The Royal Commission was, nevertheless, strongly resisted, and it took two Acts of Parliament (1854 for Oxford and 1856 for Cambridge) and two Executive Commissions to open them to non-Anglican students, to strengthen the administrative powers and teaching functions of the University over against the Colleges, and to reorganize the professoriate along professional lines. It took a further Act, in 1871, to abolish all religious tests for college fellowships and university offices, and a further Royal Commission of 1872 and the Act and Executive Commission of 1877 to abolish the celibacy rule for fellows and to put the relations between each university and the colleges on a satisfactory footing.[2] Between the legislation of the 1850's and that of the 1870's, however, a revolution had already taken place in both the work of the two universities and their role in relation to society. Mark Pattison believed that the 1850's saw 'more improvement in the temper and teaching of Oxford' than the previous three centuries.[3] In Cambridge 'the work of the Royal Commission

1 Mansbridge, *op. cit.*, p. 156.
2 A. I. Tillyard, *A History of University Reform* (1913), chaps. vi–ix.
3 Quoted by C. E. Mallet, *A History of the University of Oxford* (1927), III. 330.

appointed in 1850 bore fruit some years later, in the shape of a new and surprising increase in the number of students, and in the altered conditions of academic life and study which were brought to pass ... During the thirty years 1850–1880 the numbers of Freshmen at Cambridge were exactly doubled, rising from 400 to 800 per annum.'[1] Not only was a new race of lecturing and researching professors inaugurated, and new honours courses, such as the Moral Sciences, Natural Sciences, Theological, and Historical Tripodes at Cambridge and the serious study of mathematics and science at Oxford, introduced, but a new type of college tutor arose, typified by Oscar Browning at Cambridge and Benjamin Jowett at Oxford, dedicated to preparing their students by strenuous intellectual training not merely for scholarship but for devoted service to society outside the university. The influence of Jowett's pupils, especially such men as T. H. Green, Arnold Toynbee and Alfred Milner, and of Jowett himself, on the reform of the civil service, on the administration of the British Empire, and on social work in the East End of London, was enormous, and made Balliol one of the main springs of the professionalization of government and of the Welfare State.[2]

Yet it was not all gain. The abolition of the 'poverty clauses' for scholarships and fellowships and the opening of scholarships and exhibitions to 'merit', measured by success in expensively acquired subjects such as Latin and Greek, meant that the number of poor scholars at Oxford and Cambridge was reduced in the second half of the nineteenth century to the lowest proportion of all time.[3] The ironical consequence of Jowett and company was that there were no more Jowetts, at least until the twentieth century. The reformers, imbued with the anti-privilege and competitive spirit of the professional and industrial middle calsses, had even less consideration for the ancient rights of the poor than the self-interested property-holders by appointment whom they replaced. Fortunately, this was to be a temporary attitude, and the logic of their professionalism was to lead them on to seek to open the academic career to

---

1 J. A. Venn, *Oxford and Cambridge Matriculations*, pp. 16–17.
2 Cf. Sir Geoffrey Faber, *Jowett* (1957), pp. 165, 353, 356–65.
3 Mansbridge, *op. cit.*, pp. 108–9, 167; Hester Jenkins and D. Caradog Jones, 'Social Class of Cambridge University Alumni of 18th and 19th Centuries', *British Journal of Sociology*, 1950, I, 93f.

talent wherever it could be found. Meanwhile, even in the Victorian age the consciousness that Oxford and Cambridge had a responsibility to a wider audience than their own students found expression in such extra-mural endeavours as the Cambridge extension lectures of the 1870's, which provided the catalyst for a number of provincial university colleges, and the Balliol tradition of contact with working men which culminated in the university tutorial classes of the Workers' Educational Association in 1907.

Enormously important to higher education and to society as was the professionalization of university teaching both at Oxford and Cambridge and in the new civic universities, it was still in 1900 on a very small scale. In spite of the enormous increase in student numbers, in England and Wales from 1,128 in 1800 and only about 5,500 as late as 1885 to 16,735 in 1899,[1] there were still less than 2,000 university teachers in Great Britain, about half of them, approaching 1,000, at Oxford and Cambridge. By 1910 when the figures are firmer there were 1,478 outside Oxford and Cambridge: 202 in London colleges, 730 in the civic universities and university colleges, 143 in Wales and 403 in Scotland.[2] By any standards it was still a tiny profession, little more than a tenth of the size of today's 20,000 or more. But it was already, especially outside Oxford and Cambridge, beginning to exhibit some of the vices as well as the virtues of professionalism. While at first practically all the teachers in the civic universities and university colleges had been professors, by the Edwardian age they had acquired a substantial number of underpaid and underprivileged 'assistants', with almost no rights and often only temporary appointments. In Manchester, the largest of the provincial ones, for example, the original six professors of 1851 had grown by 1900 to 24, but there were now 43 non-professorial teachers, only 7 of whom were permanent.[3] In British universities as a whole, excluding Oxford and Cambridge, professors in 1910 were less than a third (31.4 per cent) of the total, and the assistants thus outnumbered them by two to one.[4] In such a

1 Mansbridge, *op. cit.*, p. xx n.; Armytage, *op. cit.*, p. 233; A. N. Little, 'Some Myths of University Expansion', *Sociological Review Monograph No. 7: Sociological Studies in British University Education* (Keele, 1963), p. 196.
2 Halsey and Trow, *op. cit.*, chap. i, pp. 6–9, 12–14.
3 H. B. Charlton, *op. cit.*, p. 183.
4 Halsey and Trow, *loc. cit.*

situation the opportunities for exploitation in the form of low pay and the premature discontinuance of their cheap labour were almost irresistible. It was out of a revolt of these academic helots that the Association of University Teachers was to be born.

Chapter 2

The Foundation of the A.U.T.

In a world increasingly dominated by economic pressure groups, of which the occupational interest groups are amongst the most typical and powerful, it was inevitable that sooner or later the university teachers should form their own professional association. Many of the professions to which individual academics belonged had long had their professional societies or institutions. The civil engineers had had their Institution since 1818, the solicitors and attorneys their Law Society since 1825, the doctors the British Medical Association since 1856 which in the form of the Provincial Medical and Surgical Association dates back to 1834, the architects their Institute, later the R.I.B.A., since 1834, the mechanical engineers their Institution since 1847, the chemists their Royal Institute since 1877, and the librarians their Association from the same year.[1] The cognate profession of school teaching had had its College of Preceptors since 1846, its Headmasters' Conference for the public schools since 1869 and its National Association of Elementary Teachers (later the National Union of Teachers) since 1870, and for those in between, the Associations of Head Mistresses since 1874, and Assistant Mistresses since 1884, of Head Masters since 1890 and Assistant Masters since 1891.[2] What is perhaps surprising, in a profession like university teaching where remuneration was not, as in the case of the fee-taking doctors and lawyers, self-determined but imposed mainly by university Councils composed predominantly of laymen and where favourable conditions of service were so vital to the creative functions of teaching and research, is that it should have taken so long.

1 Millerson, *Qualifying Associations*, pp. 121, 126.
2 A. M. Carr-Saunders and P. A. Wilson, *The Professions* (Oxford, 1933), pp. 253–6.

The reasons for the delay are not hard to find. In so variegated a profession, in which every man thinks of himself as a specialist first – a classicist, a historian, a chemist or an engineer – many university teachers already belonged to professional bodies, ranging from the straight learned societies like the Modern Languages Association to powerful 'trade unions' like the B.M.A., to which they felt they owed their first allegiance. Medical teachers are still difficult to recruit to the A.U.T. because they feel, rightly or wrongly, that the B.M.A. is a more adequate defender of their interests. A more important reason is that for long university teachers were scattered in small isolated pockets which were not only difficult to organize on a national scale but felt they had sufficient control or influence over their pay and conditions of work to determine or negotiate them locally and on an informal basis. There were large groups of several hundred only in Oxford and Cambridge, and there the allegiance of the fellows was to the individual colleges which were not only small, rarely exceeding a score or so of dons, but also autonomous corporations determining their own 'dividends' and living conditions. Elsewhere, most of the civic universities in the nineteenth century were tiny institutions with one or two dozen staff, mostly professors who, although ostensibly employed by lay-controlled governing bodies, had sufficient influence through Senate and their representatives on Court and Council to mitigate most of their grievances. Connected with this was a third reason, the very real autonomy of the universities and colleges which led to a great variety of pay and conditions and, in the absence of a national paymaster, made it pointless to organize nationally, especially since individual institutions were often too ill-endowed to afford higher salaries or better equipment and research grants than they actually provided.

Yet these same reasons also made it inevitable that the pressure for national organization, when it finally came, should come from the non-professorial staff of the civic universities and university colleges. The assistant staff were generally appointed at an earlier age than the professors and were less likely to have acquired long experience of and firm allegiance to another professional body.

They were not represented at that time on the governing bodies of their institutions – which in itself was one of their major complaints – and had no sense of being in a position to air their grievances or to influence their pay and conditions. Indeed, they had originally come into existence as temporary assistants, often of individual professors and sometimes paid by or through them, and the very safeguards which protected the professors from interference or dismissal were a cause of their insecurity and lack of rights. Finally, the autonomy and poverty of the individual university or college were to them a frustrating oppression, since they more than anyone else had to bear the burden of it. Any plea for higher pay, more permanent appointments, better facilities or larger research expenses could always be met by the unanswerable argument that 'the university cannot afford it', against which, unlike the professors on Senate or Council, they had no avenue of appeal.

As long as the assistant staff were truly temporary and could look forward with reasonable confidence to joining within a few years the ranks of the professors, their position was perhaps tolerable. But, as the lecturers' Memorandum to the Governing Bodies of Universities and other Colleges of University Rank was to put it, quite accurately, in 1918,

The newer universities have grown out of a number of small departments, in which the whole work of teaching and administration was undertaken by the Professors in charge. The large increase in the size of the various departments and in the scope of University teaching has been generally met by the appointment of Assistants, usually at a low salary and with limited tenure.

So long as the Assistants had a reasonable chance of obtaining academic promotion, this policy may have been unobjectionable; but in recent years the prospects of the Junior Staff have become discouragingly inadequate. The number of Assistants is now very much larger than the number of professorial posts, and their opportunities of promotion have correspondingly diminished.

On account of the increasing specialization in most branches of knowledge, many subjects of instruction have been entrusted to members of the staff, who have had considerable independence and responsibility in their work, and who, while retaining the title and status, and receiving the remuneration of Assistants, have had duties virtually co-ordinate with those of Professors.

The present grading of the academic staff is inequitable, in that it preserves an undue distinction of status between the professorial members, which no longer corresponds to a real difference in the character of the educational work and responsibilities assigned to them respectively.[1]

These feelings of frustration were coming to a head amongst the non-professorial staff of the larger civic universities well before the First World War. In Liverpool in 1909 a young lecturer in zoology, R. Douglas Laurie, who was to play much the largest role in the foundation and subsequent development of the A.U.T. down to his death in 1953, took the initiative, along with a colleague in the same department, of calling a meeting

To consider a proposal to form an Association for bringing the members of the Junior Staff more into touch with one another and with the life of the University.[2]

The meeting included such later well-known names as Patrick Abercrombie, Cyril Burt, P. M. Roxby and R. Stenhouse Williams. The Junior Staff Association it founded was ostensibly a dining and discussion society, but there was no doubt from Laurie's remarks from the chair at that first meeting – that while the professors were represented on Council, Senate and Faculties and the undergraduates through their Guild, 'the Junior Staff alone had either been omitted or had omitted itself from any organized participation in the corporate life of the University' – that a new pressure group had come into existence which was determined to make itself heard. Although their discussions ranged from F. J. Marquis (later Lord Woolton) on the Liverpool University Settlement to Miss Horniman on repertory theatres, they invited the Vice-Chancellor, Sir Alfred Dale, to their first dinner, and later opened the question of representation on the Faculties, which they obtained in 1910.

At first their aims were purely local, and they were unaware of similar developments in other universities. They soon learned that parallel groups had been formed or were in process of forma-

1 Association of University Lecturers, *Memorandum to the Governing Bodies of the Universities, University Colleges and Colleges of University Rank in England, Wales and Ireland*, 1918.
2 'A History, giving the Origin and Work of the A.U.T., by its Hon. General Secretary, R. Douglas Laurie (Professor of Zoology, University College of Wales, Aberystwyth), up to the time of his death in April 1953', pp. 1–2. Copies of these invaluable MS notes were typed and supplied to me by Miss D. K. Davies, his personal secretary from 1921 and later Chief Assistant Secretary of the A.U.T. until her retirement in 1963. (Subsequently referred to as *Laurie*.)

tion in Bristol, Sheffield, Birmingham and Cardiff, and in January 1910 they entertained to dinner representatives of the junior staffs from these and from Manchester.[1] Whether stimulated by this contact or not, the Manchester junior staff conducted their own campaign in the next few years for improved status and remuneration.[2] In 1913 fifty-eight members of the Manchester assistant staff, including J. S. B. Stopford, later Vice-Chancellor and Lord Stopford, J. E. Myers, later Sir James Myers, Principal of the College of Science and Technology, T. H. Pear, the educationist, and H. B. Charlton, later Professor of English Literature and historian of the University, sent a 'Memorial' to the University Council 'respectfully requesting' reconsideration of their pay and grading:

The present commencing salaries of £150 in Arts and £125 in Science are unanimously considered inadequate to the requirements of University teachers at a period when they should be actively engaged in the conduct of research and in increasing their general efficiency. . . . It is in fact found that the junior members of the Staff are in many cases unable to live on their salaries, and are compelled to supplement them from private income, by advances from parents, by outside work, or even by borrowing.

They suggested that the initial stipend should be substantially increased, a definite scheme of regular increments introduced, salaries of long-serving members allowed to rise above the 'customary limit' of £250 per annum, and that, since 'it is clear that the majority of Juniors can never attain to professorial rank,' readerships and assistant professorships similar to those in certain other universities should be instituted.[3]

The Council replied that, although they had agreed that 'eventually the stipends of Junior Assistant Lecturers and Demonstrators should be fixed at £160,' present finances

1 *Laurie*, pp. 2–3.
2 The Manchester representative at the Liverpool dinner in 1910, Dr. J. H. Shakeby of the Physics Department, is not on the list of those who signed the 1913 Manchester 'Memorial' below.
3 Manchester A.U.T. Archives, 'Memorial from the Members of the Assistant Staff to the Council of the Victoria University of Manchester', 1913. (These very full archives, in my possession, which include for the earlier years copies of all documents emanating from the national body, are subsequently referred to as 'Mcr. A.U.T.').

rendered this immediately impossible, that the alteration of salaries could not be considered apart from the annual estimates, that financial considerations prevented a rise above the customary limit except in a few individual cases, and that readerships and other senior posts already existed. They agreed, however, to a meeting of junior staff representatives with the Vice-Chancellor, as a result of which they appointed a committee to consider the raising of stipends on reappointment of individual lecturers.[1]

These discussions, with their usual frustrating outcome, were cut short by the War. Meanwhile, it is only fair to the authorities of the universities to say that their plea of poverty was quite genuine. They were in a real dilemma, unable to pay adequate salaries for their greatly expanded staffs without drastically curtailing the large extension of their range of subjects and of their services to the community which had been thrust upon them by the spontaneous internal development of learning and science and by the increasing demands of the public. The initial endowments of Victorian founders, however generous, were never intended to support such greatly enlarged activities, and were quite incapable of sustaining, still less of further extending, the universities' new roles. The obvious, indeed the only ultimately adequate saviour from this dilemma was the State. Even barring ancient royal endowment of particular colleges and regius chairs, State aid to universities has a longer history than is often thought. At the Union of England and Scotland in 1707 the Crown took over the Scottish Government's responsibility for assisting the Universities of St. Andrews, Glasgow, Aberdeen and Edinburgh, and these small Crown grants were replaced by an annual parliamentary vote, of £5,077 in 1832. The examining University of London chartered in 1836 received Government aid from its earliest years to meet the deficiency over and above fee income in the cost of conducting the examinations and awarding prizes and honours, a grant which was reduced from £4,170 to £3,370 in 1841. Small parliamentary grants of about £4,000 each were made to the new or recently founded Welsh University Colleges of Cardiff, Bangor and Aberystwyth in 1884.[2] By then both the

1 Mcr. A.U.T., 'Pre-War Memorandum', note of reply from the University Council, 22 January 1914.
2 University Grants Committee, *University Development, 1957–62* (Cmnd. 2267, 1964), pp. 170–1; R. O. Berdahl, *British Universities and the State* (Cambridge, 1959), pp. 48–50.

public and the Government were beginning to be disturbed by the so-called 'Great Depression' and by the increasing trading competition of Germany and America, whose industrial success was seen to be based on their superior education systems. James Bryce, now Professor of Civil Law at Oxford, pointed out that while Germany with a population of 45 million had over 24,000 university students, England with 26 million had only 5,500: 'Nothing could more clearly illustrate the failure of the English system to reach and serve all classes.' The Royal Commission on the Depression in Trade and Industry of 1885–86 underlined the active help which the German and American governments gave to higher technical education. T. H. Huxley warned in 1887 that 'We are entering, indeed we have already entered, upon the most serious struggle for existence to which this country was ever committed', and together with Sir Bernhard Samuelson, A. J. Mundella and Sir Henry Roscoe set up the National Association for the Promotion of Technical Education. Benjamin Jowett, Master of Balliol, urged the claims of the University Colleges at Leeds, Newcastle, Sheffield, Nottingham and Bristol:

They have proved their value, and, like every other educational institution, they have proved that they cannot live without external help. The only help that is likely to be permanent and that will enable them to feel secure is help from the State; and, in a moderate degree, it will be worth the State's while to give it.

Sir Henry Roscoe, who had been Professor of Chemistry at Owens' College, Manchester, for twenty-eight years and was now a Liberal M.P., declared:

The localities have in almost all cases now practically exhausted the power of raising funds from private sources ... We cannot afford to wait until public opinion has reached the point at which ratepayers generally are convinced that it is to their advantage to support such colleges. The only alternative, therefore, is that the State as a whole shall, through the Government, acknowledge its obligation.

In 1887 a public meeting in Southampton in connection with the extension of the Hartley Institution into a University College called for a State grant of £50,000 a year for the English university colleges.[1]

The result of this campaign was the Technical Instruction Act,

1 Armytage, *Civic Universities*, pp. 233–5.

1889, and the famous 'whiskey money', diverted by the temperance lobby from the parliamentary compensation for discontinued publicans' licences to the support of technical education by the new County and County Borough Councils. At the same time a small grant, of £15,000 a year, was made to the university colleges in England and Scotland. The money was distributed by a Committee on Grants to University Colleges in Great Britain, in which can be seen the remote origin of the University Grants Committee founded in 1919. The grant was made on a five-yearly basis, like the present quinquennial system, but the Committee was not a permanent one, a fresh *ad hoc* Committee being appointed every fifth year to apportion the grant for the next five. By 1904, after five *ad hoc* Committees had done their work, the number of aided institutions had risen from eleven to fourteen and the annual grant from £15,000 to £27,000. In that year, in the enthusiasm generated by imperialism and the arms race with Germany, the Chancellor of the Exchequer, Austen Chamberlain, promised to double the grant for 1904–05 and to redouble it in 1905–06, and to this end appointed a rather more high-powered committee, called the University Colleges Committee, under a leading Opposition statesman, R. B. Haldane. Haldane, a keen supporter of civic universities, was to play a leading part in the reorganization of London University as chairman of the Royal Commission of 1909. The *Third Report* (23 February 1905) of his Committee laid the foundations of the present (or, more strictly, the recent) system by recommending a permanent advisory body which should itself receive from the Exchequer and disburse the grant to the colleges, reporting annually via the Treasury to Parliament. The grant for 1905–06 was duly increased to £100,000, and in 1906 the first permanent Advisory Committee on Grants to University Colleges was appointed with, as chairman, Professor (later Sir) William M'Cormick of Dundee University College, then secretary of the Carnegie Trust for the Universities of Scotland, and later first chairman of the Advisory Council to the Department of Scientific and Industrial Research from 1915 and of the U.G.C. itself from 1919 to his death in 1930.[1]

After an unsuccessful bid to wrest control of all grants to universities, a large part of which (32 per cent) came from the

1 U.G.C., *op. cit.*, pp. 171–4; Berdahl, *op. cit.*, pp. 50–4.

Board of Education principally for teacher training, this Committee was replaced in 1911 by an Advisory Committee on University Grants composed entirely of academics or ex-academics, still under the chairmanship of Professor M'Cormick, but responsible not to the Treasury but to the Board of Education, and concerned only with the English civic universities, the Scottish and Welsh remaining under the aegis of the Treasury. The vote, now covering the eleven universities and university colleges of Manchester, Liverpool, Durham (for Armstrong College, Newcastle), Birmingham, Leeds, Bristol, Sheffield, London (for five institutions), Southampton, Nottingham and Reading, was increased to £149,000 per annum, exclusive of Treasury grants of £31,000 to the Welsh colleges and £1,000 to Dundee University College. The grants were made for a five-year period from 1 April 1911, were paid over without earmarking to the universities' general income to be expended at their discretion, though only for recurrent, non-capital purposes of teaching and research of university standard, and not for scholarships, awards or subsidies to students. The Committee initiated much of the U.G.C.'s later procedure, assessing the universities' claims on the basis of *ad hoc*, especially quinquennial, statements and annual returns, and inaugurating the informal 'visitations' which have continued since. The only major difference from the later system was that ministerial responsibility lay with the President of the Board of Education rather than the Chancellor of the Exchequer – anticipating the present responsibility of the Secretary of State for Education and Science – and it was to the war-time President of the Board (1916–22), the ex-Oxford historian H. A. L. Fisher, that the university lecturers were to address their grievances.[1]

The growth of Government finance, although potentially a threat to university autonomy, was the assistant staff's best hope of ameliorating their condition. One problem was that of superannuation, which in the diverse schemes operated by the different universities was often inadequate, not easily interchangeable, and for temporary and low-paid staff usually non-existent. The Committee on University Grants took a long stride towards solving this problem by setting up in 1914, after consultation with a joint committee of the universities, the Federated

1 U.G.C., *op. cit.*, pp. 174–7; Berdahl, *op. cit.*, p. 54–5.

Superannuation System for Universities. Under this scheme the university teacher and his institution each paid an annual premium equivalent to 5 per cent of his salary to one of the insurance companies on the panel of the F.S.S.U. Central Council, on an endowment or deferred annuity policy, at the choice of the member, guaranteeing an annuity or lump sum at age 60 or on later retirement or earlier death.[1] Although a great improvement on earlier arrangements, F.S.S.U. had three drawbacks. It did not cover temporary appointees, nor any university teacher earning less than £160 a year, and it was not compulsory for those earning less than £300 a year. It was not proof against inflation, a flaw which became important during and immediately after the War. And, compared with the scheme which was to be offered to the school teachers in 1918, it had the disadvantage of having to be paid for partly out of salary.[2] For these reasons, and one still more vital one, that a man's pension rights affect his whole career and therefore unite the interests of professors and non-professors, the question of superannuation was to play an important part in the founding of the A.U.T.

Another effect of the growth of Government aid, of ultimate advantage to the unification of the academic profession, was the dim yet growing realization on the part of university chief administrators that unity had advantages when facing a common paymaster. The principle of absolute autonomy of universities, which has always meant first and foremost autonomy for Vice-Chancellors and governing bodies, died hard – indeed, it has kicks left in it yet – but it relaxed sufficiently at the (second) Congress of Universities of the Empire in 1912 to permit the establishment of a Universities Bureau of the British Empire, to publish a *Yearbook*, exchange information, and hold periodical imperial conferences. It grew out of the imperialism of the Edwardian age and was concerned more to unite the far-flung Empire than the British universities. It was hypersensitive about university autonomy, and at its first meeting in 1913 passed a resolution 'that it will at no time be the business of the Bureau Committee to pass judgement on University policy'. But the representatives of the home universities, who acted as a per-

---

1 U.G.C., *op. cit.*, p. 176; Berdahl, *op. cit.*, p. 55.
2 Cf. Association of University Lecturers, *Report drawn up by the Pensions Committee of the Conference of University Lecturers, 1919.*

manent executive between conferences, found themselves work to do, especially during the enforced isolation of the War. A Conference of British Universities in May 1917 'to consider the situation arising out of the closing of the German and American universities to graduate students from the countries of the Allies' discussed the establishment of a research doctorate; and met again a year later at the instance of A. J. Balfour, the Foreign Secretary, and Fisher of the Board of Education, when it not only recommended the institution of the Ph.D. but appointed a standing Committee consisting of 'the Vice-Chancellor or Principal of each university, or a deputy appointed by him, together with the Executive Committee of the Universities Bureau.'[1] This was in effect the Committee of Vice-Chancellors and Principals, formally constituted as such in 1919, the same year that the University Grants Committee was set up on its modern basis, and that the A.U.T. was founded. Thus, by one of those historical coincidences which would not be allowed in respectable fiction, the three bodies whose subsequent intercourse has constituted the national history of the universities in the twentieth century came into existence in the same year.

The coincidence has an explanation, however. It grew out of the post-war difficulties of the universities, the demand for a much-expanded Government grant, and the consequent need for a body to advise the Treasury (rather than the Board of Education) on the size of the grant and control its disbursement, and for two other bodies to watch the interests respectively of the universities as institutions and of their academic staffs as employees and professional men. The immediate origins of the last can be traced to the effects of the War on the living standards of those junior lecturers who had not, for various reasons, been called into the armed forces. The outbreak of the War had cut short their efforts at amelioration and had frozen salaries, but by 1917 inflation was beginning to hurt. At Liverpool Douglas Laurie, the Secretary of the Junior Staff Association, called a meeting and drew up a memorandum for presentation to the Board of Education. As an after-thought the Liverpool Association decided to approach the assistant staffs of all the universities

1 Sir Eric Ashby, *Community of Universities: an Informal Portrait of the Association of Universities of the British Commonwealth, 1913–63* (1963), chap. i; U.G.C., *op. cit.*, pp. 177–8.

in the British Isles with a view to a meeting and a joint memorandum. So unpremeditated was this move that Laurie, without contacts in all the universities, addressed many of the invitations to 'a senior member of the non-professorial staff' and sent them via the Registrars. The meeting was held on 15 December 1917 at the Exchange Hotel, Liverpool, and was the first of a series of conferences of what was to become the Association of University Lecturers. It was attended by representatives from Belfast, Birmingham, Bristol, Durham, Leeds, Liverpool, Manchester, Sheffield, St. Andrews and its affiliated College at Dundee, Aberystwyth, Cardiff, and the London Colleges, Bedford, King's and University. Letters of support also came from Aberdeen, Edinburgh and Glasgow, and from the University Colleges at Dublin, Cork and Galway. Bangor's invitation had gone astray, and it only joined the later Conferences.[1] Laurie was elected to the chair, and the meeting rapidly passed the following motion by 19 votes to 5 (Manchester, Bedford College and University College, London, opposing it for procedural reasons which will appear):

That action be taken to improve the status and salary of full-time University teachers of non-professorial rank by approaching the President of the Board of Education (or other authorities in the case of Scotland or Ireland) and that the governing bodies and Senates of each University concerned be in the first instance invited to support such action.

The Liverpool memorandum to the latter was accepted as the basis of discussion, and the meeting got down to detailed re-drafting of it, including Schedule A, 'a scale of salaries to be presented as an absolute minimum', ranging from £200 to £300 in Grade 3 (equivalent in modern terms to the assistant lecturer grade), £300 to £450 in Grade 2 (equivalent to lecturer), and £450 to £600 in Grade 1 (equivalent to senior lecturer and reader). The heads of the memorandum read like the minutes of any subsequent meeting of the Council or Executive of the A.U.T.: tenure, status, grading, salaries, opportunities for research, superannuation scheme. So instantly did the perennial preoccupations of the professional interest group spring to mind. Finally, at Laurie's suggestion the meeting decided, on the

1 *Laurie*, pp. 3–5.

following (Sunday) morning, to form an inter-university association with the name 'the Association of University Lecturers'.[1]

The name caused misgivings amongst some of the representatives from the first. Even before the Liverpool Conference the Manchester junior staff in electing delegates had instructed them, while conveying their cordial sympathy, to oppose as 'highly undesirable . . . an immediate appeal to the Board of Education, without the co-operation of the Senates and Councils of the several Universities'. That was the reason for their vote, along with three of the London delegates, against the main resolution at the Conference. On their return the Manchester delegates, C. B. Dewhurst and George Hickling, reported back to a meeting of junior staff in January 1918 which reaffirmed the view that it would decline to take part in a separate approach to the Board of Education, and prepared a memorandum addressed to the rest of the Association, putting the case for acting 'in the most loyal and sympathetic co-operation with its fellow-teachers' and with the governing bodies, and declaring that

While it would desire to do all in its power to promote the successful issue of the inter-university Conferences representing the Junior Staffs . . ., it would deprecate the foundation of a permanent Association which should exclude any group of University teachers.

As an earnest of their belief in co-operation they 'appointed representatives to discuss the whole question with the University Council, through the Vice-Chancellor, so that the most fully-informed representations may be made by the Council to the Board of Education.'[2]

Some other junior staffs felt similarly. Bedford College (for women), London, strongly deprecated 'any cleavage of professorial and non-professorial staff in any action taken to secure this improvement' in status and remuneration, and Leeds thought the Liverpool memorandum so divisive that it drew up another, supported by Manchester and, with additions, by Bedford

1 Mcr. A.U.T., Minutes of 'Conference of University Lecturers held at the Exchange Hotel, Liverpool, 15 December 1917'.
2 *Ibid.*, Minutes of 'General Meeting of Junior Staff, 18 January 1918', and 'Memorandum from the Junior Staff of the University of Manchester in reference to the Resolutions of the Conference of Delegates held at Liverpool on 15 December 1917'.

College.[1] At the second Conference of University Lecturers, at Liverpool on 9 March 1918, however, the Leeds and Manchester proposal to accept the Bedford College version as the basis for discussion was rejected, and the Liverpool memorandum, with verbal amendments, was accepted for presentation to all governing bodies, soliciting their support for a deputation to the Board of Education early in June. At the same time an 'Application to the Rt. Hon. the President of the Board of Education and to the Lords Commissioners of His Majesty's Treasury with reference to Augmented Grants for the purpose of Increasing the Salaries of University Lecturers' was approved, with a blank space for listing those university governing bodies which supported it. The dissidents, however, were able to persuade the rest to leave open the question of membership, and carry a unanimous resolution 'that this Conference continue as a Conference of Delegates of University Lecturers until such time as it is merged into an Association of University Lecturers or Teachers.'[2]

They were not able to prevent another sort of split:

It was intimated to this meeting that the Scottish members had decided that, largely owing to matters of internal organization, it would be convenient for them to proceed with a separate movement. They sent their good wishes and hoped that the two movements would keep in touch with each other.[3]

Although the Scottish Association did not come into formal existence until 1922 – the first joint Council of the four Scottish Local Associations met in Edinburgh on 6 May of that year – this was the origin of the separate A.U.T. for Scotland which was not re-united with the southern body until 1949.[4]

During the summer of 1918, while the last great German offensive on the Western front spent itself in exhausted defeat and was slowly turned into victory for the Allies, Laurie and the university lecturers were fighting another sort of battle, collecting

---

1 *Ibid.*, 'Leeds Memorandum', and 'Draft Memorial (based on the Draft drawn up by the Junior Staff of Leeds University) embodying the views of the Staff of Bedford College for Women'.
2 *Ibid.*, Minutes of 'Second Conference of Delegates of University Lecturers (England, Wales and Ireland) at the Exchange Hotel, Liverpool, on 9 March 1918'.
3 *Laurie*, p. 5.
4 T. R. Bolam, 'The Scottish Association of University Teachers', *British Universities Annual*, 1964, pp. 77, 82.

sympathy, though rarely committed support, for the details of their salary claim, from university governing bodies, and trying, through a group of M.P.s led by Sir Philip Magnus and Alfred Bigland, to bring H. A. L. Fisher of the Board of Education to a confrontation. In the last few weeks of the War Sir Philip Magnus managed to pin him down to an agreement to receive a deputation, only to have it snatched away again when Fisher and the Chancellor of the Exchequer arranged to receive one 'from the Universities' – that is, from the Vice-Chancellors and governing bodies – instead. He asked Magnus to let the question of a deputation from the non-professorial staff 'stand over for the present' and, unkindest cut of all, referred to them as 'the *Assistant* Lecturers'.[1] This rebuff must have driven home to many the weakness of the junior staff if they chose to 'go it alone'.

Fisher did, however, agree to receive further written evidence in support of their case, and Laurie seized the opportunity to send him a mass of papers, including the Memorandum to Governing Bodies and copies of their individual sympathetic replies, and a fat survey of the salaries and length of service of the lecturers in fifteen universities and university colleges.[2] This remuneration survey, of a kind which the A.U.T. was to make at regular intervals in support of salary claims, was an impressive document, replete with tables, graph and comparisons with other professions. It showed that the average salary of 330 lecturers, with service ranging from 4 to 13 years, and mostly 7 to 10, was £206, little more than that of secondary schoolmasters of 3 years' standing, and less than most. It also showed the wide and arbitrary range of salaries in the same and between different institutions, bearing little relation to qualifications and length of service, from £100 or less to £500 or more – further underlining the need for common action, not only by the lecturers but in co-operation with the university authorities, to solicit increased Government aid.

1 Mcr. A.U.T., Copy of letter from H. A. L. Fisher, President of Board of Education, to Sir Philip Magnus, M.P., 1 November 1918.
2 *Ibid.*, Copy of letter from Laurie to Fisher, 8 November 1918; 'Memorandum to Governing Bodies' cited above; Copies of Resolutions from Councils or other Governing Bodies of the Universities and University Colleges of Aberystwyth, Cardiff, Durham, Leeds, Sheffield, King's and University Colleges, London, and Cork, Dublin and Galway; 'Remuneration of University Lecturers re Deputation to the President of the Board of Education.'

The Board of Education replied on 11 November, the day the War ended, officially postponing the question of a deputation until the President had met the representatives of the universities.[1] Laurie pondered what to do next. The next meeting of the lecturers' representatives was to have been at the meeting with Fisher, which was also to have provided an opportunity for a further Conference to found the Association of University Lecturers and to adopt the rules being drawn up in preparation for it by F. Raleigh Batt, lecturer in law at Sheffield University. Laurie had also heard, early in October, of a crisis impending on another question vital to university teachers, that of superannuation. It became clear that the Teachers' Superannuation Bill which Fisher was piloting through the House of Commons did not after all cover university teachers.[2] At all events, Laurie, after some hesitation, decided to call the third Conference, by telegram at three days' notice, on 30 November at King's College, London.[3]

The meeting was in form a double one, a continuation of the conferences concerned with the agitation over salaries, and the first meeting of what the agenda called the Association of University Lecturers. The Conference business was taken first, and Laurie as chairman was instructed to write to the President of the Board of Education asking the result of the University Deputation of 23 November, offering further evidence in support of the salary claim, asking for part of the universities' grants to be specifically allocated to salary increases, and repeating the request for a deputation to be received. The meeting then resolved itself into a provisional committee of the Association of University Lecturers, to consider the agenda motion 'that an Association be and is hereby formed, for, among other purposes, the promotion of the interest of University Lecturers'. Manchester, along with six other institutions, was not represented at this emergency meeting, but Hickling's telegram was read out:

Manchester supports proposals to accelerate action of Board but main-

1 *Ibid.*, Copy of letter from Fisher's Private Secretary to Laurie, 11 November 1918.
2 *Ibid.*, Copies of letters, Laurie to Fisher, 28 September, and Fisher's Private Secretary to Laurie, 2 October 1918.
3 *Ibid.*, Telegrams from Laurie to Hickling, Manchester, 27 and 28 November 1918.

tains former attitude regarding Association and strongly reaffirms need for united university front.[1]

To avoid an open split Laurie moved from the chair a resolution which referred to an Association to promote the interests of university teachers, leaving the definition of membership to the discussion on the constitution. This was passed with only one dissentient, Bedford College, which would not commit itself until the basis of membership was known. The rules as drafted by F. Raleigh Batt said very firmly that 'Membership . . . shall be open to all persons not being professors who are members of the teaching bodies of any University or other Institution hereinafter mentioned.'[2] Imperial College and Bedford College moved that the words 'not being professors' be omitted, and this was carried, against the opposition of Liverpool, Sheffield, Birmingham, Bristol, and University College, London. With this and other minor amendments, and a subscription set at 7s. 6d., the draft rules were sent for ratification to the junior staffs of the institutions.[3]

Meanwhile, the meeting, once again turning itself into a Conference, set about pursuing its campaign for better salaries by appointing Laurie and A. J. Monahan of Leeds to draft a letter to Parliamentary candidates for university constituencies and university towns in the imminent general election, and asking the London group of colleges to appoint a Publicity Committee to make the Association's views known. On superannuation all that could be done was to ask the Sheffield and Leeds Associations, who had raised the matter, to form a Pensions Committee to report to a further Conference which, because the question was so urgent, should be called before the one to finalize the name and constitution of the Association.[4]

Laurie in his notes on the history of the A.U.T. seemed to think, from the standpoint of thirty-five years later, that the third Conference settled the question of membership in favour

1 *Ibid.*, Copy of telegram, Hickling to Hazlitt, Lecturers' Conference, King's College, London, 30 November 1918.
2 *Ibid.*, Draft Rules of Association of University Lecturers (duplicated).
3 *Ibid.*, Minutes of 'Third Conference of Delegates of University Lecturers (England, Wales and Ireland) and first meeting of the Provisional Committee of the Association of University Lecturers, at King's College, London, on 30 November 1918'.
4 *Ibid., op. cit.*

of including professors,[1] but this was by no means the case at the time. The question was not finally settled until the fifth meeting, in June 1919, at which the draft rules, printed for the occasion, were headed, 'An Association to promote the Interests of Teachers in Universities', and Rule 1 read, 'The name of the Society shall be . . . (to be settled at a future date).'[2] Meanwhile, two developments were to occur which were to be decisive in swinging opinion towards a wider definition of membership. The first was the crisis over superannuation which, since it affected the whole of an individual's career as lecturer and professor, was designed to unite the profession, and which evoked a joint conference between the university lecturers, representatives of the professorial and administrative staff of the universities, and of the Association of Directors and Secretaries for Education, in April 1919. The second was the constructive opportunism of the Manchester junior staff, who seized the opportunity offered by this obvious unity of interests to approach their Senate with a view to forming an association of university teachers of all ranks, and so pre-empting, as it were, the decision on the question of membership.

The Conference on superannuation took place at Sheffield on 11 April 1919. Laurie had sent invitations to Registrars via the junior staff associations stating that

As the matter is obviously one of joint concern to all University Teachers, the Lecturers of England, Wales and Ireland hope that Senates will send representatives to the meeting referred to, in order to decide upon a joint plan of campaign for the purpose of obtaining a Bill in Parliament to deal with the matter.[3]

Twenty-one of the twenty-five universities and colleges represented sent Senatorial delegates, including a Vice-Chancellor (Dr. J. S. G. Pemberton of Durham) and two Principals (Nottingham University College and East London College), and no less than four Fellows of the Royal Society. The Association of

1 *Laurie*, pp. 5-6.
2 Mcr. A.U.T., *An Association to promote the Interests of Teachers in Universities: Draft Rules passed provisionally by the Provisional Central Committee of the Association of University Lecturers at their meeting at King's College, London, 30 November 1918* (printed).
3 *Ibid.*, Copy of letter, Laurie to Registrars of Universities and University Colleges, 24 February 1919.

Directors and Secretaries for Education was represented in a consultative capacity by James Graham, Director of Education for Leeds, and A. R. Pickles, Secretary of Education for Burnley, on the initiative of their Chairman, Austin Keen, who had written to Laurie regretting that the Teachers' Superannuation Act had not been extended to the administrative staffs of the Local Education Authorities. The Council of the Federated Superannuation System for Universities was also represented by its Chairman, A. J. Hobson, whose Executive had sent a deputation to the President of the Board of Education on 4 April to ask for funds to improve the pensions under their scheme.[1]

The Conference addressed itself to the printed report of the Pensions Committee, the burden of which was that the Teachers' scheme, being contributory and granting both an annuity and a lump-sum payment based on the average of the last five years of service, and also taking into account for calculation of pension all years of 'recognized service' whether formally under the scheme or not, was decidedly superior to F.S.S.U. and ought to be extended to all university staff, including administrators, librarians and museum staff. Mr. Hobson, the Chairman of the F.S.S.U. Council, made a strong plea for the scheme put by his Executive's deputation to the Board of Education, which asked for an increase in the F.S.S.U. premium from 10 to 15 per cent of salary, of which 10 or even $12\frac{1}{2}$ per cent would be paid by the university out of Government grant. He was opposed by J. L. S. Hatton, Principal of East London College, who had also been on the deputation and had come away feeling very disappointed and with the conviction that the interests of existing staffs were not being properly considered. The upshot of the discussion was that the Conference rejected an improved F.S.S.U. and passed by a majority of 22 to 1 the motion

that this Conference wishes to urge strongly that the Teachers' (Superannuation) Act, 1918, be extended so as to include the staffs of Universities and University Colleges.

In case that proved impossible, it was also agreed to communicate immediately with the President of the Board of Education

1 *Ibid.*, Minutes of 'Meeting of the Fourth Conference of University Lecturers in conjunction with representatives from the Professional and Administrative Staff of the Universities and University Colleges and from the Directors and Secretaries for Education, held at Sheffield, 11 April 1919'.

urging that before any modification of F.S.S.U. was adopted all sections of university staffs should be allowed to state their views to him and to the Treasury. Although, as we shall see, this joint conference did not achieve its objective of extending the Teachers' Superannuation Act to universities, it did display an extraordinary unanimity on a question which profoundly affected the whole profession, and so marked a long step in the direction of formal unity.[1]

Next day, Saturday, 12 April, the lecturers continued their fourth Conference without their guests, passing a series of resolutions forwarding their campaign for better salaries, and updating their proposed scales, which had been based on pre-war values, to take account of rising prices. The revised scales ranged from £200 to £300, over three years, for Grade III, from £300 to £550, over six years, for Grade II, and from £550 to £800, over a further six years, for Grade I. The significance of this was that, for the first time, non-professorial salaries were demanded which rose within sight of the professorial level. At the end the Leeds delegate brought forward the matter of the Association, urging that it be put on a definite footing without delay; and it was agreed to do this at the next Conference, if possible by the end of May.[2]

Now, many of the local Associations were still strongly in favour of restricting membership to non-professors, and the Manchester delegate, H. B. Charlton, believed that if some extraordinary effort were not made to avoid it the next Conference would found an exclusive Association of University Lecturers. On his return he and his alternate delegate, George Hickling, later Professor of Geology at Newcastle, wrote a report to the Vice-Chancellor and the Senate appealing to them to support a wider association. After reporting on the joint Conference on superannuation, they continued:

It is in our opinion desirable to take this occasion to draw the attention of the Senate to another matter which has occupied a permanent place in the discussions at each of the four Conferences of non-professorial staffs during the past 15 months, and which has now reached a crucial stage, viz., the proposal to found an Association of University teachers.

1 *Ibid., op. cit.*
2 *Ibid.*, Minutes of 'Fourth Conference of University Lecturers, held at Sheffield, 12 April 1919'.

The Foundation of the A.U.T.

The original proposal, put forward at the Liverpool Conference in December 1917, was for the immediate formation of an inter-University Junior Staff Association. Mainly in response to the representations of the Manchester delegates, the proposal was postponed for fuller consideration. At a later Conference, it was urged and carried, though in face of strong opposition, that a wider association, which might embrace university teachers of all ranks, would be both stronger and more generally useful than any sectional association, while it would at the same time avoid the obviously undesirable suggestion of divided interests among university staffs, which the original scheme implied. The successive Conferences have shown a steadily growing conviction that some association must be founded, and at the second session of the Sheffield Conference it was resolved that a further Conference should be called before the end of the present term, for the definite purpose of completing the foundation of such an association and fixing its constitution ... We are convinced that further opposition on our part to the formation of an association will have the effect of giving the association which will be formed a sectional and partisan character. On the other hand we are of opinion that a wide association, open to all members of University staffs, might prove to be of great value as a medium of intercourse and for the more effective formulation of general university ideals. We therefore appeal for the approval of the Senate to the foundation and trial of such an association.[1]

This cunningly devised appeal had its desired effect. Not only did the Senate appoint the Vice-Chancellor, Sir Henry Miers, and four other members to meet five representatives of the junior staff to discuss superannuation, but two leading professors, T. F. Tout, the great historian, and F. E. Weiss, an ex-Vice-Chancellor, joined with Charlton and Hickling in calling a meeting of all staff, senior and junior, for 5 June.[2] The meeting cordially approved the proposal to found an Association of University Teachers of all ranks, appointed Professor Lapworth and Dr. Hickling to express its views at the next Conference at Bristol, amended the Draft Rules of the national Association to accommodate them, including the insertion of the name 'Association of University Teachers', and gathered the signatures of the Vice-Chancellor, the Registrar, the Principal of the College of Science

1 *Ibid.*, 'Report to the V.C. and Senate, 25 April 1919' (MS copy).
2 *Ibid.*, Letter from H. P. Turner, Registrar, to H. G. A. Hickling and H. B. Charlton, 27 May 1919; and Notice and Minutes of 'Meeting of the Teaching Staff of the University of Manchester, 5 June 1919'.

No Hickling.

and Technology, 28 professors and 46 lecturers to a declaration signifying their intention to constitute themselves a Manchester Branch of the Association. To clinch the matter the Junior Staff held a separate meeting on 19 June appointing Hickling as their official delegate to the Bristol Conference and instructing him to state that 'the Junior Staff of Manchester would not join an Association of University Lecturers if such should be formed.'[1]

Whether or not this piece of moral blackmail was necessary, it manifestly worked. At the Bristol Conference on 27 and 28 June 1919 professorial delegates were admitted, nine of them, from Bristol, Durham, Liverpool, Nottingham, Southampton, Bangor and Cardiff as well as Manchester. Laurie from the chair 'pointed out that the idea which had brought the Association into being was of a trade union character, but he expressed the hope that, when material conditions had been satisfactorily improved, educational matters generally would form the essential points on which discussion would take place.' In view of the division of feeling on the matter the decision on the name of the Association was postponed until after the objects and membership had been determined. There was no difficulty in amending the objects to read: 'the advancement of University Education and Research and the promotion of common action among University teachers in connection therewith' (at the next meeting in December 'in connection therewith' was replaced by 'and the safegurding of the interests of the members'). But there was a lengthy discussion about the second, 'with special reference to the inclusion or non-inclusion of Professors', and an attempt was made to re-insert the words 'not being Professors' before the wider formula was finally accepted. The rest of the Friday session was taken up with amending and approving the rest of the Rules, which made the Association a federation of Local Associations, electing representatives to a Central Council which in turn elected an Executive Committee (exactly as today). It was therefore on the Saturday

1 *Ibid.*, 'Resolutions passed at a Meeting of Junior Staff, 19 June 1919'. It was not strictly the first Local Association to be formed: at a meeting at the London School of Medicine for Women on 27 May 1919 it was proposed and carried unanimously that 'An Association of Teachers in the London Medical Schools should be formed, with the idea of affiliating to the Central Association now in process of formation', with Professor Frazer of St. Mary's Hospital School as President, and Miss Laycock and Miss Bond of the London School of Medicine for Women as Secretary and Treasurer – London Medical Schools Local Association archives, in my possession.

R. D. Laurie   Dr. Arrald

The Foundation of the A.U.T.

morning, 28 June 1919, that the motion, proposed by R. J. Tabor of Imperial College and seconded by George Hickling of Manchester,

That the name of the Association be 'The Association of University Teachers'

was 'carried *nem. con.* after various alternatives had been rejected'.[1]

R. D. Laurie was fittingly elected President of the new-born Association, Professor F. E. Weiss, F.R.S., ex-Vice-Chancellor of Manchester, the distinguished Vice-President, F. Raleigh Batt of Sheffield, drafter of the constitution, later Professor of Commercial Law at Liverpool and later still a County Court Judge, appointed Secretary, and R. J. Tabor of Imperial College, Treasurer. To mark the admission of professors, resolutions were proposed and carried, by Professors Lapworth of Manchester and Swimmerton of Nottingham respectively, that 'the minimum salary of the Professor in charge of a small department be £800' (which happened to be the top of the salary scale proposed for Grade I of the non-professorial staff) and that 'adequate secretarial assistance be provided for Heads of Departments'.

'We count this as the first meeting of the A.U.T.,' Laurie wrote in 1953 of this Bristol Conference, and the Minutes are printed under the heading 'Association of University Teachers'.[2] The first Council meeting called as such, however, was, appropriately enough, held at Manchester University on 12 and 13 December 1919. Dr. Hickling for the Local Association organized the arrangements for the meeting, and the members were entertained to dinner and a reception on the Friday evening by the Council of the University.[3]

It would be fitting to be able to record an equally appropriate laurel wreath for that other midwife of the A.U.T., the super-

1 'Association of University Teachers: Minutes of a meeting of representatives of the professorial and non-professorial Staffs of the Universities, University Colleges, and Colleges of University rank, in England, Wales, and Ireland, held at the University of Bristol, on Friday, June 27th, and Saturday, June 28th, 1919'.
2 *Laurei*, p. 6.
3 'A.U.T., Minutes of a meeting of representatives, etc. . . . at the University of Manchester, on Friday, December 12th, and Saturday, December 13th, 1919'; the meeting is referred to as 'this Council' throughout.

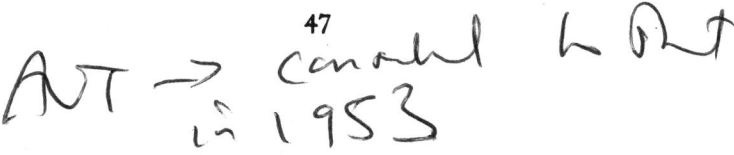
AUT → council in 1953

annuation question. Unhappily – or, as it turned out in view of the school teachers' experience, perhaps happily – the campaign to get the Teachers' Superannuation Act extended to the universities completely failed, and the A.U.T. had to be content with the improved F.S.S.U. urged by its Chairman, by which the universities' contribution was raised from 5 to 10 per cent of salary, the member's share remaining at 5 per cent. This, however, along with the outcome of the salaries campaign, we may leave, with the A.U.T. safely brought to birth, to its infancy and adolescence between the Wars.

Chapter 3

An Amateur Professional Body
1919–39

1 THE INFANT PRESSURE GROUP

The Association uniting the professorial and non-professorial levels of university teaching which came into existence on 28 June 1919 was inevitably, and for long remained, a professional body run by amateurs. In the first place, since it was a very small profession, it was inevitably a very small association. In 1919–20, its first full year of existence, there were only 2,277 full-time university teachers in Great Britain, excluding Oxford and Cambridge which took no part in the A.U.T. until the 1930's, and these had risen only to 3,819 by 1938–39 (3,994 including professors and readers at Oxford and Cambridge).[1] Not all of these were at first considered eligible for membership, since they included temporary assistants, demonstrators and the like, of doubtful academic status, and in June 1920 the first Honorary Secretary, Professor Raleigh Batt, reported that the membership was 1,163, and that a further 371 university teachers were eligible to join. Seventeen institutions had formed Local Associations. (*The University Bulletin* for April 1923 reported 1,319 'branch members' for 1919–20 in 24 institutions, but these included four in Ireland, all of which except Belfast later seceded, and it is not clear whether the 'branches', or Local Associations as they strictly were, admitted members from the 'others' category who were not eligible for national membership.) Membership fluctuated during the 1920's, reaching a nadir of 1,035 in 1926–27 and rising to 1,360 in 1928–29, and rose steadily in the 1930's to 1,899 in 28 Local Associations by 1938–

---

1 Halsey and Trow, *op. cit.*, chap. i, p. 8; U.G.C., *University Development from 1935 to 1947* (1948), p. 103.

1939.[1] Even excluding Oxford and Cambridge the A.U.T. between the Wars attracted into membership rather less than half of an already small profession.

In the second place, the Association was run on a shoe string. Whether because of the traditional penury (or thrift?) of academics or because of the need to keep the subscription low for recruiting purposes, university teachers have always paid less for the support of their professional organization than the doctors, the lawyers, the school teachers and indeed most other professional men, and even than most trade unionists. The subscription, set at 10s. *per annum* in the original Rules in 1919, was increased to 15s. in 1921, where it remained until after the Second World War. Consequently the income of the Association remained exiguous: less than £1,000 in 1921–22, and still under £1,500 in 1938–39.[2] In view of these stringently limited resources the amount of activity sustained by the A.U.T. can only be described as astonishing.

The achievement was due to a dedicated band of men and women who were amateurs in the best sense of the word, giving freely of their time and talents in the service of their fellows. The academic profession is, of course, supremely fortunate in being able to call on a greater variety of trained intelligence than any other, and the A.U.T. took every advantage of this. Its first Secretary and drafter of its constitution, Professor F. Raleigh Batt, was a lawyer who, even when he became a County Court judge, continued to offer free legal advice to the A.U.T. Another of the founding fathers, Dr. S. Brodetsky of Bristol, a Russian-born Zionist and supporter of Chaim Weizman, the Manchester professor who became first President of Israel, was Professor of Mathematics at Leeds from 1924, and from 1932 until he went to become President of the Hebrew University in Jerusalem in 1945 he was the A.U.T.'s brilliant, explosive and immensely persuasive negotiator on salaries. He was succeeded as Convener of the Salaries and Grading Committee by his Leeds colleague, Mr. W. A. Wightman, whose tenure of the office, and of the Convenership of the Superannuation Committee, was even longer. The first Honorary Treasurer, R. J. Tabor of Imperial College, long Assistant Professor of Botany there, served in that onerous

1 Council Minutes, 1919–39, *passim.*
2 *Ibid., passim.*

office until 1946, and was President of the Association for most of the Second World War. He in turn was succeeded as Treasurer by Professor H. V. A. Briscoe, also of Imperial College, who served until his death in 1961. His successor, another chemist, Dr. T. G. Halsall of Oxford, is still in office. Only three treasurers in half a century is a record of which few voluntary associations could boast. Since the first few numbers which were symposia by the Editorial Committee, the Association's journal, *The University Bulletin* (1922-28), *The Universities Review* (1928-62) and the *British Universities Annual* (1962-), has had only half a dozen editors, the reign of the remarkable blind editor C. M. (later Professor) MacInnes lasting no less than 35 years, from 1926 to 1961.[1] And there are many other devoted unpaid servants of the A.U.T. whose names will appear later in the story.

The greatest and most devoted amateur of them all, the man who not only did more than anyone else to found the A.U.T. but to hold it together and guide its development for no less than thirty-four years, was its first President, Professor R. Douglas Laurie, who in 1920 stepped down from the Presidency to become, until his death in 1953, its lynch-pin as Honorary General Secretary. He was described, quite accurately, by one of the early Presidents, as 'the life and soul of the movement'.[2] For two-thirds of its history the A.U.T. administratively was a one-man concern. It was run from a room in his private house in Aberystwyth, where he transferred from Liverpool in 1920 as senior lecturer and head of department and soon as Professor of Zoology. At first he did not even have any full-time secretarial help, but in 1921 the Association allowed him to engage a personal secretary. This was Miss D. K. Davies, who until after the Second World War was the only full-time paid employee of the A.U.T., finally retiring as Chief Assistant Secretary only in 1963. She too possessed, inspired by Laurie, the dedication of the true amateur. On the eve of his death in 1953 Laurie wrote of her in the context of the devoted contributions of other leading members:

I have had previous occasion in these records to say that I found it difficult to speak too highly of the services rendered to it by certain

1 *Laurie*, p. 7, and obituaries in *Universities Review*, 1952-58.
2 Professor J. W. McBain, 'Presidential Address', *University Bulletin*, November 1922, p. 3.

of its members; in speaking of Miss Davies I find it verging on the impossible to adequately record my appreciation. Her untiring loyalty and the much more than conscientious fulfilment of the many duties which have devolved upon her have always commanded my admiration and gratitude.[1]

It is not too much to say that from its foundation until 1953, if not until 1958 when the first professional Executive (now the General) Secretary was appointed, Professor Laurie and Miss Davies between them, as far as its central headquarters organization was concerned, *were* the A.U.T.

For the rest the central organization meant the Executive Committee of fourteen (from 1923–24 sixteen) members elected by the Central Council and reporting back to it at its twice-yearly meetings, as they became after the first few hectic years, generally in May or June and November or December. The Executive, as it was usually called for short, was, and is, the 'cabinet' of the system of government, and its members, especially those key members who were Conveners (combined chairmen and secretaries) of the leading Sub-committees, were in effect departmental ministers, responsible through the Executive to the 'parliament', the biannual Council. In view of the division between professors and non-professors which played so large a part in the foundation of the Association, and of the latter's primary objective of unifying the profession – 'A great beginning has been made,' declared its third President in 1922. 'It is painful to recall the disunion of a few years ago, – the deep gulf between lecturers and professors is now obliterated in most institutions'[2] – it is interesting to see in what proportions the two sections were represented on the Executive. Although professors were less than a third (31.4 per cent) of the profession at the beginning of the inter-war years and less than a fifth (19.6 per cent) at the end, and declined from about a quarter of the membership of the A.U.T. in the 1920's to about a fifth in the 1930's, they formed a majority of the Executive throughout the period, with the exception of the single year 1922–23. The majority was never large, averaging approximately 9 to 7, and was partly due to a strong tendency to elect professorial Officers, who outnumbered the non-professorial ones on average by slightly more

1 *Laurie*, p. 49.
2 McBain, *loc. cit.*, p. 3.

than 4 to 3, while there were fifteen professorial Presidents to only five non-professorial ones.[1] There was also a tendency for the Conveners of the leading Sub-committees to be professors: of the first twelve internal Sub-committees formed, seven were headed by professors.[2] None of this was surprising or divisive, however, but merely the natural tendency for the older and more prestigious members of the profession to be chosen to speak for it to the outside world, and particularly to the vice-chancellors and governing bodies of universities and to the U.G.C., the M.P.s and members of the Government with whom it was desirable and necessary for the Association to have dealings.

For the A.U.T. was nakedly and unashamedly a pressure group, seeking to influence public opinion and, either through it or by more direct means, the Government and the universities, in the interest of its members. In this it differed scarcely at all, except in the lateness of its birth, from such successful professional organizations as the British Medical Association or the National Union of Teachers noticed in the last chapter. Its methods were the same as theirs: to keep itself fully informed on every topic and issue which affected the interests of the profession and the well-being of its members, to arrive by study and discussion at a considered view or policy on each of these, to publicize the policy by all available means, and to bring its influence to bear by representation and discussion on those who made the operative decisions on them in the university institutions, the University Grants Committee and Government Departments. In this dual process of public education and pressure behind the scenes the role of the Conveners and their Sub-committees was crucial. As Professor J. W. McBain of Bristol, one of the early Presidents, clearly foresaw, in addition to 'economic questions' (salaries, superannuation, grants for buildings, and so on)

The Universities are faced with all sorts of problems ranging from entrance requirements to standards of post graduate degrees and facilities for advanced study and research . . . We envisage a long programme of these major problems on which a considered judgment is necessary . . . Briefly our proposed method of dealing with each of these subjects is to appoint a small representative committee to collect

1 Council Minutes, 15 December 1939.
2 *University Bulletin*, November 1922, pp. 15–18.

information and prepare an agendum or provisional report which will be sent to each of the local associations, but finally it will come to the Central Council to be hammered into shape, and then placed on record as our opinion for the benefit of the public both within and without the Universities ... We are endeavouring to make our Sub-committees as strong as possible by securing the co-operation of those of our members who can advise with authority, and, further, by enlisting distinguished representatives from Universities outside our membership, in Oxford, Cambridge, and Scotland. Among those who have already been invited in this way I may mention the names of Sir Charles Sherrington, Sir Ernest Rutherford, Principal Irvine, Professor Firth, Professor Myres, and Professor Stanley Gardiner. These reports and discussions should provide ample material not only to bring us all together, but also to provide results which will be fruitful in the advancement of University education and research.[1]

Of these Sub-Committees, the most important, then as now, were those dealing with 'economic questions' – the Salaries, Grading, and Superannuation Sub-committees; with conditions of service and working facilities – the Sub-committees, under various names, on tenure and conditions of service, on Facilities for Advanced Study and Research, on Libraries and Library Co-operation, and with the Representation of Members of Teaching Staffs on University Bodies (later broadened to include the whole of University Government); with publicity in various forms – the important Parliamentary and Parliamentary Representation Sub-committees of the 1920's, the Editorial Sub-committee responsible for the Association's journal, *The University Bulletin* launched in 1921 and renamed in 1928 *The Universities Review*, as well as *ad hoc* Sub-committees from time to time mounting or co-operating with special campaigns for the support of higher education; and with more purely educational matters, such as the important Sub-committee on Student Affairs (later the Sub-committee on Student Welfare and Maintenance) and various Sub-committees on University Entrance Requirements, Initial Degrees, Post-graduate Degrees, Student Awards and Grants of various kinds, and so on. There were also hard-working Sub-committees on Income Tax matters, which struggled for years to persuade the Inland Revenue that university teachers need to spend money on books, learned journals, travel for research purposes, and the maintenance of a

1 McBain, *loc. cit.*, p. 5.

study at home, and on Concessions, which negotiated discounts for members on a whole range of goods and services from insurance to Boots' Booklovers' Library. Most of the above were standing committees, and in addition the Executive appointed as and when they were needed *ad hoc* Sub-committees on a very wide range of subjects, from Family Allowances to Academic Hospitality (for refugees from Hitler's Europe) and Action in a National Emergency (to make plans for keeping the universities running and to contribute to the national effort in time of war).

In addition to all these internal or exclusively academic professional Sub-committees, albeit with non-A.U.T. members, the Association also consciously sought to appoint a whole range of joint committees with other bodies and organizations sharing a common interest. Foremost amongst these was the series of joint committees with the representatives of the vice-chancellors and university governing bodies appointed to organize the joint conferences and deputations to members of the Government, especially the Chancellor of the Exchequer and the Prime Minister, which were one of the most important activities of the Association's early years, as we shall see. Then there were the joint committees with parallel or overlapping professional bodies, which had a direct or indirect interest in university salaries and conditions of service, such as the Joint Committee with the British Medical Association on the salaries of university teachers of medicine, that with the National Union of Scientific Workers which both overlapped in membership and was concerned with the University technicians vital to the operation of laboratory subjects, or those with the various school teachers' organizations which had common interests in educational matters and in such material concerns as the interchangeability of superannuation schemes. Thirdly, there was from the earliest days a Joint Committee with their 'junior colleagues' of the National Union of Students, ranging over the whole of student affairs from grants to residential and recreational facilities. Finally, there were increasing contacts with Colonial, Dominion and foreign university teachers which developed via Joint Committees to organize conferences and exchange visits into a full-blown, if rather loose, international association, as we shall see.

These methods, of preparation and study by Sub-committees

and Joint Committees with other bodies, of discussion by the Local Associations followed by the determination of policy by the Central Council, and of publicity and parliamentary and other pressure by the Officers and the Executive, are the same as have been used ever since. Only once did the Association go beyond the methods of the pressure group, and try the more direct means of getting its own independent representation in Parliament, as distinct from having friends there in the orthodox political parties. This was in the General Election of 1922, when the President, Professor John Strong of Leeds, stood as an Independent candidate for the two-member Combined Universities constituency. He came third, polling 819 votes against 1,093 for Sir Martin Conway, Coalition Unionist, and 1,008 for H. A. L. Fisher, Coalition Liberal.[1] After that, although the A.U.T. has had many friends on both sides of both Houses, it gave up the forlorn attempt to be a political party and was content to be what it was, a professional pressure group.

2. THE PROBLEMS TO BE FACED

This then was the carefully planned and efficient but essentially amateur apparatus with which the infant A.U.T. faced the manifold and difficult problem of the inter-war years. Those problems were formidable indeed, and exacerbated by contrary pressure not only from the outside world of popular opinion and government finance (or, rather, lack of finance) but also from within the universities themselves, in the shape of contradictory and incompatible views of what universities were and what they were for. Together these contrary pressures set up a kind of organizational neurosis in the academic world, which makes the history of the profession between the Wars, like that of the country and indeed of the world, a history of paradox and uncertainty, of opportunity and frustration.

Externally, from the great world of society and the State which in the final analysis called the universities into existence and supplied their *raison d'être* and their means of life, there was, on the one side, an enormous pressure for expansion, not so much in numbers of students – although contemporaries found even here an 'astonishing' growth – as in the range of subjects and

1 *Laurie*, pp. 53-4; Council Minutes, 25 November 1921 and 4 March 1922.

ever more varied services to society which they were expected to provide. This expansion continually impressed the University Grants Committee. In its 1936 Report, for example, it remarked:

Paradoxically enough, the difficulties and deficiencies, such as they are, of the Universities in the past have been due largely to their own success and to the sensational and unforeseen rapidity of their expansion. Thus, between the beginning of the century and the War, . . . there was a great increase in numbers; and since the War there has been renewed tumultuous growth, together with a multiplication of new subjects of study and a sub-division of old subjects, presenting a bewildering variety of problems. In such conditions the University authorities were of necessity occupied breathlessly in a day-to-day endeavour to meet each new need as it arose. Large-scale and long-term planning were virtually impossible. Now, however, there is something of a lull . . .[1]

The 'great increase in numbers' before the War was from 20,249 students in 1900–01 to 27,728 in 1910–11, a percentage increase in fact considerably larger than in either of the inter-war decades. The 'rush of war students' remarked by an earlier Report contributed to the post-war peak of 48,452 students of 1920–21, which declined to 42,892 in 1923–24, and then rose to 47,826 in 1930–31 and 50,638 in 1934–35, where it levelled off, remaining at 50,246 in 1938–39. Moreover, in spite of the self-conscious emphasis of the period on sex equality most of the inter-war increase was amongst men students; the numbers of women, having doubled since before the War to 11,453 in 1920–1921 and rising to 13,072 in 1930–31, fell back again to 11,689 in 1938–39.[2] In general, student numbers were from 60 to 80 per cent greater than they had been before the First World War, but the 'tumultuous growth' of the inter-war period itself was at best (from the post-war trough of 1923–24) only a little over 25 per cent, and at worst (from the temporary post-war peak of 1920–21) barely 4 per cent. Given the falling birth-rate of the twentieth century, however, and the economic crises of the inter-war period, this higher and still rising level of student numbers was a source of problems and difficulties for the Universities and their staff.

On top of the expansion in numbers was a very real proliferation of the subjects taught in and the services rendered by the

1 U.G.C., *Report for period 1929–30 to 1934–35* (1936), p. 11.
2 *Ibid.*, pp. 52–3; *University Development, 1935–47*, p. 103.

universities. Under the combined pressures of the internal logic of learning and the sciences and the external demand for new courses of training, particularly vocational training for new and fissiparous professions, the range of subjects taught and studied continuously widened, as the U.G.C. constantly remarked, for example in its 1925 Report:

As the bounds of knowledge have extended, the Universities have been steadily improving and expanding their courses in all Faculties, and every year has seen the institution of a few new professorships, readerships and lectureships to meet the growing needs of the various departments. It may give some idea of the variety of these needs if we mention that, to take only two institutions, recent additions to the staff range from Professorships of Logic and Scientific Method and of the Tropical Diseases of Africa, to Lectureships in Comparative Philology and in Reinforced Concrete Construction.[1]

In a world increasingly specialized and professional the universities were increasingly looked to to supply professional experts, from the ever-widening varieties of engineers, chemists and physicists to the social workers and administrators required for the rapidly expanding Welfare State which grew up between the National Insurance Act of 1911 and the Beveridge Report on Social Insurance of 1942.

At the same time the universities were increasingly expected to provide a growing variety of services both for their students and for the public at large. The U.G.C. in its Reports constantly badgered them to provide for their students more and better tutorial care, both academic tuition in smaller groups and 'pastoral' or moral guidance, larger and improved union, common room and refectory accommodation and sporting and recreational facilities, health centres and/or medical treatment schemes, halls of residence, and appointments boards or careers advisory services.[2] It equally encouraged them to extend their blessings to the general public in the form of adult education lectures and classes, summer schools and the like, both independently and in co-operation with the Workers' Educational Association and the Local Education Authorities, and by means of their museums, exhibitions and public lectures.[3] Other Government organs

1 *Report . . . 1929–30 to 1934–35*, p. 4.
2 *Report . . . 1923–24*, pp. 24–6; *Report . . . 1929–30 to 1934–35*, pp. 14–33.
3 *Report . . . 1923–24*, pp. 27–8; *Report . . . 1929–30 to 1934–35*, pp. 47–8.

besides the U.G.C. looked to them to carry out research projects in the national interest and provided the necessary funds, notably the Medical Research Council (founded in 1911), the Department of Scientific and Industrial Research (founded in 1915), and the Ministry of Agriculture which since before the War had been financing agricultural research institutes and farm advisory services based in the universities, a function partly taken over by the Agricultural Research Council in 1931.[1] In addition, increasing numbers of business firms and of the new research associations which were coming into existence in various industries were anxious to get research work done for them in the universities and were offering research contracts and consultancies for that purpose.[2] Not that these multiple demands on their services were unwelcome to the universities and their staffs. Far from it: they were only too glad to extend their activities in any interesting and intellectually profitable direction, provided only that the money was available to support them.

There, however, was the rub. For the Government and the public which demanded so much and increasingly more from the universities was less than willing to pay adequately for it. On the other side from the constant public pressure for expansion there was, paradoxically, an equally constant public pressure for retrenchment. Whatever the universities did by way of development and service was too little, whatever they asked for by way of financial support was too much. There was in the public and still more in the politicians of that epoch an extraordinary detachment in dealing with the universities. The notion of university independence was raised to such a stratospheric abstraction that, while the universities were lauded for their 'national usefulness' as an integral and essential part of the education system, they were treated as autonomous entities, which ought, with a little charitable aid from the State, endeavour like the medieval monarchy to 'live of their own'. From this point of view expansion, especially in new directions, was a species of self-indulgence to be puritanically deprecated. This attitude is

1 Berdahl, *op. cit.*, pp. 55–6, 62.
2 Cf. V. E. Cosslett, *The Relations between Scientific Research in the Universities and Industrial Research in Great Britain* (published by I.A.U.P.L. with the assistance of U.N.E.S.C.O., London, 1955), Appendix II, list of Research Associations set up by Industry with the aid of the D.S.I.R. up to 1951.

epitomized in the reply of the Chancellor of the Exchequer, Austen Chamberlain, to a deputation of representatives from the universities, including the A.U.T., in 1920:

The Universities have extended beyond their means. They have been more anxious to extend than to pay their existing staffs properly; and, accordingly, the salaries are much too low. My opinion is, you ought not to extend into new fields until you have been able to pay decently, I do not say extravagantly or richly, because I think it will never be a well-paid profession; but until you have been able to pay adequately the staffs which you already employ, you ought not to seek to extend.[1]

Not a word about providing the money, either for adequate salaries or expansion, nor even for pensions comparable with those of school teachers for which the deputation asked and was refused! It was as if the universities were spendthrift poor relations living beyond their means an utterly irrelevant and useless life and needing to be hectored into paths of self-respect and rectitude again.

The same tone can be found in many of the politicians and public figures of the period, including some in the universities themselves. Behind it lay something more sinister, partly fear, reminiscent of the early nineteenth-century fear of elementary education for the poor, of over-educating the nation, or of educating too large a proportion of its children for the socially tragic and politically dangerous consequence of high graduate unemployment – a consequence which proved to be disastrous in contemporary Germany; and partly a pervasive anti-intellectualism which threw doubt on the whole value of university education and research, and caused the Bishop of Ripon to suggest to the British Association in 1931 that science should 'take a ten years' holiday', and Aldous Huxley in *Point Counter Point* to mock at the intellectual's life as 'child's play; which is why intellectuals tend to become children – and then imbeciles and finally, as the political and industrial history of the last few centuries clearly demonstrates, homicidal lunatics and wild beasts.'[2] Such attitudes even pervaded the universities and their

---

1 *Deputation to the Rt. Hon. Austen Chamberlain* (*Chancellor of the Exchequer*). *of Representatives of the University Colleges of England and Wales on Superannuation for University Teachers, 17 June 1920* (printed transcript from shorthand notes of Harry Counsell and Co.), p. 7.

2 Quoted Armytage, *Civic Universities*, pp. 262, 266 (and cf. chap. xii for this whole discussion).

leading members and freshest products. Sir Ernest Barker, then Principal of King's College, London, warned in 1927:

There is a danger in modern times of what might be called the clericalisation of society. The general spread of education, if it works by books and directs itself only to intelligence, readily produces a great supply of would-be clerical workers, which pours a flood towards every grade of clerical service. The channels are not adequate for its flow; the discontented product of a clerkly system may become a revolutionary force.[1]

And H. G. G. Herklots, himself a fresh product of the system, argued in 1928:

This should be a period of retrenchment and reform: it should not be a period of further expansion. One cannot but deprecate the attempts that are being made to found universities up and down the country . . . if matters continue as they are at present we are promised a spate of new universities. These will either lower the standard of education in the universities that are already in being, and widen further the breach that exists between the old and the new, or else they will form a new and surely unnecessary type, perhaps most like the American small town college.[2]

'More means worse' has a much longer pedigree than Kingsley Amis.

As to the first fear, of graduate unemployment, Britain suffered much less from this between the Wars than most other advanced countries. As the U.G.C. put it in 1936,

For a variety of reasons not all countries have been able to ride the economic storm since the War as successfully as our own, with the result that the University student abroad has experienced hardship in the way of unemployment on a scale to which there has been no parallel here.[3]

As to the second, the fear of elephantiasis of the intellect and the evil consequences of scientific research, this is a matter of opinion and temperament. Whether economic development and the rise

1 E. Barker, *National Character and the Factors in its Formation* (1927), p. 244.
2 H. G. G. Herklots, *The New Universities: an External Examination* (1928), pp. 87–8.
3 *Report . . . 1929–30 to 1934–35*, p. 29.

of living standards are seen as the onrush of philistine materialism or as the liberation of the human being for cultivated leisure,
whether science is seen as producing the benefits of atomic
energy or the universal destruction of the nuclear holocaust, the
golden reign of the elders in *Back to Methuselah* or the sybaritic
idiocies of *Brave New World,* lies in the optimistic or pessimistic
eye of the observer. Yet in a sense the question is irrelevant:
the country – the advanced country that is, already dependent on
applied intelligence for its living and its survival – which opts
out of scientific, industrial and economic development opts out
also not only of power and influence in the world but of survival
itself, both as a political entity and as a civilized society. And since
trained intelligence comes to depend more and more on the
universities, or whatever institutions of higher education stand in
their place, the nation which neglects them strangles its own
future.

The contradictory pressure for expansion and retrenchment,
for universities as the growth points of a new, professionally
scientific and technological world or as communal ivory towers of
an élite culture, divided university teachers themselves. One
section followed Julien Benda (translated in 1928) in attacking
the *Trahison des Clercs* by abandoning the search for abstract
truth in favour of the utilitarian pursuit of material gain, and the
American Abraham Flexner who lectured at Oxford (least guilty
of the sin) in 1928 on the myopia and absurdity of teaching any
technology, from brewing or automobile engineering to social
work or domestic science, in a university.[1] Sir Charles Grant
Robertson, Principal of Birmingham University and Chairman
of the Committee of Vice-Chancellors, warned against producing
'a highly competent mediocrity' and urged the universities to
'narrow the gates of entry'.[2] Members of the A.U.T. like
Professor R. C. McLean of Cardiff declared in *The Universities
Review*:

Go on as we are going, and we shall sink under sheer weight of the
mediocrities who have diluted and deteriorated the universities they
have so copiously invaded;

1 J. Benda, *La Trahison des Clercs* (trans. as *The Great Betrayal* by R. Alding-
ton, 1928); A. Flexner, *Universities, American, English, German* (1930), pp.
255–6.
2 Sir Charles Grant Robertson, *The British Universities* (1930), p. 75.

and his colleague Professor Mansell Jones, that 'Where the Modern Universities are wrong' was that they had become machines 'devised to produce graduates furnished with qualifications which will help them earn a livelihood'.[1] These comments all belonged to an ancient view of the universities as communities of learning placed apart from and above the everyday world of the factory and the market-place for the sole purpose of pursuing truth and preserving the high culture of society, a view epitomized by F. R. Leavis in his *Education and the University*:

> The universities are recognized symbols of tradition ... of cultural tradition conceived as a directing force, representing a wisdom older than modern civilization and having an authority that should check and control the blind drive onward of material and mechanical development, with its human consequences.[2]

The competing sections of university teachers saw no such dangers in expansion and the teaching of vocational subjects and useful technologies. They too belonged to an ancient tradition, one even older than their rivals', since they claimed descent from the original medieval university with its vocational schools of theology, law and medicine. Less eloquent and more pragmatic than the guardians of unitary truth and culture, they concentrated on developing new institutions and new subjects wherever they felt they were needed. Such men founded the few new universities of the inter-war period, the University Colleges of Hull (1926), and Leicester (1927) and the only full University, Reading (raised from collegiate status in 1926), and the many technical colleges, evening institutes and day continuation schools which served British industry as American and Continental were served by their universities and technical high schools. Within the universities they also founded a vast range of new sciences and technologies, aeronautics at Cambridge, building construction at London and Manchester, fuel technology at Leeds, London, Sheffield and Nottingham, industrial relations at Cambridge and Leeds, naval architecture at Newcastle and Liverpool, oil technology at Birmingham and London, technical optics at Cambridge and London, and so on.[3] The

---

1 Quoted by Armytage, *op. cit.*, p. 11.
2 *Op. cit.*, (1943), pp. 15–16.
3 Cf. Armytage, *op. cit.*, p. 272.

irony of the contempt in which their 'materialism' was held is that without the contributions of these and similar technologies we should not have won the Second World War, and the guardians of truth and culture would have had nothing left to defend.

F. R. Leavis in a characteristic oversimplification saw these competing ideals as attaching themselves not merely to the arts (and more specifically the critical study of English literature) versus the sciences but even to Oxford and Cambridge versus the rest of the universities. He continued the above quotation:

The ancient universities . . . may fairly be called foci of such a [cultural directing] force, capable by reason of their prestige and their part in the life of the country of exercising an enormous influence.[1]

Now, although the A.U.T. was overwhelmingly representative of the civic universities – there was no Cambridge Local Association until 1935 and no Oxford one until 1939 – and although the Association continually stood for expansion of the universities in general and of science and technology in particular, it would be an equally gross oversimplification to equate the A.U.T. with one side in this controversy. For one thing, as we have seen, the controversy invaded the pages of the *Universities Review*, where members like Professors McLean and Mansell Jones took the anti-expansionist, anti-utilitarian side. For another, as we shall see later, a very large proportion of university teachers before 1945, and almost certainly a majority in the arts faculties of English and Welsh civic universities, were themselves trained at Oxford or Cambridge. Moreover, A.U.T. policy on university government was closer to the collegiate ideal of a community of scholars than to the civic tradition of a professorial-dominated hierarchy: from 1922 the Sub-committee on the Representation of Teaching Staffs on University Bodies never ceased to press for a share by non-professors as well as professors on Councils, Courts and Senates.

Nevertheless, there is a sense in which the A.U.T. stood more for the professional approach to university teaching and research as evolved by the Scottish and the new English civic universities of the nineteenth century, and less for the more leisurely ideal of the 'gentleman and scholar' (in that order) which still survived most typically at Oxford and Cambridge. Without the ample

1 *Op. cit.*, pp. 16, 17–18.

endowments of their Colleges, their complete academic autonomy and freedom from lay control, or the level of remuneration afforded by their dividends, the bulk of A.U.T. members at the civic universities were bound to spend much of their energy in seeking larger funds for salaries, buildings, libraries and research equipment from the State, and to justify their demands on the national purse by pointing to their usefulness to society. It was in the logic of their situation that their Association should devote a large part of its efforts to putting pressure on the Government and the universities to allocate more material resources to teaching and research.

It was also in the logic of their situation that it should fail, or rather that it should not succeed in gaining all its objectives. All pressure groups concerned with the allocation of scarce economic resources are bound to fall short of their objectives, since the allocation is bound to be a matter of compromise between incompatible claims, and even if one group's share should begin to approach its ideal it would either have to raise its sights or abandon its *raison d'être* and go out of existence. Hence frustration and a sense of at least partial failure are inevitable. To this 'pressure-group psychology' the A.U.T. was not immune, and has borne throughout its existence a characteristic conviction of frustration and failure, only slightly mollified from time to time by some partial and belated success. Whether that diffident conviction was justified the readers of this history will have to judge for themselves. The A.U.T. could at least claim what classical economists like McCulloch claimed for the early trade unions, that although they could not raise wages above the market rate they succeeded in raising them more rapidly than they would otherwise have done *to* the market rate. In other words, the A.U.T. helped to gain for its members and for the universities in general a larger and more promptly allocated share of national resources than they would otherwise have received.

A modern wage economist would, in fact, go further than this. Guy Routh in his *Occupation and Pay in Great Britain, 1906–60* has shown that the differential rise of unskilled over against skilled wages in the face of much higher unskilled unemployment, especially between the Wars, is the reverse of what demand-supply relations would suggest, and the same paradox applies to the narrowing differential between all the non-manual classes, except industrial managers, and manual workers. He hypothesises that the rigidities of the national pay structure, and the tendency to level up those at the bottom, are due not so much to market forces, except in so far as these express socio-psychological expectations, as to the intuitive conviction by occupational groups of what their level of remuneration should be in relation to that of other groups, and, by extension, to their success in convincing others, notably employers and the State, of what is an equitable rate for the job which they do.[1] This normative or sociological explanation of wage rates is supported by industrial psychologists like Elliott Jacques, economists like Lady Wootton, and sociologists like W. G. Runciman, whose *Relative Deprivation and Social Justice* bases the whole theory of relations between the social classes on the same principle.[2] Thus the task of any occupational interest group, a professional body or a trade union, is to 'educate' the rest of the public, their employers and, where relevant, the Government, to their own view of their rightful place in the hierarchy of incomes. Hence the continuous concern in pay claims with comparability with other occupations and grades, both to demand equal remuneration with those considered to be equivalent in status and value to the nation and to insist on specific differentials over those considered inferior.

In the case of the university teachers, as in that of any other profession supplying a State-aided service (as, for example, the doctors under the panel system of 1911 or the National Health Service since 1948), the task of the professional body becomes wider than the narrow question of remuneration. It becomes essential, whether from the 'altruistic' point of view of the good of the service or from the 'self-interested' point of view that a highly valued service will provide better rates of pay, to educate the public and the Government in the value of the service to society and the nation. Even if the A.U.T. had not had the value of higher education at heart it would have been politic for it to act as if it had. In fact, the vast majority of the members, like the vast majority of university teachers, whether they subscribed to the utilitarian or cultural traditions of the university's purpose,

1 *Op. cit.*, (Cambridge, 1965), pp. 14–54.
2 Elliott Jacques, *The Measurement of Responsibility* (1956); Barbara Wootton, *The Social Foundation of Wages Policy* (1954), esp. p. 162; Runciman, *op. cit.* (1967).

sincerely believed that the universities were vital to the well-being if not indeed to the survival of the nation and its civilization. They could without hypocrisy uphold the objects of the Association, which placed 'the advancement of University Education and Research' before 'the safeguarding of the interests of the members'. As Laurie put it at the foundation meeting in 1919,

the idea which had brought the Association into being was of a trade union character, but he expressed a hope that, when material conditions had been satisfactorily improved, educational matters generally would form the essential pointer on which discussion would take place, and he expressed further his conviction that the Association would become a factor of real importance in helping to determine educational policy.[1]

Yet, since academic salaries were much the largest item of university expenditure, and since, as the University Grants Committee put it in 1922, 'The best men and women will neither enter nor continue in the profession at the rates of salaries at present within the competence of the Authorities to offer, nor can a teacher under the perpetual shadow of financial anxieties give his best to the work of instruction and research,'[2] it was inevitable that the Association should give priority to the improvement of salaries and to the increased Government grants which alone could make this possible. Laurie's first recruiting letter to university teachers stated plainly:

The aim of the Association is twofold, educational and economic. Those who have been promoting its formation consider both functions as of fundamental importance. It is the economic factor which has brought the Association into existence . . .[3]

3. 'THE ECONOMIC FACTOR'

How and with what success did the A.U.T. set about the delicate task of educating the public and the Government to the values of higher education, and of university teachers' services, in the

1 Council Minutes, 27 and 28 June 1919.
2 U.G.C., *Report . . . 1919–22* (1922).
3 Circular letter, Laurie to university teachers, 22 October 1919.

climate of contradictory and even paradoxical pressures described above? The first and most obvious step was to win the
confidence and support of the vice-chancellors and governing
bodies of the universities so as to present a united front to the
public and the Government. This was not always easy, for it was
in the nature of things that, since the authorities in the civic
universities were both fellow workers and employers of the
teaching staff, there should always be an ambivalence in their
dealings with each other, a love-hate relationship akin to certain
sorts of marriage, in which mutual affection and suspicion were
equally mingled, and co-operative zeal blew now hot, now cold,
according to the climate of internal opinion and the hostility of
the world outside. When the issues agitating university teachers
were internal ones, concerning university government or the
autonomy of vice-chancellors and university Councils, relations
grew cold and strained; when they were external ones, concerning
academic freedom or the provision of public finance, they grew
warm and friendly. Fortunately for both sides, they never came
anywhere near approaching marital breakdown; family quarrels,
yes, but divorce or separation, no, since the latter would have
been suicidal.

In the early years the A.U.T.'s relations with the universities
were exceptionally good, since the crisis which brought it to
birth was a shortage of finance which both the Association and
the universities knew could only be supplied by the Government.
The first act of the fully constituted A.U.T. was to take over the
programme of activities of the Lecturers' Conferences, including
the joint deputations with the university authorities to the
Chancellor of the Exchequer and the President of the Board of
Education on salaries and superannuation. The way had been
paved for the first of these, on superannuation, by the Joint
Conference of University Lecturers and Professorial and Administrative Staffs of the Universities at Sheffield on 11 April 1919,
which we noted in the last chapter. The deputation was eventually
arranged for 17 June 1920, when twenty-two vice-chancellors or
other representatives of the universities and five representatives
of the A.U.T. were introduced by Sir Philip Magnus, M.P., to
the Chancellor of the Exchequer, Austen Chamberlain, and the
President of the Board of Education, H. A. L. Fisher, to put
their case for extending the Teachers' Superannuation Act, 1918,

to the universities. They were met by what can only be described as an arrogant and ill-tempered rebuff by Chamberlain, who continually interrupted the delegates with remarks such as 'The whole grievance is, that somebody else has had more cake than you', and ended by accusing the deputation of ingratitude:

> in fact, it is worse than ungrateful, it is unwise – to come to the Government at a time of great financial strain and difficulty, when you cannot open a paper without seeing the Government in general, and the Minister you are addressing in particular, ... denounced for his improvident handling of national finance, and ask for more money without any limit, without saying one word until the last speaker [Sir Michael Sadler, Vice-Chancellor of Leeds] of recognition of anything the Government has done.

He pointed out that he had raised the Treasury grant to the universities from under £500,000 to over £1,000,000 a year, warned that further dependence on State aid might entail a loss of university autonomy, and wound up by suggesting that they should find more money from their own resources, in particular by raising students' fees.[1] The deputation came away empty-handed, though the Government later made a grant of £500,000 to supplement the pensions of older university teachers whose service under the F.S.S.U. scheme of 1914 was necessarily short; and funds were made available to raise the universities' contribution to F.S.S.U. from 5 to 10 per cent of salary (the member's remaining at 5 per cent), where it remained down to and beyond the Report of the Maddex Committee in 1967.

On the second issue, that of salaries, the newly-constituted A.U.T. invited the heads of all university institutions together with a lay member of each governing body to a Conference at Bedford College, London. This met on 18 June 1920, the day after the deputation to the Treasury on superannuation, the overtones of which dominated the proceedings and helped, in spite of the inevitable differences of attitude between employers and employed, to produce a sense of unity in adversity. In preparation the A.U.T. had produced a Report on Salaries (the second of the series of surveys if we count that of the Association of Lecturers in 1918), which showed that the median salary of professors was £800 as against the A.U.T.'s proposed minimum

---

1 *Deputation ... 17 June 1920.*

of £1,100, that of assistant professors, readers and lecturers of £366, as against A.U.T. scales of £400 to £650 for Grade II and £650 to £900 for Grade I, and that of assistant lecturers £250 as against an A.U.T. scale of £300 to £400.[1] Laurie was voted into the chair on the nomination of Dr. Russell Wells, Vice-Chancellor of London University, and read a resolution passed unanimously that morning by the A.U.T. Council:

That the Council of the Association of University Teachers, realizing the critical situation of the Universities, and having deeply at heart the best interests and prosperity of the Universities, are anxious to co-operate to the utmost of their power with the Administrative University bodies in any steps that can be taken to improve the situation.

In the course of the proceedings the Vice-Chancellor of London stressed the harmony of interests between the A.U.T. and the university authorities:

I cannot help feeling that this move of yours, in asking those who are in official positions in the University, the Vice-Chancellors and the like, is a very wise one. In all vocations it is necessary that some should occupy the position of employed, and some the position of employer, and right through the country one of the great difficulties at the present time is getting those two classes together to see one another's point of view. Now in University circles there is no social distinction between the two classes, ... consequently we are very much more in accord and far better able to meet round a table, and to take a point of view, than in other labour movements ... We are ... so identically the same as to social class, so nearly identical in regard to our previous training, and with regard to courses we have been through, that I cannot help thinking that the Universities may show the way of meeting difficulties about salaries by Conferences like these, to other branches of human activity.[2]

Employers and employed managed to disagree considerably, nevertheless, about both the substance and the feasibility in the current financial stringency of the A.U.T.'s scales. Some vice-chancellors thought the minima much too high, others were particularly hostile to any increments in the probationary grade of assistant lecturer, while all firmly believed after the previous

1 *Report on Salaries*, 1919 (duplicated).
2 A.U.T., *Proceedings of a Conference on Salaries, between the Council of the A.U.T., Heads of University Institutions, Non-academic Members of University Governing Bodies at Bedford College, London, 18 June 1920*.

day's experience at the Treasury – in spite of a colourful intervention from Alderman Thomas Burt representing the Council of Bristol University, 'an old agitator', ex-President of the T.U.C. and one of the first two working-class M.P.s, to urge the A.U.T. not to lower their standard but to 'ask for more than you want' – that there was no immediate prospect of wringing a further penny out of the Exchequer. The Conference therefore seized eagerly on the Chancellor's suggestion about raising students' fees, and Professor Tout of Manchester moved a resolution that fees should be raised all round by 25 per cent. At this point the natural caution of vice-chancellors took over, various objections were made, especially from Birmingham where fees were already thought too high and from Wales where fees had been pegged in exchange for a grant of a penny rate, amounting to £50,000 a year, from the Local Authorities, and the insuperable argument was raised that, since the Conference was not empowered to pass any resolutions without a mandate from the governing bodies, such a course of action would require a further conference.[1]

In fact, a series of three Joint Conferences followed, under the chairmanship of Sir Michael Sadler, the well-known pioneer of educational enquiries and reports for the Education Department and Board of Education, now Vice-Chancellor of Leeds, who proved a good friend to the A.U.T. until his retirement as Master of University College, Oxford, in 1934. At the first of these, on 17 February 1921, a Committee of both university administrators and A.U.T. Executive members was set up, under Sadler's chairmanship, to draw up a Memorandum on Salaries, which was discussed at the second, on 4 July, and, after ratification by the governing bodies, approved at the third, on 26 November 1921.[2] The scale of minimum salaries and the system of grading proposed, known as the 'agreed scheme', became the basis for the A.U.T.'s policy, publicity and pressure on the question of pay throughout the inter-war period. It differed from the A.U.T.'s 1920 proposals only marginally, except at the top, where the

1 *Ibid.*
2 A.U.T., *Memorandum on the Salaries of Full-time University Teachers in England and Wales, approved by the Conference of Heads of University Institutions, Non-academic Members of University Governing Bodies, and the Council of the A.U.T. at Bedford College, London, on 4 July 1921 and ratified at a further similarly composed Conference at Bedford College, London, on 26 November 1921.*

minimum demanded for professors was '£900 or £1000', the other differences being a flat rate for Grade III (assistant lecturers on probation) in the first two years (of £300 instead of £300 and £350) and £350 in the third year instead of £400; and a slightly higher starting point for Grade I (senior non-professorial posts) of £700 (to £900) instead of £650. The Committee estimated that to put the scheme into operation for the 1,875 teachers at the thirteen universities and university colleges in England and Wales (including London and Wales as single institutions and excluding Oxford and Cambridge) would cost £375,424 a year if the minimum for professors were £1,000, and £338,952 if it were set at £900.

Far from providing the additional money, the Government took away part of what it had already promised. For this was the period of the first post-war economic crisis and the notorious 'Geddes axe', when cuts were made in all public expenditure, including a 20 per cent cut in the U.G.C. (recurrent and non-recurrent) grant of £1,500,000. Two days before the Joint Conference which approved the 'agreed scheme', the A.U.T. Council, noting that 'owing to the large demands made upon them by all classes of society the Universities were at the present time in a state of financial embarrassment unequalled in their history', unanimously passed the following resolution:

This Council of the A.U.T. has heard with dismay the proposal of the Lords Commissioners of the Treasury to reduce the annual grant-in-aid of University education by £300,000, and protests against the proposal on the ground that it will seriously impair their efficiency, and in consequence retard their development in the future, to the great loss of the nation.[1]

The Association drew up a Memorial against the cut, addressed to the Prime Minister, the Chancellor of the Exchequer, the President of the Board of Education, and the rest of the Cabinet, and collected 400 signatures supporting it from the governing bodies of the universities. A letter was also sent to every M.P., and the Parliamentary Committee, convened by the President, Professor John Strong of Leeds, spent some considerable time in the smoke-room of the House of Commons lobbying the politicians.

1 Council Minutes, 25 November 1921.

It was all in vain. The cut was made, and it was not until 1924 that it became politically opportune to get it restored. In the spring of that year the Standing Committee of Vice-Chancellors and Principals seized the opportunity of a change in Government to press for a deputation to the Prime Minister and the Chancellor of the Exchequer, now Ramsay MacDonald and Philip Snowden. Sir Michael Sadler, now Master of University College, Oxford, and no longer a member of the Vice-Chancellors' Committee, wrote to them reminding them of the 1921 Joint Conferences and suggesting a joint deputation with the A.U.T. By now, however, relations had cooled since, for one thing, the A.U.T. had been pressing some of the more backward institutions to use what funds they had to bring salaries up to the general, if still inadequate, level and to establish a separate salaries fund for the purpose, and the request was rejected. Sir Michael, accompanied by Laurie, Strong and McBain for the A.U.T., therefore descended on the Vice-Chancellors' Committee and threatened to mount a separate deputation under the mandate of the old Joint Conference, whereupon the Committee relented and invited the President and ex-President of the A.U.T., Professors Alexander Mair of Liverpool and F. C. Lea of Birmingham, to accompany them. The deputation was received on 27 November 1924 by the new Prime Minister and Chancellor, Stanley Baldwin and Winston Churchill, and the cut was restored in 1925. The A.U.T. immediately sent a letter to all university governing bodies, signed by the President, Professor Mair, Laurie as Honorary General Secretary, and the two distinguished Vice-Presidents, Professor Dame Helen Gwynne-Vaughan and Professor F. E. Weiss, F.R.S., pressing that the money should be used to improve salaries, especially at the senior non-professorial level where the need was greatest.[1]

That the universities should need this kind of pressure is a reminder that they were far more autonomous in salary matters then than now, and the rates they paid varied enormously from one institution to another. The Association spent a lot of effort in the 1920's and 1930's trying to persuade laggard universities to bring their salaries up to the general level. In this they found an ally in the University Grants Committee. The Vice-Chancellors' Committee always resisted any joint approach with the A.U.T.

1 *Ibid.*, 7 March, 3 July, 28 November 1924, 6 March 1925; *Laurie*, pp. 10-12.

to the U.G.C., jealously guarding their 'special relationship' with the fountain-head of Government funds. The Association, therefore, was forced to seek separate recognition, and was able to send deputations at quinquennial intervals in 1924, 1929, and 1934 to discuss such matters as salaries, cases of superannuation hardship, and conditions of service. At one institution on its quinquennial visitation of 1929 where no staff deputation had been arranged, the U.G.C. had asked to meet representatives of the Local A.U.T. In 1934 the U.G.C. consulted the A.U.T. on the questions of family allowances supplementary to salary and the ratio of Grade I to Grade II appointments.[1] Whether as a result of A.U.T. pressure or not, the U.G.C. continually lectured the universities in its reports on the virtue of paying the rate for the job, while delicately withdrawing from any notion of coercing them.

One of the A.U.T.'s techniques for dealing with the laggards was to publish the scales paid by individual universities and colleges, and this they did in a Report on Salaries in 1929. In one case, that of University College, London, the Secretary refused to supply the information, and the Report printed on an otherwise blank page, the following:

University College (University of London) The Secretary of the College writes: 'The documents relative to these matters are confidential, and have therefore not been communicated.' February 18th, 1929.[2]

The device had its effect, and no institution has ever since refused to supply information. The Report revealed that the grading system approved by the 1921 Joint Conferences had been generally adopted, but that 'In no Institution has it been found possible to pay the full salaries attaching to the several grades in the Agreed Scheme, although in some cases, for example, Imperial College, Birmingham and Bristol, a substantial degree of approximation thereto has been attained.' It was at this time that the U.G.C. in its Report for 1928–29 declared:

It is not perhaps to be expected that universities will find it possible at one stride to put salaries and libraries beyond the reach of criticism and complaint, but we shall be profoundly disappointed if, at the end of

1 Council Minutes, 28 November 1924, 31 May 1929, 30 June 1934.
2 *Report on Salaries and Grading*, February 1929, p. 18.

another quinquennium, we have once more to inform your Lordships that it is for expenditure upon these two items that additional income is in general most urgently required.[1]

It was at this time, too, that relations between the A.U.T. and the Vice-Chancellor's Committee reached their nadir for the inter-war period. The Association's continuous pressure on the universities to bring their salaries into line with the 'agreed scheme' of 1921, and its declared belief, expressed to the Government, that the universities had not carried out the recommendations of the U.G.C., did not endear it to the Vice-Chancellors' Committee. It was not surprising, therefore, that the chairman, Sir Charles Grant Robertson of Birmingham, should have refused the A.U.T.'s request to be represented on their deputation to the new Chancellor of the Exchequer, Philip Snowden, on 29 November 1929, and it required pressure via the Financial Secretary of the Treasury, Mr. Pethick-Lawrence, to get the President, Assistant Professor E. F. D. Witchell of Imperial College, invited to accompany them.[2]

After that relations improved again, partly as a result of renewed adversity. During the great slump, in 1932, the Government grant to universities was cut again, this time by £150,000 a year, but joint pressure was successful in getting it restored in 1933. The next time the Vice-Chancellors' Committee planned a deputation to the Treasury, in 1935, the Chairman, Dr. T. Loveday of Bristol, quite readily agreed to invite three A.U.T. representatives, Professors Laurie, Brodetsky (Convener of the Salaries and Grading Committee) and G. C. Field of Bristol (Senior Vice-President) to accompany them.[3] The way was thus prepared for a renewal of the joint conferences with which the inter-war period had started. Once again, in 1938, the Association produced a large Report on Salaries and Grading, and invited the heads of university institutions to a conference to discuss it. The Report, 70 pages long, analysed in great detail the distribution of salaries throughout the profession and in individual institutions, and compared them with salaries in the civil service, military colleges, State secondary schools, and public schools, and concluded that 'the general standard of university

1 *Report . . . 1928–29* (1930), p. 51.
2 *Laurie*, pp. 12–13.
3 Council Minutes, 26 May 1933, 13 December 1935.

salaries is definitely lower than what is considered suitable by the Government for similar services, or indeed for services to which the academic is certainly superior in qualifications and responsibility.'[1]

The Joint Conference met on 6 May 1939 under the shadow of the rape of Czechoslovakia and the gathering certainty of European war. The President of the A.U.T., in moving Dr. Loveday, Vice-Chancellor of Bristol, to the chair 'by acclamation', suggested that 'however difficult the times it was our duty as faithful servants of the community to maintain the efficiency of our university institutions, and to state as clearly as possible what was needed for their well-being'. Professor Brodetsky presented the Report on Salaries and suggested that in view of the forthcoming quinquennial visitations by the U.G.C. it would be useful to form a joint committee to provide a united basis for submissions and encourage action by the Government. Sir Ernest Simon, head of two Stockport engineering firms and lay Treasurer of Manchester University, resisting immediate detailed discussion of the Report, said, 'This is the first time that we Treasurers and Administrators have met together in the same room for twenty years, and it is the first time we have had an opportunity of discussing the broad principles of salaries.' He suggested that 'it was rather unfortunate that there was not some organized arrangement for meeting and exchanging experiences, apart from the Committee of Vice-Chancellors, whose primary function was academic rather than financial.' But he also expressed the view that this was the very worst time for discussing increased salaries, and suggested as an alternative family allowances for university teachers with children such as had long been operative at the London School of Economics and had been favoured by the A.U.T. Report produced at the suggestion of the U.G.C. in 1936. Sir Henry Tizard, Rector of Imperial College, and later renowned as a war-time scientific adviser to the Government, was also opposed to raising salaries, doubting whether in view of the already heavy expenditure per head on British students ($£150$ a year for each science student) the money would be forthcoming; objecting to comparisons with the civil service on the grounds that 'People in universities had a freedom which nobody in the technical or administrative

1 *Report on Salaries and Grading*, May 1938, p. 27.

branches of the Civil Service enjoyed, and university people could use this freedom to make additions to their salaries'; and opposing uniformity in scales of pay between institutions as impracticable. Other university representatives were doubtful about a separate salaries fund which would unnecessarily hamper a university's freedom of manœuvre, and Sir Robert Waley Cohen of University College, London, even opposed the limitation of Grade III to a probationary period, and saw no reason why teachers fit only for routine work should not remain there (at a level of salary lower than that of most school teachers!).

The A.U.T.'s spokesmen, notably Brodetsky and Professor E. R. Dodds of Oxford, were able to deal with most of these objections, controverting, for example, Tizard's misleading statement of university teachers' freedom to earn large outside incomes, which in few cases rose as high as an additional 10 per cent on their salaries, and won sufficient sympathy to gain not a joint committee but a promise to put the question on the next agenda of the Vice-Chancellors' Committee.[1]

The Conference was in effect a double one, and went on in the afternoon to discuss superannuation, and particularly an Actuarial Report on F.S.S.U. drawn up by the A.U.T.'s consultants, Bacon and Woodrow, which particularly recommended a breakdown pension for cases of total disability, representation for the A.U.T. on the Council of the F.S.S.U. (composed exclusively of representatives of the institutions), and negotiation with the insurance offices on the panel to gain better terms for the members. The discussion produced only flat opposition to all these, and was remarkable only for the extraordinary naive statement by the Chairman of the Finance Committee of Leeds University that 'no attempt should be made to negotiate with the offices, as the result could only be an increase in rates and a decrease in bonuses'![2]

In the event Dr. Loveday, the Chairman of the two Conferences, did lay the Report on Salaries and Grading before the Vice-Chancellors' Committee, which agreed to institute a comparison of the differing scales and the practices concerning

1 A.U.T., *Proceedings of a Conference of Representatives of University Institutions and of the A.U.T. on Salaries and Grading of University Teachers, 6 May 1939.*
2 A.U.T., *Proceedings of a Conference . . . on F.S.S.U., 6 May 1939.*

grading and promotion in the universities and colleges.[1] About two months later, however, the country was at war, and the matter, apart from the payment of war bonuses, was shelved for the duration.

The question naturally arises, what had the A.U.T. gained, in material benefits, from twenty years of pressure and agitation? At first sight, not a great deal. The Treasury grant to universities had increased, slowly but fairly steadily, as shown in Table 1.

TABLE I

Recurrent and Non-recurrent Treasury Grants, 1919–39

R = Recurrent   NR = Non Recurrent £000

	R	NR		R	NR
1919–20	692	372	1929–30	1550	99
1920–21	798	252	1930–31	1798	–
1921–22	1085	273	1931–32	1828	–
1922–23	1153	45	1932–33	1828	–
1923–24	1208	19	1933–34	1828	–
1924–25	1238	79	1934–35	1828	–
1925–26	1513	–	1935–36	1828	–
1926–27	1517	103	1936–37	2035	35
1927–28	1523	55	1937–38	2035	29
1928–29	1535	0·5	1938–39	2078	125

Source : U.G.C., *University Development, 1957–62* (1964), p. 183 (the cuts of £300,000 in 1923 and £150,000 in 1932 are partly concealed by the accounting procedure of spreadover of grants from year to year).

These grants, however, had to cover an increasing number of institutions – Oxford and Cambridge were added to the list in 1922–23 – and still more an increasing number of students, from 36,709 (excluding Oxford and Cambridge) in 1920–21 and 42,892 (including Oxford and Cambridge) in 1923–24 to over 50,000 from 1933–34 onwards. As a percentage of university income, therefore, the recurrent grant was almost stationary, rising from 28·8 per cent in 1919–20 to 34·5 per cent in 1928–29 and declining again to 31·0 per cent in 1938–39, while the total inter-war non-recurrent grant for building and other purposes, less than £1·5 million (to which we should add £0·5 million for retrospective

1 *Laurie*, p. 15; Council Minutes, 26 May, 15 December 1939.

F.S.S.U. benefits in 1921) was described by a post-war U.G.C. report as 'insignificant'.[1]

Meanwhile, the improvement in average salaries was also modest, as shown in Table 2.

TABLE 2

Average Salaries of University Teachers, 1923–39

	Professor	Reader, Asst. Professor, Independent Lecturer	Lecturer	Assistant Lecturer
	£	£	£	£
1923–24	977	582	444	307
1928–29	1,068	627	455	310
1934–35	1,094	661	471	310
1938–39	1,115	671	477	313

Source : U.G.C., *Reports*, 1925, 1936, 1948.

These moderate increases for professors and senior non-professors and almost negligible ones for the rest can scarcely be described as impressive.

Yet, considering the economic climate of the inter-war period, the high unemployment, and the almost continuous economic crises and financial stringency, it was perhaps no mean achievement to keep the figures moving in the right direction, and perhaps a more pertinent question to ask is, what would have happened to them if the A.U.T. had not existed? The cuts of 1922 and 1932 and their restoration under pressure are an indication of what might have happened if no pressure had been applied. Moreover, since this was a period, from 1920 at least, of declining prices, the purchasing power of salaries was continuously rising. The Ministry of Labour index of retail prices (1914=100) showed a decline from 249 in 1920 and 174 in 1923 to 140 at the trough of the slump in 1933 and 156 at the peak of recovery in 1938.[2] Thus in round terms the purchasing power of the average professorial salary rose between 1923–24 and

1 *University Development, 1957–62* (1964), pp. 114, 179.
2 B. R. Mitchell and P. Deane. *Abstract of British Historical Statistics* (Cambridge, 1962), p. 478.

1934–35 by 39 per cent, or, more fairly, between 1923–4 and 1938–39 by 27 per cent; that of the lecturer over the first period by 33 per cent, and over the second by 20 per cent; and that of the assistant lecturer over the first by 28 per cent, and over the second by 14 per cent. These figures should be compared with a rise in real national income per head over the first period of 22 per cent and over the second of 36 per cent, and with a rise in real wages over the first by 19 per cent and over the second by 20 per cent.[1] In other words, while over the shorter period academic salaries in real terms pulled ahead, over the longer (and for purposes of comparison, fairer) period the senior ranks of the university teaching profession failed to keep up with the rise in other middle-class incomes, while the lower ranks lagged well behind.

The figures also illustrate another and in some ways more significant point: like other secure professions, university teachers were less vulnerable to economic depression, which disproportionately depressed national income and wages in the early 1930's, and in their security stood to gain more from the falling prices of hard times than the non-salaried business men and manual wage-earners, whose earnings tended to fall more in aggregate than they were raised in value by the fall in prices. Conversely, university teachers gained less from economic recovery and boom conditions than the business men and manual workers, since their salaries then tended to lag behind the rise in prices. The security and stability of professional salaries were, in fact, an advantage in a period of unemployment and falling prices like that between the Wars, and the university teachers suffered much less than they might have done from their apparently weak bargaining position. That weakness, at bottom, was due to the attractiveness of the academic life, to the security and freedom to 'do one's own work' which pulled able men and women from higher-paid jobs elsewhere, and thus had a 'negative economic value' which had to be paid for in lower salaries. But freedom and security, though absolutely necessary to productive teaching and research at the frontiers of knowledge, were not always and everywhere to be taken for granted, and had also to be fought for from time to time, as we shall see.

1 Calculated from *Ibid.*, pp. 345, 368.

4. SECURITY, FREEDOM AND PARTICIPATION

The professional interests of university teachers include not only material rewards but also conditions of service, notably security of tenure, the basic academic freedom to teach and to study one's subject as one sees fit in the light of intellectual truth and moral integrity without any political or other outside interference, and, as a corollary of these, the right to some share in making the decisions determining the conditions of life and work and the content and methods of teaching and research in the institution to which one belongs. Traditionally, British university teachers have enjoyed a freedom and security and a degree of participation in university government second to none. Fellows of Oxford and Cambridge Colleges and the professors of Scottish and of English and Welsh civic universities were appointed until the age of retirement, usually 65 or 70, and could not be dismissed except for complete incompetence or gross immorality, and only then after lengthy enquiry with a right to be heard in defence and to appeal. Resident M.A.s at Oxford and Cambridge, at least since the mid-Victorian reforms which reduced the power of the 'Heads of Houses', were the ultimate authority in those universities, and professors at the other universities were, through the Senate (Academic Council in Scotland), the ultimate academic authority, and were in practically all cases represented on the governing bodies with financial responsibility and sovereignty, Council and Court (Court and Conference in Scotland). Although in theory the professors could be overruled by the lay majorities in the latter bodies, in practice custom declared that they should reach their decisions by consensus, and a straight vote of laymen versus academics was almost unheard of.

It might be thought, therefore, that the A.U.T. would have found little or nothing to do on this front. Far from it: the Association originated, it will be remembered, in a movement to safeguard the rights of the under-privileged non-professorial staff of the civic universities, and there was a great deal to be done before they all obtained reasonable security of tenure and a modest share in the running of their universities. Very occasionally, moreover, even professors fell foul of university governing bodies, and in two celebrated cases in the 1930's the A.U.T. had to bring pressure to bear in defence of victimized or threatened professors.

The most continuous and serious effort on this front was naturally on behalf of the security of junior non-professorial staff. When the Association of University Lecturers was mooted in 1917 the great majority of the members had no security of tenure, but were appointed under a variety of contracts ranging from three to five years down to three to six months' notice. No doubt like farming tenants-at-will and short leaseholders most of them could expect to continue indefinitely by a sort of unwritten custom of the manor, but the psychological insecurity was there, and could become a reality if the incumbent fell out with the lord of the manor (the professorial head of department), especially when a new one appeared with new ideas on how to farm the estate. It was not unknown for men and women in middle life with no training for any other career suddenly to find themselves out of a job: Laurie instances one such case at Liverpool before the First World War, of a man of 40 who was 'incompatible' with his professor and did not have his appointment renewed.[1] The problem was complicated by the question of probation, since no one could expect security for life before he had proved himself capable of doing the job satisfactorily, and by the practice in many universities of limiting the number of established lectureships and using the probationary Grade III as a source of cheap labour, and either dismissing perfectly satisfactory assistant lecturers at the end of three of four years because there was no vacancy in Grade II or keeping them on as semi-permanent temporaries at the same assistant lecturer's salary. As we have already seen, there were university administrators, like Sir Robert Waley Cohen of University College, London, who publicly defended these practices for those teachers 'who were not going to be distinguished in the profession',[2] and still more who apologetically clung to them to save their institutions' finances.

The Association of University Lecturers' Memorandum to the Governing Bodies in 1918 declared that 'The tenure of the Lecturer's post remains, in many cases, limited and insecure, and, as a result, much of his work is restricted and made less effective'; and recommended that 'The tenure of probationary appointments should extend over not more than three years, and

1 *Laurie*, p. 19.
2 *Proceedings of a Conference . . . on Salaries and Grading, 6 May 1939.*

thereafter the appointment should have a certain security of tenure. Probationary appointment should be confined to Grade III.' It also asked that 'Lecturers should have adequate representation on the bodies which exercise control over the teaching in their University or College'.[1] The A.U.T. inherited these demands, and continued to press for them year in and year out, with steady progress but never in this period with complete success. The Memorandum of 1920 repeated the complaint, and slightly extended the remedy:

Where the first appointment of a teacher to a full-time University post in any University or University College in the United Kingdom in Class A [Grade III] there should be a probationary appointment of three years; a similar appointment in Classes B, C or D [Grades II, I and Professors] should be probationary for not more than one year. [There would not be many in Class D who would agree to probation of any length whatever!] After the probationary period has been completed dismissal should only be possible upon grounds of neglect of duties, improper conduct or incapacity.[2]

The Association managed to persuade the university representatives at the Joint Conferences in 1921 to accept Grade III as a three-year probationary grade (in exchange for a flat rate of pay for the first two years), which the A.U.T. Council in 1922 took to mean that 'Whilst such appointment carries with it no promise of the promotion of any individual to Division II on termination of service in Division III, yet in the interest of University education the most capable teachers in Division III ought normally to be appointed to Division II on the termination of their probationary period.'[3] The A.U.T. found, however, that although the majority of English universities had the same understanding of the agreement, a number, notably university colleges of London and Wales (to which should be added the Scottish Universities, which long remained the worst offenders), took it to mean that they could employ as many assistant lecturers as they liked, irrespective of their prospects of promotion, as long as they sacked them after three years.

1 Association of University Lecturers, *Memorandum to Governing Bodies* . . . *March 1918.*
2 *Memorandum issued by the Council of the A.U.T.*, 27 March 1920.
3 *Memorandum on Salaries . . . ratified . . . 26 November 1921*; Council Minutes, 3 and 4 March 1922.

The 1929 Report on Salaries and Grading again complained of '*cul-de-sac* employment' in 'a very few Institutions', and found an ally in the University Grants Committee, whose 1925 Report, after noting an average salary of £307 for assistant lecturers and demonstrators who 'are learning the work of university teaching and proving their fitness to undertake it as a career', commented:

we wish to make it clear that low salaries of this kind are only defensible on the assumption that the posts are in fact probationary, and that the holders will not, at the end of the probationary period, be retained from year to year doing the work of a permanent Lecturer on a probationer's salary.[1]

The 1938 Report on Salaries and Grading still found that 'the average number of years of Service in Grade III is practically five', which was 'clearly inconsistent with the policy of the Joint Conference'. It quoted the A.U.T.'s submission to the U.G.C. in 1934:

In our submission, appointment to a teaching post at a university means that the person so appointed has been recognized as possessing such academic qualifications as justify his reaching, in due course, the normal Grade II stage of full lecturer. A university teacher who, after three years' service, is not worthy of promotion to the position of Lecturer should not in the first instance have been appointed to a university . . . We would urge that the greatest care should be exercised in the making of Grade III appointments, in order that, after the probationary period is over, the teachers concerned may be worthy of promotion to Grade II, and not be either turned adrift at an age when a change of profession is fraught with serious difficulties, or be tempted to remain indefinitely in posts intended only for beginners.[2]

The U.G.C. reported in 1936 that 'We fully appreciate the dilemma in which the Universities must have been placed' in the depression years between prolonging temporary appointments and throwing young probationers into unemployment, but insisted that the rule must be enforced, both for the sake of the unsuitable teacher himself who should not be allowed to drag on until he was unfit for an alternative career, and to avoid any risk of general 'exploitation of cheap labour'.[3] The fact that such

1 *Report on Salaries and Grading*, February 1929; U.G.C., *Report . . . 1923–24*, p. 16.
2 *Report on Salaries and Grading*, May 1938.
3 U.G.C., *Report . . . 1929–30 to 1934–35*, p. 39.

representations and warnings had to be repeated at intervals down to and beyond the Second World War shows that, although the majority of assistant lecturers in England and Wales, as opposed to Scotland and Northern Ireland, were promoted to lecturer in their own university, there were still institutions which exploited the cheap labour of a continuing series of young, and sometimes not so young, men and women before 'throwing them on the scrapheap' of the overcrowded intellectual labour market.

Meanwhile, however, much had been gained for the lecturers and more senior non-professorial staff who had passed the probationary grade. Some of them it is true, still had to serve a further three years' probation on promotion to lecturer, and in some universities anyone appointed from outside to a non-professorial post, however senior, had to serve up to three years' probation. Beyond that, however, most assistant professors, readers, senior lecturers and lecturers became in the course of the inter-war period almost as secure in practice as the professoriate. There might not be the same right of inquiry and appeal on dismissal, but appointment to age of retirement became the norm.

How secure, on the other hand, were professors? The clauses safeguarding them in their contracts of service and in university charters and statutes seemed at first sight to be incontrovertible, but they were in fact full of vague phrases about 'immorality', 'scandalous conduct', and 'good and sufficient cause' which might prove barricades of straw when put to the test. They were not often put to the test, but there was one outstanding case in the early 1930's, that of Professor H. J. Hutchens, Professor of Bacteriology at the College of Medicine, Newcastle-upon-Tyne, which was, along with the adjacent Armstrong College, one of the Colleges of Durham University. Following a dispute between the two Colleges as to which of them should teach the premedical subjects, including bacteriology, Hutchens received six months' notice from the Registrar of the College of Medicine on behalf of the College Council. The Local Association took the matter up with the national A.U.T., which collected £1,000 for legal expenses, engaged Norman (later Lord) Birkett and H. S. G. Buckmaster, junior, as counsel, and instituted legal proceedings. The dispute became a *cause célèbre*, watched throughout the university world for its implications for the whole profession, and it dragged on for two and a half years. In the course of it

Lord Londonderry, the Chancellor of Durham University, appointed a committee of inquiry under a judge, Lord Kirkley, not only into the circumstances of Hutchens' dismissal but into the administration and constitution of the College of Medicine. To make way for this inquiry the Professor withdrew from the legal proceedings. The result was that Hutchens, who was nearing retirement age, was given the title of Professor Emeritus and an annuity of £650, and the constitution of the College of Medicine was completely reformed. That outcome, and the notoriety achieved by the College throughout the university and medical worlds was a sufficient guarantee that no other institution would in future lightly contemplate dismissing a professor without very good reason indeed.[1]

An even more celebrated, though less dangerous, case concerned the attack made in 1934 by the Vice-Chancellor and Principal of London University on a speech given in Moscow by the famous left-winger, Professor Harold Laski of the London School of Economics, which seemed to threaten the academic's freedom of speech. It came at a time when academic freedom was under attack on the Continent, above all in Hitler's Germany, and the outcry was accordingly all the stronger. The Council of the A.U.T. at its December meeting in 1934 passed the following resolution:

The Association of University Teachers affirms the right of University teachers to the full exercise of their functions and privileges as citizens. It maintains that the public expression of opinion, within the limits of the law, on controversial matters is in no way incompatible with the position and responsibilities of a University teacher, it being understood that such expression is personal and does not commit the Institution to which he belongs.

The Association of University Teachers recognizes that a special responsibility rests on a University teacher to weigh his words carefully when making public pronouncements. But the application of this principle in particular cases must, in the final resort, be left to the judgment of the individual concerned, and the Association of University Teachers would resist any attempt by University Authorities or by outside bodies to impose restrictions on such expression of opinion.

1 *Laurie*, pp. 21–2; Mcr. A.U.T., file labelled 'Hutchens Case' (containing copies of correspondence, newspaper cuttings, and formal opinion of A.U.T.'s Honorary Legal Adviser, Professor F. Raleigh Batt).

A London professor referred to a recent case at Leeds and pointed out that the position was much more serious for non-professorial staff than for professors, whose position was more secure.[1] The Executive circularized Local Associations, but found no evidence of the infringement of the rights of either. It also approached University M.P.s and candidates, and got letters of agreement from most of them, and of 'guarded agreement' from all but one of the rest.[2] There was in fact little danger of political interference with academic freedom in this country, and as the U.G.C. pointed out in a contemporary report, 'The universities of Great Britain rightly set store by the maintenance of that healthy spirit of independence with which they have grown up; and the recent experience of the universities of some other countries has only served to strengthen this attitude.'[3] The attack on academic freedom in Nazi Germany naturally gave much more cause for concern, and to the A.U.T.'s response to this we shall return.

The demand for participation in university government which the A.U.T. inherited from the Association of University Lecturers received powerful and continuous support from the University Grants Committee. In their 1925 Report, for example, they put the case and summarized the current situation with great clarity, and it is worth quoting in full:

The importance of securing to the professors a proper share of influence in the management of a University's work has long been recognized. Everywhere they sit upon the supreme advisory authority in academic matters – the Senate or Academic Board; and they are almost always directly represented on the executive body – the Council, or, in Scotland, the Court. Most of the constitutional instruments under which the Universities are governed took shape at a time when students were much less numerous, and when the teachers of infra-professorial rank played a smaller and less important part in the work of the University than they do now. In recent years, however, most Universities and Colleges have grown greatly in size, and the numbers and responsibilities of the lecturers have correspondingly increased; it is therefore reasonable that they should now regard themselves as deserving a more clearly recognized position in the government of the Universities. In some places the non-professorial staff is already represented on the Senate or Academic Board, but the practice is at present by no means general. It must of

1 Council Minutes, 14 December 1934.
2 *Ibid.*, 31 May, 13 December 1935, 29 May 1936.
3 Quoted by *Laurie*, p. 45.

course be remembered that the value of such representation may vary a good deal from institution to institution; where, for example, owing to the multiplicity of subjects and departments, the Senate is already a numerous body with functions mainly of general supervision and review, and where a large amount of power and responsibility is devolved upon Faculties or Boards of Studies which include the lecturers, representation of the lecturers on the Senate, as well as on the smaller bodies, may be a matter of comparatively minor importance. Each institution will naturally approach this problem in the light of its own peculiar circumstances, and it is of little consequence which particular method is adopted, provided that it enables the non-professorial staff to feel that they are given the opportunity of taking a reasonable share in the guidance and organization of the institution's work. It was with the object of meeting this point that we suggested, in our previous Report, that the lecturers as well as the professors should be represented on the executive governing bodies, and we have been a little disappointed to find how rarely this suggestion has been adopted. Where the experiment has been tried, it has, we are told, proved wholly successful, and its effect has been precisely what we had hoped. The presence of one or two representatives of the junior staff can in no way disturb the balance of power and authority on the executive body, while it certainly serves to spread throughout the staff a knowledge of the financial and other reasons which underlie a particular decision or line of policy, and to remove suspicions which ignorance of those reasons often tends to breed.[1]

The 'guidance' of the U.G.C. and the pressure of the A.U.T., especially at local level, gradually took effect, and the Sub-committee on Representation of Teaching Staffs upon University Bodies which made an analytical and tabulated study in 1927 was able to report that non-professorial staff were elected or appointed to the Faculties in the Universities of Birmingham (except the Faculty of Science, where they were members of departmental Boards of Studies), Bristol, Leeds, Liverpool, Manchester, Reading, Sheffield, Durham, Wales, and the University Colleges of Exeter, Nottingham and Southampton; though in some cases the elected representatives were too few to have much influence or to cover the whole span of academic interests. They were represented on the Senate by two members at Aberystwyth, Bangor, Exeter, Reading and Swansea, and on the Council by two members at Leeds and Manchester, and similar arrange-

[1] U.G.C., *Report . . . 1923–24*, pp. 20–1.

ments were being discussed at other universities. The Council of the A.U.T. welcomed these reforms, and moved that they be extended to all universities.[1]

By 1936 the U.G.C. could report:

We believe that in most cases, though not in all, the non-professorial staff are now represented on the Senate or the Academic Board. On the other hand, in a number of cases no steps have so far been taken to afford the non-professorial staff any representation on the Governing Body. We cannot but think, judging from the admirable results in those cases where such representation has been arranged, that this policy might with great advantage be more widely followed.[2]

A further A.U.T. Report in 1943 commented that 'In recent years the great majority of University institutions have taken steps to implement these recommendations in some degree'. This Report, based on three questionnaires sent out during 1940–42, can be taken to represent the position at the end of the inter-war period. It showed that in eleven out of twenty-seven institutions in England, Wales and Northern Ireland (excluding Oxford and Cambridge) permanent full-time non-professorial staff were members of Faculties or Boards of Studies, subject in two cases to a certain length of service in the permanent grade, and that in a number of others they served by election or in rotation. In twenty-three there were non-professorial members of staff on the Senate, either elected or *ex-officio* (Heads of Department, etc.) or both, in the remaining four there were a few places reserved for the Librarian, non-professorial Deans of Faculties, or other co-opted members. In all cases there was academic representation on the Council, and though only five made separate provision for the election of non-professors it was found that in most cases one or two were so elected in practice. At all seventeen institutions possessing Courts there was academic representation on that body, at eight separate provision was made for non-professorial representation, and at only one was it impossible for non-professors (other than non-professorial Deans of Faculties) to be elected. The Report concluded that there was now, with few exceptions, adequate non-professorial representation on Faculties and Boards of Studies; that satisfactory

1 Report on the Representation of Teaching Staffs upon University Bodies, October 1927; Council Minutes, 3 June 1927.
2 U.G.C., *Report . . . 1929–30 to 1934–35*, p. 41.

progress had been made in achieving such representation on Senates, but that there were still five of the larger institutions without it; and that, although it was now theoretically possible for non-professors to be elected to Council and Court, election was too often controlled by the professorial majority on the Senate. On the whole it could look back with satisfaction to the progress made in the inter-war period, not for the sake of further-ing the interests of one class of teacher against the other, but for the sake of the unity of the profession:

We believe that the value of the co-operation of the great body of readers and lecturers which the expansion of the last twenty years has brought into being is generally acknowledged by the professors whose claims to a share in the government have been recognized from the first. We agree whole-heartedly with the University Grants Committee that 'the right view surely is that governing body, professors and lec-turers are all united in a common bond of service to their University, and that it is to the interest of all that means should be found to use and develop to the best advantage the powers of each individual member of those groups' (Report, 1930).[1]

5. 'THE EDUCATIONAL FUNCTION'

Laurie's first recruiting letter in October 1919 stressed the educational function of the Association as of equal importance with 'the economic factor': 'Universities may be expected to take their due place in the educational world more fully as the efforts of University Teachers become more co-ordinated ... The Association may be expected to interest itself in, among other matters, the relation between Universities and Schools, the relation of the Universities to the working man, and the inter-relations between Home and Colonial Universities.'[2] Although like any professional interest group it had to give a high priority to remuneration and conditions of service, it could claim in 1938 that 'the Association of University Teachers does not concern itself only with the professional interests of university teachers, and in fact devotes most of its energies to the study of

1 *Report on the Representation of Teaching Staffs on University Governing Bodies*, November 1943.
2 Circular letter, Laurie to university teachers, 22 October 1919.

the wider problems of academic life.'[1] How far this claim was justified can only be gauged from the minutes of the Executive and the Council, from the reports of the Sub-committees and the Joint Committees with the school teachers' associations and other bodies, and from the pages of the *University Bulletin* and the *Universities Review*. It cannot, of course, be denied that salaries, superannuation, income tax allowances, security of tenure and other material concerns were constantly on the agenda, and that Beatrice Webb's caustic observation on the materialism of London 'society' could with aptitude be applied to university teachers, as to any other professional interest group, sitting in conclave: 'Mention money, and every face lights up.'[2] Nevertheless it is only fair and equally true to say that from the start educational questions bulked as large on the agenda as economic ones. Amongst the more important of these were student welfare, university entrance requirements, the content and structure of degree courses, facilities for advanced study and research, library provision and co-operation, and co-operation through conferences, exchanges of staff and the like with Commonwealth and foreign universities. The last became so important in the 1930's that it deserves a section to itself, but the rest will be dealt with, all too briefly, in this one.

On the side of student welfare most of what was done was done in co-operation with the National Union of Students. The latter only came into existence in 1922, as a body co-ordinating the activities of the various Students' Unions, Guilds and Representative Councils of the universities and colleges (including many non-university colleges) of England, Wales and Northern Ireland and promoting the educational, social and general interests of students. In its early years it mostly occupied itself with international contacts and student travel, but gradually extended its range to cover all student affairs. In 1927 the A.U.T. and the N.U.S. set up a Joint Standing Committee of four members from each Executive, and it was arranged that the A.U.T. would circulate to Local Associations the Annual Reports of the N.U.S. and information concerning exchange and other visits of foreign students, that the N.U.S. would supply the Editor of the *University Bulletin* with a regular article on their

1 *Report on Salaries and Grading*, May 1938.
2 Beatrice Webb, *My Apprenticeship* 1926.

activities, and that A.U.T. members were welcome to use the facilities provided by the N.U.S. such as foreign travel schemes.[1] From time to time the N.U.S. representatives raised for discussion such matters as matriculation standards, students' grants, examination, tutorial and lecture systems, and for example objected to compulsory attendance at lectures, which was very general at provincial universities until after the Second World War. In 1930 they began to press for what has ever since been a perennial demand, student representation on university governing bodies, especially the Council and the Faculties, and for the creation of joint Staff-Student Committees in each university institution. The A.U.T. attitude at that time was that membership of the first two would prove to be useless and a disappointment, but that Staff-Student Committees would be a useful innovation.[2] The most fruitful co-operation was in the field of student health. In 1934 the N.U.S. published a report on the availability of schemes for medical treatment in universities and colleges, and the Council of the A.U.T. resolved that 'the Association should give the National Union of Students every assistance in its power in regard to the consideration and development of medical schemes.'[3] The most concrete proposal in student health was the setting up of an International University Sanatorium scheme for students suffering from tuberculosis. This grew out of the International University Conference on Student Health at the Universities of Geneva and Lausanne in July 1938, the fourth in the series of international conferences which, as we shall see later, the A.U.T. took the lead in organizing.[4] The project, however, was interrupted by the War, a Pilot Centre at Pinewood in Berkshire was opened only in 1952, and the scheme was wound up in the 1960's as a result of the conquest of tuberculosis by antibiotics.

One of the first contacts made by the A.U.T. with other professions was at the Conference of National Associations of Teachers called by the Teachers' Registration Council in London in May 1920, at which resolutions were passed calling for 'united action for the benefit of education and of the profession as

1 Council Minutes, 3 June 1927.
2 *Laurie*, p. 50; Council Minutes, 12 December 1930.
3 Council Minutes, 14 December 1934.
4 *Ibid.*, 27 May, 16 December 1938.

a whole' and for 'consultation by both Central and Local Authorities on all important questions, administrative and other, affecting education.'[1] Although the A.U.T. has always resisted amalgamation with any other professional organization, whether of teachers, technical college lecturers, scientific workers, or the like, fearing to be swamped by bigger battalions, it has always sought to co-operate with them on specific and especially practical issues. The most practical common issue affecting the schools and the universities was the question of university matriculation (or entrance) requirements, which naturally influenced both the work of the schools and the level at which university study could begin. The A.U.T. set up a Sub-committee of three in July 1922 on Entrance Requirements to liaise with the Secondary Schools Association. At that time matriculation in most universities (other than the Scottish) was based on the School Certificate introduced in England in 1918 and in Wales in 1920, although entrance to particular departments or courses might require passes or credits in two or three subjects in the Higher School Certificate as well, but not only did the entrance standards differ from one university or department to another but some universities would not accept the examinations of other University Examining Boards. The result was confusion and duplication of syllabuses for the schools, and for the universities the difficulty of teaching students with very different educational backgrounds and standards, which was one reason for the large differences in many of them between the pass and honours degree courses.

In 1928 the Sub-committee drew up a Report on the Machinery governing Matriculation Requirements of Universities which stated as the problem that

The burden placed on schools when pupils wishing to enter different Universities have to be prepared for different examinations is often intolerable; that many subjects should be taught is stimulating both to school and pupils but much time and energy is wasted when the same subject has to be taught in different ways at the same stage to suit the specific requirements of different Examining Boards.

It called for a common policy, but resisted a single national examination as too unwieldy and stereotyped, preferring instead

1 *Ibid.*, 19 June 1920.

the existing system of separate Examining Boards, but with more co-ordination as to timing and standards under a central body with advisory powers, and more willingness on the part of universities to recognize the Certificate of other University Examining Boards.[1]

A more constructive Report in 1930, pointing out the growing gap between bare matriculation and the much higher attainments of the majority of students who stayed on at school until 18, and its consequences in the demand for specialized (rather than general) honours courses in the universities and in too early specialization in the schools, suggested that the School Certificate as a test of general education at age 16 should be separated from matriculation, which should be based on a modified Higher School Certificate at 17 or 18, testing a broad range of subjects including an obligatory test in the use of English, together with a certificate from the actual school teachers on the candidate's power and interests. It also suggested that scholarship awards should not be based on this qualifying examination, and, as we shall see in a moment, that universities should reform their degree schemes so as to enable honours to be awarded for a more general course.[2] By 1936 the Association could

justly claim that the suggestions made in that Report have had a marked effect on the lines along which constructive criticism and experiment have proceeded in the six intervening years. There is now for example, very general acceptance of the principle that Matriculation should be separated from the ordinary School Certificate, and one important body, the Joint Matriculation Board of the Northern Universities, has taken steps to differentiate the two qualifications in the near future. The need for a 'reformed' Higher School Certificate and the method of determining the award of scholarships are receiving increasing attention; and several universities are exploring the possibilities of providing Degree courses of an Honours standard but of a less specialized character than those usually offered by the single-subject Honours School.

The 1936 Report spelled out these reforms in more detail, and in its 'draft scheme for a general university entrance examination at a higher standard' recommended that it should test a general

---

1 *Report on the Machinery Governing Matriculation Requirements of Universities*, April 1928.
2 *Report on Entrance Tests and Initial Degrees*, October 1930.

education, not a specialized or narrow one, that it should cover a minimum of four subjects, plus the test in the use of English, two years after School Certificate, so that entrance to a university should not, in general, take place before the age of 18.[1] It is possible to see in this scheme the seed of the General Certificate of Education of 1951, and the discussions with the teachers' organization which helped to germinate that seed will be dealt with in the next chapter.

The Report of 1930 dealt with initial degrees as well as entrance tests, as we have seen. It pointed that, because of the rising standard of entrance, the pass degree intended for the barely matriculated student had lost its previous status, and almost every student wished to become an honours graduate. The honours courses at the civic universities, originally intended for those who had already received a broad education either for the pass degree or outside the university, had, however, become highly specialized. 'There is thus a difficulty in obtaining a broad general training at the university, with a good and respected degree at the end.' The Sub-committee therefore recommended that there should be two types of degree courses, both capable of the award of honours, 'a more general course leading to a *General Degree*, and a more specialized course leading to a *Special Degree*.' Both courses should last three years, and be built on approximately the same first-year scheme of studies, so as to facilitate transfer between them at the end of the first year.[2] Again it is possible to see in this the seed of post-war developments, not only in the general honours degrees in the civic universities, as in arts at Birmingham in 1948, or in social studies at Manchester in 1960, but in the whole educational philosophy of the new post-war universities from Keele in 1950 to the new universities of the 1960's.

The Association also took an interest in the development of higher degrees as a training for postgraduate students. Before the First World War postgraduate students had been few, and until the 1917 Conference of British Universities, mentioned in the last chapter, which endorsed the adoption in Britain of the Ph.D.,[3] there was no doctorate by research but only those

1 *Report on University Entrance Requirements*, November 1936.
2 *Loc. cit.*
3 Ashby, *op. cit.*, pp. 16–23.

crowning glories of a long and distinguished academic career, the D.Litt., LL.D. and D.Sc. Between the Wars there was still a sharp difference of opinion in the academic profession between those, mainly on the arts side, who thought that new knowledge and original research worthy of a doctorate could hardly be attained before long experience and a mature age, and those, mainly on the science side, who felt that there was real need for an incentive to research in the years immediately following graduation. The A.U.T. appointed a Sub-committee on Higher Degrees with a star-studded cast, including Sir Ernest Rutherford, O.M., F.R.S., Sir James Irvine, F.R.S., the chemist and Vice-Chancellor and Principal of St. Andrews, Dame Helen Gwynne-Vaughan, Professor of Botany in the University of London, four other F.R.S.'s and some eminent arts professors, which reported in 1926. After a sensible statement of general principle, that all university work should be characterized by a liberal outlook and a spirit of enquiry, that degrees in themselves simply marked successive stages of development and scholarship, and no higher degree should be awarded without evidence of the candidate's ability to think for himself, it recommended

That the higher doctorates, D. Litt. and D.Sc., should be conferred only upon candidates whose work both shews conspicuous ability and originality and constitutes a distinguished and sustained achievement.

That the degree of Ph.D. should be conferred only upon candidates who show ability to study a problem systematically and to relate their results to the general body of the knowledge of their subject, and who make a definite contribution to knowledge or scholarship.

That the degree of Master, whether M.A., M.Sc., or others, should be conferred only upon candidates who produce evidence of such definite training as equips them to carry on independent investigation. In effect the degree should be a certificate in the technique of investigation.

It went on to embody these principles in suggested regulations, and to submit further considerations on the requirements of theses, the minimum time required for full- and part-time research degrees, the problem of research done by candidates in collaboration with their seniors, and the need to facilitate the migration of postgraduate students between universities for the benefit of their research.[1] Whether or not this Report helped to

1 *Report on Higher Degrees*, November 1926.

bring it about, these admirable principles certainly anticipated the enormous development of postgraduate studies which has since taken place.

The Association was also continuously concerned with facilities for advanced study and research, especially by the academic staff themselves, and had a Sub-committee on the subject from 1922. In a sense, of course, much of its work concerned the economic rather than the educational function alone, since research costs money in staff time, equipment, travel, and so on; but then every educational activity has some cost. In 1925 the Sub-committee reported that, although the advancement of knowledge was a primary function of the universities and suitable conditions for the pursuit of advanced study and research were therefore essential, the evidence was that such conditions did not in general exist in the universities at that time. More free time and improved salaries were required, and routine duties took up too much of the working day. A regular system of study leave was recommended, together with a research fund in each university for travel and other expenses, and the value of a generously equipped library and of a university press for publication of research work was stressed.[1] They were supported by the U.G.C. who in their 1929 Report pointed out that

teaching at the University level is not likely to possess or to retain the essential qualities or freshness and vitality unless it is given by teachers who are themselves engaged in original work in their subjects. It is therefore of very real importance to a University that it should be able to provide its staff with favourable opportunities for the prosecution of research and advanced work. The first and most obvious need is for a reasonable amount of time free from the pressure of their ordinary duties;

and in 1936 they were 'glad to know that the system of sabbatical leave, first instituted (we believe) in the Universities of America and in certain of the Dominion Universities, is generally approved in principle and is being adopted by the Universities of this country in so far as their finances permit'.[2] Unfortunately the finances of many universities did not permit, and study leave

1 *Report on Facilities for Advanced Study and Research*, March 1925.
2 U.G.C., *Report . . . 1928–29*, p. 34; *Report . . . 1929–30 to 1934–35*, p. 42.

and other facilities for research were long to remain on the agenda of the A.U.T.

One of the most important facilities for research is an adequate library or, failing that, some means of obtaining reasonably quickly the literature one needs. When the A.U.T. was founded the university libraries of this country were separate entities with no means of pooling their resources. The Association therefore set up in 1923 a Sub-committee on Library Co-operation, and this was shortly joined by F. E. Sandbach, Professor of German at Birmingham, who came to be the moving spirit in inaugurating the modern system of inter-library loans. As Convener he invited representatives of all the universities to a Conference on Library Co-operation on 6 January 1925, which tentatively adopted a scheme to place before the individual university authorities, and set up a Joint Standing Committee of Librarians and A.U.T. representatives to carry it out. Professor Sandbach was chairman of the Conference and of the Joint Committee until his death in 1946, and Laurie was its Honorary Secretary until 1950 and Treasurer until his death in 1953. A member of the University Library staff at Birmingham, Mr. Oldaker, was appointed as a part-time Enquiry Officer to run it, outside library hours, on an experimental basis, and year after year the growth of the number of enquiries for books was reported to the Joint Conference in January and to the A.U.T. Council in the following May, rising from 117 in 1925 to 5,353 in 1938. The Carnegie United Kingdom Trust made a grant of £150 a year towards expenses for the first three years, and renewed it at £250 a year for the next three. It also guaranteed the cost up to £2,500 of the Enquiry Office's great contribution to bibliography, the *Union Catalogue of Periodicals in University Libraries* published in 1936. (This lists humanities periodicals, not covered by the already existing *World List of Scientific Periodicals*.) The Catalogue was the work of Mr. Newcombe, Librarian of the Central Library for Students in London, to which in 1931 the Enquiry Office was transferred from Birmingham.[1] As the National Central Library this still carries on the invaluable work started by Profes-

1 *Laurie*, pp. 42–4; Council Minutes, 1923–39, *passim*; A. J. Hatley (Hon. Treasurer of Joint Standing Committee on Library Co-operation), 'The Role of A.U.T. in Library Co-operation', *British Universities Annual, 1964*, pp. 74–6.

sor Sandbach and the A.U.T., perhaps the most useful and concrete example of the Association's exercise of its 'educational function'.

6. INTERNATIONAL RELATIONS

From the earliest days the Association came into contact with foreign and colonial academics and universities, who exchanged correspondence on matters of common interest and sometimes, like the American Association of Professors founded in 1915, invitations to each other's Council meetings and regular copies of their respective journals. In the inter-war period, too, the Scottish Association of University Teachers founded in 1922, which, as we saw in the last chapter, decided to go its own way, was in effect a foreign Association. From 1927 it was invited to send a fraternal delegate to A.U.T. Council meetings, where its representative, the Honorary Secretary, Mr. T. A. Joynt, became a familiar figure, and the A.U.T. was similarly represented by a series of delegates to the Scottish Council. The Scottish Association followed a parallel development, discussing much the same topics of salaries, superannuation, conditions of service, and so on, sending a deputation to the U.G.C. on its visit to Scotland in 1929, pressing from 1931 for non-professorial representation on university governing bodies, and opening negotiations with the four Scottish Universities in 1939 on behalf of the hard-pressed and underprivileged 'Assistants', as they were still called there. All this was done without an Executive, the affairs of the Association being conducted between Council meetings largely by the Secretary, Mr. Joynt, and it was not until 1941 that a Standing (War) Committee was appointed, which was replaced by an Executive Committee only in 1946. By then the main issue before the Association was whether or not to join forces with the southern A.U.T., which in fact occurred in 1949, as we shall see later.[1]

In 1922 the A.U.T. was approached about affiliation by the Secretary of a newly-formed Association of University Teachers at the University of Hong Kong, and set up a Sub-committee on Relations with Teachers in Colonial Universities to consider the

1 T. R. Bolam, 'The Scottish A.U.T.', *British Universities Annual, 1964,* pp. 77–82.

whole question of membership by both individuals and colonial associations, and as a result of its report corresponding member-ship (at a 5s. subscription) was offered to teachers in colonial university institutions, subject to the endorsement of the local Association (if any) and the approval of the home Central Executive.[1]

In 1924 the Sub-committee was reconstituted under Professor F. E. Weiss and widened in scope to cover relations with all overseas universities, in order in the first instance to discuss a system of exchange of staff adopted recently by the University of Basle.[2]

Not much seems to have come of this, but in 1929 there was a resurgence of interest in international affairs when Professor W. Stanley Lewis represented the A.U.T. as an observer at a Conference of Inter-University Student Societies held at the Board of Education in March at the request of the British National Committee on International Intellectual Co-operation, and when the Executive was approached by the British Universi-ties League of Nations Society to support an International Congress which it was organizing in 1930. Professor Lewis was asked to act as Liaison Officer for the latter, and also to convene a new Standing Sub-committee to consider ways and means of international intellectual co-operation.[3] This was the beginning of two important and related developments: a series of A.U.T. 'commissions of investigation' into the university systems of various Continental countries, and a series of international conferences which eventually led to the founding, during the War, of the International Association of University Professors and Lecturers.

The commissions of investigation began with a visit by fifteen members of the A.U.T., led by Professors Laurie and H. J. Fleure, to the French Universities of Lille, Dijon and Paris, in consultation with M. A. Desclos, Assistant Directeur of the Office National des Universités, Paris. The members paid their own expenses, though they received a good deal of hospital-ity from the three universities. Their 29-page Report is still worth reading as a brief and informative guide to the French

1 Council Minutes, 27 June, 25 November 1922.
2 *Ibid.*, 7 March, 23 July 1924.
3 *Ibid.*, 31 May 1929.

university system in all its aspects, from relations with the State and the general educational system to the housing and cost of living of students.[1] There were similar visits to and reports on the German Universities of Berlin, Hamburg and Göttingen in 1931, the Swiss Universities of Basle, Berne and Zurich and the Federal Institute of Technology at Zurich in 1935, and the Scandinavian Universities of Copenhagen, Lund, Uppsala, Stockholm and Oslo in 1937.[2]

Meanwhile, the Sub-committee on International Relations had turned its attention to the need for an international federation of organizations of university teachers, and suggested to the December Council meeting of the Association in 1932 that representatives of other countries be invited to an informal discussion of the proposal in conjunction with the next Council meeting. So it was that at Exeter University College on 26 and 27 May 1933 representatives of university teachers from Germany, Holland, Italy, the Irish Free State, Poland, Sweden, U.S.A. and the United Kingdom met (with letters of support and interest from Australia, Czechoslovakia, Denmark, France, Switzerland and Yugoslavia). They were addressed by Professor R. C. McLean of Cardiff, the main driving force behind the proposal, who said that his ideal was to draw closer together those who were actually engaged in the work of universities all over the world. Political and social changes in many countries were pressing upon the universities, and urging them away from their ancient ideals. Universities must adapt to a changing world, but it would be dangerous not only for themselves but for the civilizations of which they were, or should be, the leaders if these changes were along purely local (meaning national political) lines, with consequent estrangement between them. He therefore proposed 'some kind of loose grouping of the university associations which already existed in several countries, and of university committees, formed or to be formed, in others'. The proposal was welcomed by speaker after speaker, and it was agreed that the International Relations Sub-committee of the A.U.T. should convene another Conference at which it was

1 *The French University System, being Report of the A.U.T. Commission of Investigation, 1930*, October 1930.
2 *The German University System*, October 1931; *The Swiss University System*, October 1935; *The Scandinavian University System*, November 1937.

hoped the delegates would be empowered by their national associations to set up an international federation.[1]

This first International University Conference, as it came to be called, was held under the chairmanship of Professor McLean from 29 June to 2 July 1934 at University College, Oxford, where the Master and host was the A.U.T.'s old friend, Sir Michael Sadler. 110 delegates attended, including 44 from 35 university institutions in 20 overseas countries, together with the Council of the A.U.T. and representatives from the Scottish A.U.T. and the British Federation of University Women. The first session was devoted to addresses on the constitution and work of those Associations already in being, in Britain north and south of the border, America, France (two), Germany, Hungary and Mysore. The second split into four commissions to discuss overcrowding in the universities, vocational instruction, the interchange of university teachers, and adult education. The third took up the question of future action, and it was agreed to set up an International Conference Committee, with McLean as Secretary, to organize future conferences in different countries.[2]

The second International Conference was held in Grenoble on 9–11 June 1935, where the main work was in three separate commissions, on professorial exchanges and the status of the international federation; the organization of university extension and the responsibility towards the student; and overcrowding of university careers, graduate unemployment, and women in universities. Both the commission dealing with the question of the international federation and the Conference thought that this was still premature, and appointed instead an International Committee, with McLean again as Secretary, to draft a constitution, to be submitted to the next Conference, at Heidelberg in 1936.[3]

It was at the Third International Conference at Heidelberg, 24–27 June 1936, that a permanent constitution was adopted for the Conferences, in the form of a Standing Executive Committee

1 *International Relationships of Universities; Preliminary Report of a Conference held at Exeter, 26 and 27 May 1933.*

2 *International University Conference, Oxford, 1934: Report issued by the A.U.T. of England, Wales and Northern Ireland.*

3 *Second International University Conference, Grenoble, 1935: Report issued by the A.U.T. . . . translated from the French text to be published by the Fédération Française des Associations de l'Enseignement Supérieur.*

with McLean as International Secretary.[1] But a dark shadow lay across the proceedings. Nazi persecution of Jews and political opponents was already affecting German university teachers, who were being forced increasingly to choose between support of the régime and dismissal. Up to March 1936 1,300 German scholars had been displaced. The International Conference was immediately followed by the celebration of the 550th anniversary of the University of Heidelberg, which the Nazis were turning into a propaganda affair. The British Vice-Chancellors and the A.U.T. were invited to send representatives, but both refused in protest against Nazi denial of academic freedom, and the A.U.T. delegates to the International Conference walked out the day before Hitler arrived.[2]

A Fourth International Conference was held in Switzerland, 6–10 July 1938, when the discussion on student health took place which led to the project for an International Sanatorium scheme, already mentioned.[3] The Fifth Conference was invited to meet in Rome in 1940, but the A.U.T. Council in May 1939 strongly opposed the venue, and suggested instead a meeting-place in one of the smaller 'neutral' countries (they were all neutral, but war was imminent, and the prospective belligerents were known).[4] In the event, of course, no conference was held. Instead, therefore, of a straightforward and harmonious evolution via the International Conferences to an international federation, the latter began, like the United Nations, as a by-product of war and on one side only. Early in 1942 was formed an Association of University Professors and Lecturers of the Allied Countries in Great Britain, which in conjunction with McLean's International Committee called the Fifth International University Conference at Oxford in July 1943. How this grew into the International Association of University Professors and Lecturers we shall see in the next chapter. Of this, however, there can be no doubt, that without the driving force of R. C. McLean and the initiative and persistence of the A.U.T.

1 *Report of the Third International Conference* (at Heidelberg, 24–27 June 1936.)
2 *Laurie*, p. 47; Council Minutes, 29 May, 11 December 1936.
3 *Report of the Fourth Meeting of the International University Conference* (at the Universities of Geneva and Lausanne and at the Swiss University Sanatorium, Leysin, Switzerland, 6–10 July 1938).
4 Council Minutes, 26 May 1939.

there would be no international association of university teachers.

One more 'international' activity of the A.U.T. needs to be mentioned, of greater human significance than all the rest. The displacement of German university teachers mentioned above evoked an immediate response from British university teachers, not merely of condemnation of any threat to academic freedom but of practical sympathy and support. As early as May 1933 the Council resolved

That the A.U.T. is ready to co-operate, with a view to the temporary accommodation and provision of special facilities at British universities, for teachers deprived of their posts in German and other universities on grounds inconsistent with the principles outlined [of freedom of opinion and teaching] . . ., it being understood that such facilities be provided out of monies made specially available and that the usual channels of promotion in the profession be not thereby affected.[1]

The Executive was instructed to take suitable steps to arrange hospitality and other help for German academics who might come, and it set up an Academic Hospitality Committee under Assistant Professor Tabor which co-operated with the Academic Assistance Council (Secretary, Sir William Beveridge, Director of the London School of Economics), later the Society for the Preservation of Science and Learning, which in five years collected over £10,000 to help resettle academic refugees. In due course it and the equivalent American Committee were able to report that out of 700 displaced scholars who had left Germany 363 had been permanently placed and 324 were being temporarily maintained in universities and other learned institutions. Contributions were also made by the A.U.T. to Australian, Czech and Chinese relief.[2]

In 1938 as the international skies grew darker the Executive set up a Sub-committee on Action in a National Emergency, convened by Professor H. V. A. Briscoe of Imperial College. On its advice resolutions were sent to the Vice-Chancellors' Committee and to the Lord Privy Seal

That the Association of University Teachers is gravely concerned that there appears to be as yet no concerted Government plan for the

1 *Ibid.*, 26 May 1933.
2 *Ibid.*, 16 December 1938.

utilization of the Universities and their personnel in a National Emergency and considers that such a plan should be drawn up forthwith by the Government in consultation with the appropriate University Authorities;

and that the plan, which the Association would be glad to do all in its power to assist, should include the continuation of university teaching for the purpose of maintaining a supply of essential technically trained people, such as doctors, engineers and chemists, of preserving intact the national education system, of maintaining general culture, and of keeping the universities in readiness for the resumption of full activities. In fact, the Committee of Vice-Chancellors and Principals had submitted to the Lord Privy Seal the previous month a memorandum on the organization of the universities for war-time service, and a meeting between him and their representatives took place in January 1939. It was therefore reported to the May Council of the A.U.T. that a scheme of inter-university co-operation in the event of war was being worked out, which included the evacuation of London Colleges to other universities, the provision for students to complete courses, deferment of military service for those taking medical, scientific and technological courses, and the like.[1] It was just in time. By the next Council meeting in December the country was at war, and the Association had a new set of problems on its agenda, even more urgent than those which had stretched its amateur if remarkably active and efficient organization for the previous twenty years.

1 *Ibid.*, 16 December 1938, 26 May 1939; U.G.C., *University Development, 1935-47*, pp. 14-15.

Chapter 4

The War and Reconstruction
1939–54

1. THE IMPACT OF WAR

The Second World War affected the universities and their staffs and students, as it affected British society as a whole, more directly and profoundly than the First. Its immediate impact, it is true, was less disruptive. There was not the same wild, enthusiastic and precipitate rush of volunteers from amongst the students and the younger staff which had convulsed the universities in 1914. For one thing, the Government was already committed to conscription and began to call up the 21-year-olds from 1 September 1939, and though many did volunteer more still waited to hear when they would be needed. For another, there was a more discriminating sense than in 1914 that modern warfare needed brains as well as brawn, and that the universities and their staffs might have a more vital part to play behind rather than in the front line, while many of their students might be more useful to the war effort after rather than before they had been trained, notably of course in medicine, science and technology.

Student numbers in fact fell much less than might have been expected, from about 50,000 before the War to about 35,500 in 1943–44, a fall of only 28 per cent; but, since the number of women students rose by 13 per cent, that of men students had fallen by 41 per cent in total, and in faculties of arts by 76 per cent, from nearly 15,000 to less than 3,500. Meanwhile, the number of full-time established teaching staff fell by 32 per cent, senior administrative staff by 22 per cent and library staff by 43 per cent; altogether, 1,380 members left for the Forces or other forms of national service.[1] The bare figures, however, give little

1 U.G.C., *University Development from 1935 to 1947* (1948), pp. 17, 18.

idea of the extent of the change in the whole ethos of university work and the composition of the student body. Apart from the increased proportion of women, many of the men students were under 18, many more were in attendance for one year only before call-up, others especially in science and technology were on shortened courses achieved by means of a four-term year, still others were already enlisted officer cadets on six-month courses in applied science or enemy languages preparatory to active service in the Royal Artillery, Royal Engineers, Royal Corps of Signals, the Royal Air Force, or the intelligence branches of the three services, and very few men students were able to complete a course of pre-war duration. For the staff such time as was left from the increased teaching loads involved in these crash courses was devoted in many cases to research directly connected with the war effort, such as radar or the theoretical aspects of atomic research, contributing to the atmosphere of overwork and strain which the universities shared with the rest of the population.

Like the rest of the civilian population, too, the universities found themselves, in contrast with the First World War, in the front line. London University was the most vulnerable to air attack, and in accordance with the plan already agreed between the Lord Privy Seal and the Vice-Chancellors' Committee all its colleges and divisions except for a few postgraduate institutes were evacuated at the outbreak of war, mostly to other university towns. This proved to be a wise precaution, since damage was extensive, notably to University College, Bedford College, Birkbeck College, St. Bartholomew's Hospital Medical College and the London School of Hygiene and Tropical Medicine in the early years of the war, King's College of Household and Social Science in 1944, and the London School of Medicine for Women by rocket attack within a few weeks of the end of the war. Most other universities suffered some damage from air attack; the ones most seriously damaged were Bristol, which lost its Great Hall and Anatomy wing in the winter of 1940–41, and Liverpool where part of the Engineering Laboratories were destroyed.[1]

University buildings were often ideal for the enormously extended war-time Government administration, and were requisitioned freely by the Ministry of Works in consultation with the

1 *Ibid.*, pp. 20–1.

universities and the U.G.C. In London most of the evacuated college premises were taken over, and the main University buildings in Bloomsbury became the headquarters of the Ministry of Information, while at Oxford and Cambridge many colleges and university buildings were requisitioned for the Ministries or the Forces.[1]

The contribution of the universities and their members to the war effort can never perhaps be assessed, and much of their work was and will probably remain secret. One of the more surprising discoveries of the war was that not all dons are remote and ineffectual, and the list of university teachers who became not merely successful war officers or scientific 'back-room boys' but capable administrators in the Cabinet Office and other Ministries, is surprisingly long. A professor of philosophy became Permanent Under-Secretary of the joint Ministries of Supply and Aircraft Production, under him served economists and economic historians as eminent as M. M. Postan and the late Ely Devons, while the Ministry of Information and the intelligence services were filled with university dons. They had good reasons to support this war, more than any previous one: the imprisonment and death of many German, Czech and Austrian university teachers before the War and of still more in the Nazi-occupied countries during it, was a sufficient warning, if any were needed, of what would happen to academic freedom in Britain if the War were lost.

The impact of the War on the A.U.T. reflected that on the universities. Membership declined from 1,899 in 1938–39 to 1,480 in 1941–42, and then slowly recovered to 1,677 in 1944–45. No Council meetings were held between May 1940 and July 1943, and the Executive issued Reports for the Sessions 1940–41 and 1941–42 in lieu of Council Minutes. Perhaps stimulated by the democratic atmosphere, an Oxford Local Association, mooted as long ago as 1921, was formed in the autumn of 1939, with the Warden of All Souls, Dr. W. S. Adams, as President, and Professor E. R. Dodds, a longstanding member of the A.U.T. Executive, as Vice-President; the Secretary was immediately called up by the Admiralty and had to be replaced. Evacuated Local Associations held joint meetings with their hosts, as at Cambridge, where Professor R. S. T. Chorley of the London

1 *Ibid.*, p. 19.

School of Economics reported a successful liaison between the home Association and the three London Colleges.[1] At the headquarters at Aberystwyth one curious by-product of the War was the almost unnoticed first step in the direction of the professionalization of the A.U.T. Laurie was due to retire from university service in 1940, and in the normal course of things might have been expected to hand over the General Secretaryship to someone else. Instead, he was re-appointed Honorary General Secretary for three years with an honorarium of £200 a year – the first professional officer of the Association, as he had been its first President and first General Secretary – and cheap indeed, one might think, at the price. At any event he continued to serve until his death in 1953. At the same time Miss Davies, his personal secretary since 1921, was appointed Assistant Secretary to the Association at £250 a year, and a sum of £50 a year was voted for office accommodation, still two rooms in Laurie's house.[2] So tentatively and casually did the A.U.T. set its foot on the road towards professional administration.

The Association's main concern at the outbreak of war was to keep the universities running, albeit at a reduced level of activity, not merely for the sake of safeguarding their present integrity as institutions and preserving them for the post-war rehabilitation of learning and culture, but so that they could make their most useful and intelligent contribution to the war effort. It was for the latter reason that the A.U.T. made repeated representations to the U.G.C. and National Service Department of the Ministry of Labour (later the Ministry of Labour and National Service) for the deferment of students to finish courses, especially in subjects useful to the war effort, and of members of staff to teach them. These representations were successful, within the limits of the increasingly voracious demand of war for manpower, in obtaining the deferment of students under 25 in engineering, metallurgy, physics, chemistry, applied mathematics, geology and the biological sciences, long enough at least to get some useful training. As the shortage of manpower grew more severe the length of time allowed for honours courses was progressively reduced, to two years and three months (two years and nine

1 Council Minutes, 15 December 1939.
2 *Ibid.*, 24 May 1940.

months for the longer Scottish course) by 1943, and some courses earning War Degrees to as little as one year and nine months. Arts and other non-scientific students were not of course deferred, except as Reservists training with University Senior Training Corps or Air Training Corps for a maximum of three terms, and in some cases for the completion of (generally first-year) examinations by those who entered university before the call-up age of 18, as it became by 1943. Medical, dental and veterinary students and, until 1944, pharmacy students were placed on the Schedule of Reserved Occupations and allowed to complete their courses, subject to serving in a professional capacity in the Forces or other national service on qualification. Women students were unrestricted until 1942, when all women under 30 were submitted to a direction of labour similar to but less constricting than that of the men. Men staff were at first reserved from the age of 25, raised to 30 in August 1940, but this was raised early in 1941 to 35 for teaching staff in subjects other than medicine and science and for all administrators and librarians (the last being later dereserved altogether), and finally in 1942 the age was progressively raised to 40 for all categories, and deferment of indispensable personnel had to be arranged individually through the U.G.C. every six months. Women staff up to the age of 30 came under regulation with the rest of their sex in 1942, and the universities had to make special applications to defer their transfer to war work.[1] Every change in the regulations governing registration, call-up, deferment, and direction of labour was reviewed by the A.U.T. Executive for its implications for university service, not only of students and teachers but also of administrators, librarians, laboratory technicians, secretarial and other ancillary staff, and many minor injustices and difficulties were thus avoided and the universities kept running as well as could be expected.

One of the first effects of the War was the freezing in many universities of practically all promotion prospects even for those who for reasons of age, physical unfitness or indispensability remained on the staffs of universities. In one department in a large civic university a reader whom a Senate committee had recommended for a chair found the appointment deferred for seven years, while his assistant lecturer remained in that grade

1 *University Development, 1935–47*, pp. 94–8.

for the same period. Salary scales were also frozen, until the pressure of rising prices caused a number of universities to pay either family allowances modelled on the pre-war scheme at the London School of Economics or from 1942 small war bonuses of the order of £13 to £26 a year, or both.[1] In 1943 the position was becoming serious, and the A.U.T. sent a deputation to the U.G.C. asking for an immediate cost-of-living adjustment of £100 a year for junior lecturers and £150 for the rest. The chairman, Sir Walter Moberly, was sympathetic, but said that the Committee could not approach the Treasury for an increased grant unless requested by the universities themselves. The A.U.T. took the hint, and either wrote letters or made local approaches to most of the university authorities, with the result that in 1944 a fairly general war bonus was granted, ranging in most institutions from £50–£100 for junior lecturers to £100–£150 for professors.[2] In 1943 the Association reviewed its proposed salary scales and adjusted them to the current cost of living,[3] but this belongs more to the policy for reconstruction which will be dealt with in the next section.

The Executive continued to watch over all the other professional interests of university teachers, which could not be allowed to atrophy during six years of war. They even found time, as we have seen, to survey and report on the representation of teaching staffs on university governing bodies.[4] They discussed with the Ministries concerned the implications of raising the salary limit from £250 to £420 for Unemployment Insurance from September 1940 and for Health and Pensions Insurance from January 1942, which brought lower paid university staff into the State schemes.[5] The Superannuation Sub-committee, now under the Convenership of Mr. W. A. Wightman, continued its pressure on the Council of the F.S.S.U. to improve the terms negotiated with the insurance companies and the information disseminated to members, and prepared a report on the hardships suffered through the increased cost of living by members retiring on unsupplemented pensions, which became the basis of a deputation

1 Reports for Sessions 1941–41 and 1940–42 (with Council Minutes).
2 Council Minutes, 10 June 1944.
3 *Ibid.*, 16 December 1943: Memorandum on Salaries and Grading.
4 *Report on the Representation of Teaching Staffs on Governing Bodies* (1943); Convener, W. A. Wightman.
5 Reports for Sessions 1940–41 and 1941–42.

to the U.G.C. on 29 May 1945.[1] They took part in the Conference called in February 1944 by the Council for Educational Advance on R. A. Butler's Education Bill, supporting its aim of secondary education for all and demanding a specific date (still unattained after 25 years) for the raising of the school-leaving age to 16. They also supported the movement by the Council for Education in World Citizenship for an international organization for education which eventually took shape as UNESCO.[2] They naturally continued to foster such routine services as the library co-operation system and the commercial concessions scheme.

As might be expected, a large part of their attention was devoted to international affairs, which thrust themselves to the forefront. The Nazi arrests, deportations and executions of staff and students at Prague, Cracow, Oslo and other occupied universities, and of Jews of every profession and status, evoked resolutions of condemnation and abhorrence.[3] Professor E. R. Dodds of Oxford carried the A.U.T.'s sympathy and support to the beleaguered Chinese universities and brought back appeals for help from six institutions, and organized with Government and A.U.T. support a 'Books for China' fund.[4] As the occupied countries were liberated towards the end of the War, the A.U.T. and the Local Associations helped to arrange accommodation and hospitality for refresher visits by their university teachers to British universities.[5]

The most significant development in this field, of course, was the International University Conference held at New College, Oxford in July 1943, and the international association which sprang out of it. As we have already seen, this was in part a continuation of the pre-war Conferences, the fifth in the series, and of the loose international organization which they had stimulated, and in part a spontaneous fusion of the exiled university teachers from German-occupied countries who had reason enough for wishing to unite in defence of academic

1 E.g. Council Minutes, 10 June 1944: Interview with Mr. Shovelton, new Chairman of F.S.S.U. Council; *ibid.*, 26 May 1945: proposed deputation to U.G.C.
2 Council Minutes, 10 June 1944.
3 *Ibid.*, 1939–45, *passim.*
4 *Ibid.*, 16 December 1943 and 10 June 1944.
5 *Ibid.*, 20 December 1944 and 26 May 1945.

freedom. The Conference was called by the A.U.T. in co-operation with the Association of University Professors and Lecturers of the Allied Countries in Great Britain. Professor Gilbert Murray, O.M., the eminent Hellenist, took the chair, Professor R. C. McLean of Cardiff, the leading spirit in organizing the pre-war Conferences, again acted as Secretary, and, apart from Great Britain which supplied much the largest contingent, there were representatives from universities in Belgium, Czechoslovakia, France, Greece, the Netherlands, Norway, Poland, Sweden and the U.S.A. The President of the Association for the Allied Countries, Professor Stefan Glaser of the Polish University of Vilna, proposed that it should be reconstructed as a permanent post-war international association of university professors and lecturers, and the entire Conference was devoted to constructive proposals for its functions: to act as a clearing house and information centre on university affairs, to facilitate exchange visits of staff and students, to publish an international review, to organize further international conferences, to explore the standardization of weights and measures and the development of an international language either living or artificial, to safeguard the freedom and professional status and interests of university teachers, and even, in the ambitious proposal of Professor Glaser, to establish an international university institute as its headquarters and a centre for comparative education.[1] This was the origin of the present International Association of University Professors and Lecturers, whose provisional statutes were adopted at a general meeting on 25 September 1944, and of which the A.U.T. became the British National Group. Laurie, as willing and indefatigable as ever, became the Secretary General of the International Association, and remained so until his death.

From quite early in the War the A.U.T. began to turn its attention, if indeed it had ever lost sight of it, to the future of the universities after the War. In 1942 the Executive appointed a Sub-committee on Post-War Developments under the Convenership of Professor Roy Pascal of Birmingham, and invited suggestions. This was the beginning of a wholesale review of all

1 *Fifth Meeting of the International University Conference, Oxford, 1943: a Report issued by the A.U.T.* (reprinted in *Universities Review*, November 1944).

aspects of the Association's policy, and led to a series of three reports in 1944–45 which constituted a blueprint for the future of the universities and of the profession of such importance that it deserves a section to itself.

2. A POLICY FOR RECONSTRUCTION

From about the middle of the War, from indeed 'the turn of the tide' at El Alamein in the autumn of 1942 and even more from the publication of Sir William Beveridge's famous Report on Social Insurance and Allied Services in December of that year, the country became gripped by the fervour for post-war reconstruction. Some war leaders, and especially Churchill, deplored this as a distraction from the single-minded pursuit of victory, but in fact it played an indispensable part in maintaining the national morale and the will to victory through the long weary years of the struggle. The vision of a brave new world beyond the smoke and rubble of the present was the tiny but expanding circle of light at the end of the tunnel which raised hopes and kept dragging feet moving. The A.U.T. may be said to have anticipated this concern for the future and then to have caught its vitality and constructive zeal. Its informing spirit was a democratic zeal for a more egalitarian society in which the nation's resources, and especially its human resources of creative talent and skill, should be used to the full so as to enable all its members to share in its material and cultural benefits. This objective crystallized around the idea of the Welfare State, then a much wider concept than it has since become, and originated by Archbishop Temple and Sir Alfred Zimmerman in contrast with the 'Warfare State' of the Nazis and the Japanese to denote a State which put the whole welfare of all its citizens before the pathological military ambitions of authoritarian political leaders. The narrower modern concept of a 'social service State', with Government-organized social security, a national health service, equal educational opportunity for all, egalitarian taxation, and – a vital prerequisite after the unemployment of the inter-war period – a full employment policy, was an integral and essential part, but nevertheless only a part, of this ideal. It was in fact a high moral ideal of the creation of the good society which would apply the national unity and determination of war-time to the provision of a good life in peace and prosperity for all its citizens. The tripartite Report on University Developments which the A.U.T. issued in 1944 and 1945 was an attempt to determine the role and contribution of the universities and of university teachers in this ideal post-war society.[1] The first part was the work of Professor Pascal and his Sub-Committee, adopted by the Council in December 1943 and published in May 1944, and dealt with entry to the universities, degree courses, the structure of universities, inter-university co-operation, the staff and their remuneration, and student conditions. It began from the expectation that the main pressure for national reform would probably be directed towards the unification of the educational system, which would incorporate the universities in a national pattern. It welcomed the opportunity of extending the contribution of the universities to social advance, while at the same time insisting on their responsibility to a wider civilization than Britain and to other generations than the present for the preservation of the tradition of free study and learning. It suggested therefore that the approach to university problems be guided by four principles:

a An essential function of universities is the pursuit of knowledge not controlled nor guided by any private or corporate interest. Without this academic freedom of enquiry, learning will suffer irreparable harm. It is a part of that wider freedom of expression of opinion on all matters of public concern which university teachers claim as their right as citizens.

b Equally essential is their function of teaching: the dissemination of knowledge and culture. The instruction the universities give embraces training in the methods of thought and research, as well as factual information.

c The universities are not merely intellectual associations, but communities of people, of which young people are members during a most important formative period of their lives. They are, therefore, schools of communal living, in which the development of students as individuals is equally important with their development as social beings.

d The universities are a part of society, both morally and intellectually, and bear a direct responsibility to it. They must therefore study the application of organized knowledge to practical problems, and train men and women for particular tasks.

1 *Report on University Developments, Part I* (May 1944), *Part II* (May 1945), *Part III* (November 1945).

In keeping with these principles and with the current demand for equality of opportunity, the Report declared under 'Entry' that 'We affirm the principle that a university education should be open to all who can profit thereby'. Maintenance grants should be given where needed to all candidates who demonstrated their fitness to study, and should be generous enough where necessary to cover the loss to the family income of the earnings of a potential wage-earner. Their number should not be determined as in the past by the finance made available, but solely by need and the passing of an approved test agreed after consultation between the universities. This would undoubtedly mean increased numbers and a larger measure of State rather than Local Authority awards, but the increase would probably be of the order of 50 per cent over pre-war numbers, which would still leave the proportion of students to population in England and Wales lower than in most advanced countries, and there was an urgent social need for a larger flow of trained and educated citizens.

Under 'Mode of Entry' the Report distinguished between the needs of three types of sixth former: those who would go straight into civil employment, those of general ability intending to go to university, and those of outstanding academic ability (the 'scholar' class). It considered that they should all receive a common education as a basis for enlightened and instructed citizenship, and should all take a six-subject School Leaving Certificate, organized as now by regional examining boards, at 17-plus; the rest should go on to take a University Entrance Examination in fewer subjects, the passing of which should entitle them to a university place and, where necessary, to a maintenance grant; scholarships would be awarded to the very able on this examination, but would confer the title only and no further financial award would be necessary. Special arrangements should be made for young people who had left school to qualify, on special conditions, for university entrance at Continuation Schools and the like, and similar opportunities should be available to adults. Finally, in the interests of equality of opportunity the differences between secondary schools must be reduced, and the smaller and weaker schools brought up to the standards of the best, or some sort of concentration of the higher forms in larger units instituted.

Once at the university, the problems were the excessive specialization of most honours degree courses and their inappropriateness to the needs of the generalists, and the diffuseness and low status of, and the neglect of the students on, most pass degree courses. The Report therefore suggested experiments aimed at remodelling the honours courses so as to link up the specialist with other students and spheres of study, to reconstruct the pass degrees so as to provide an adequate intellectual training for those who did not want or require a specialist training, and to arrange the relations between the two so that one was not inferior to, and a dumping ground for rejects from, the other. They should be renamed Special and General degrees, both eligible for the award of honours. For the first one or two years both types of student should study groups of correlated subjects, though not necessarily for equal amounts of time, at the end of which it would be possible to transfer to whichever degree were the most suitable for the student. To accommodate the scheme the normal first degree course should occupy four years. Both degrees should include some study of the structure and evolution of society, of the social significance of the subjects studied, and of the main problems of philosophy. They should also promote the personal development of the student, his power of self-expression and use of English, and to this end should utilize discussion teaching with essays and other written papers in small classes to facilitate more intimate contact between teachers and students, either in tutorial classes or in 'seminars' (so unfamiliar that the word was put in quotation marks), 'a larger discussion class in which the discussion is led by a student.' General students not attached to any one department should have directors of studies, who would be responsible for allocating tutors to them.

A long section on the Structure of Universities drew heavily on the Report of the Sub-committee on the Representation of Teaching Staffs on University Governing Bodies of 1943, discussed in the last chapter. Its main concern was further to democratize the government of what it called the regional universities, that is those other than Oxford, Cambridge and London. Although it recognized that all universities now had a national function, it considered that their regional ties and associations were valuable and should be fostered. At the same time, local interests should no longer predominate in their systems of government, lay dominated Councils should not have a veto over purely academic matters, and the academic body should be represented on the Court, Council and the Finance Committee. The Senate should include all heads of departments, the librarian, and an adequate number of representatives of the non-professorial staff, who should also have a reasonable share in the work of Faculty Boards and of university committees, such as the Developments Committees which many universities had appointed during the War, and which ought to be continued during peacetime. In larger departments or groups of small ones Boards of Studies would facilitate the organization of work, but this should not preclude non-professorial participation in Faculty Boards. Researchers should not be a separate group but should be full members of staff and enjoy all staff rights. Each University should create a Research Endowment Fund controlled by a widely representative committee and accessible to all departments. Finally, students not only desired to be associated with plans for the development of universities but were also worthy of being heard. Because of their limited experience and the heavy burden of responsibility it would entail, they should not be too closely involved with government and administration, but the student body should be represented on the University Court, should have the right of direct access to Council, Senate and the Faculties, and the Student Guild or Union Council 'should bear a high degree of responsibility for student behaviour'.

A prescient section on 'Co-operation between the Universities' pointed out that

Hitherto each university has grown separately. The main task of each university has been to establish a body of instruction and research which would meet the most evident cultural and technical needs of our people. But these needs are multiplying at a vast rate, and have in some cases outstripped the development of the universities. Not only that; but it is impossible that each institution can, even in the most comprehensive plan of future development, make provision for a universal syllabus of teaching and research . . . We are faced with a new problem, decisions on which will have the most far-reaching effects on the government of universities. This problem can be summed up as the co-ordination or planning of university development.

A preliminary problem was that of the number and size of universities. A university must be large enough to justify adequate academic staffing and to have large enough departments to cover a reasonable range of teaching and research, but it should not be so large that contact between members of staff was lost, or the students segregated departmentally (though colleges or halls of residence could help maintain contacts across a larger body here). The best size could be roughly placed therefore within the range from 2,000 to 5,000 students, provided that residential accommodation was available for a substantial proportion of them. A national university policy should first build up the smaller universities to the optimum size, and transform some of the university colleges into independent universities of that size. 'We do not preclude the foundation of a new university, but consider that only special circumstances would justify this' – almost as if they had already foreseen the foundation of Keele. Secondly, it should set up a new body expressly to co-ordinate the work of the universities and encourage a rational and fruitful division of labour. Neither the U.G.C. nor the Vice-Chancellors' Committee could properly do this, since it required the direct co-operation of the people most intimately concerned, the academic staff. The Report therefore proposed an Academic Council, 'large and representative enough to be competent to discuss the work of the universities from all sides, and empowered to send recommendations to the University Grants Committee.' Its recommendations would not be compulsory on the universities, but this extension of their self-governing powers would be a surer and more efficient method of promoting their well-being than the plan of attaching them to a particular Department or Minister of State. 'The universities touch the life of the community at so many points that no single Department or Minister can deal adequately with so vast a range of activity.' The universities were already in contact with many Government Departments, and must remain so. If they were as a whole to have direct access to the Government, the most appropriate channel might be the Privy Council.

The post-war increase of students, the need for more research, and the extension of the tutorial system would require a very considerable increase in the number of staff, especially since many pre-war universities were under-staffed. The staff should have time for research and personal contact with the students, as well as teaching, and periodic release from teaching duties (the sabbatical term or year) was desirable for minds to be refreshed by sustained and undistracted intellectual effort. To attract the best candidates and promote migration between universities, vacancies should be publicly advertised, candidates interviewed by a Senate or Faculty committee (not, presumably, by the head of department alone), and in the rush period after the War care must be taken that appointments were not rashly made. First appointments especially should be carefully made of persons likely to proceed to the permanent staff after a probationary period of no more than two years. The assistant lecture grade, Grade III, should be abolished, and replaced by the two-year probation period in Grade II, by the end of which the lecturer should either be made permanent or dismissed at a full year's notice. Every person appointed to the permanent staff should be able to proceed uninterruptedly (without what is now called the merit bar) to the top of Grade II, by the age of 40 at the latest, and there should be an increased number of posts in Grade I so as to enable all who had given good service in the lower grade in teaching, administration and/or research to be promoted. Non-professorial heads of departments should have status and salaries not much below those of professors, and professorial salaries should not be kept abnormally low in certain subjects in order to pay excessively high salaries in those competing for manpower with industry and the higher professions. Above all, if the best men and women were to be attracted and kept in the profession, salary scales must be radically revised, and the Report reprinted the revised scale agreed in 1943:

Grade II: Lecturers	£400, £425, £475, and then by annual increments of £25 to £800.
Grade I: Senior Lecturers and Readers	£800, by annual increments of £25 to £1,000.
Non-professorial Heads of Departments	Should rise to at least £1,000.
Professors	£1,500 as basic salary.

Finally, superannuation under F.S.S.U. was, in consequence of past low salaries and the current rising cost of living, proving inadequate, and the pensions needed to be supplemented to a level bearing some reasonable relationship to final salary.

In the last section of Part I, 'Student Conditions', the Report repeated its recommendation that all students admitted to a university should where necessary be awarded a maintenance grant large enough to cover normal needs, purchase of books, travel in connection with study, and so on. Since a true university was a community, every student should have the opportunity of spending at least one year in a hall of residence, and the ultimate aim should be a fully residential system of university education. Simple hostels should be established in the country, for working parties of staff and students during vacations. Long vacations should be put to better use, in guided reading or practical work, appropriate occupational experience, travel abroad for language students, and summer courses and schools (though not for the extension of formal lecture courses). Library grants should be increased for the purchase of expensive textbooks, and university presses might well consider providing really cheap textbooks. Students needed advice on future occupations and careers before as well as during their time at university, and the composition and functions of Appointments Boards needed to be reviewed, so as to strengthen communication between students, employers and members, including non-professorial members, of the academic staff.

The second part of the Report, which concerned the Place of Research in the Life of a University, the Relations of Academic and Industrial Science, and the University as a Regional Focus, was adopted by the A.U.T. Council in December 1944 and published in May 1945. Under the first, chiefly the work of Professor G. C. Field of Bristol, it pointed out that research and teaching, the advancement and dissemination of learning, were inseparably linked, and that research in one or more of its many forms must enter fundamentally into the life and thought of all university departments. Both in the sciences and in the arts there were two broad types of research which supplemented and fertilized each other:

a The discovery of new 'facts' can occur in all studies, but is much more frequent in scientific or technological investigations than in other work. Much work of this kind is of great value, and will always command the services of many research workers. But it is rarely an

end in itself and its chief value is in furnishing additional material for
b that synthesis and generalization from known ideas and facts, including their critical revaluation, which bring into coherence and harmony aspects of a subject which have previously remained unrelated. This, the finest flower of research in any branch of knowledge, is common to all faculties.

In addition to these fundamental activities, the university teacher needed to keep himself well-informed of what was being done in his own and adjacent subjects by other scholars, by constant reading and discussion, and these too constituted research in the sense of the advancement of learning. The importance of the universities as research centres could hardly be overstated, both in their direct contribution to knowledge which might have far-reaching social effects, and in the indirect and no less important service of fostering the spirit of enquiry in the community as a whole. Here again the research and teaching aspects of university life were inseparably bound up and could not be divorced, and this principle should be the foundation of all development.

In making appointments to university staffs due weight should be given both to research distinction and to teaching ability, but more consideration might be given to differences in inclination and ability between individuals, and fewer teaching hours required from dedicated researchers, for whom special readerships and personal chairs, though not headships of departments, might be earmarked to crown their careers. More thought should be given to the integration of postgraduate research with the staffing of departments, and postgraduates might be required to give a limited number of hours of teaching both to gain experience and to help their departments, which might otherwise be tempted to make an excessive number of temporary Grade III appointments. The individual university teacher was always confronted by the conflicting claims on his time of teaching, administration and research, and it should be accepted as a principle of departmental staffing that every member, including the professor, should be able to devote roughly half his time to research. Adequate funds should be made available for research expenses. The individual must have freedom of choice and conduct of his personal research, and not be coerced by the head of department, who should ensure an equitable distribution of duties and facilities amongst all members of his staff. A radical increase of library grants was required to support research. Every university, as stated in Part I of the Report, should have a Research Endowment Fund, administered by a large committee, from which all departments and individuals could draw money, including where necessary the expenses of publication of research results. Undue pressure such as the withholding of promotion should not be brought to bear for premature publication of work which required maturity of thought and outlook – 'the risk of a few idle Professors would be a lesser evil than the certainty of a flood of inferior published work done to order.' Since universities could not be closed institutions in the matter of research, there should be greater facilities for the exchange of staff between universities and other research institutions, and members of staff and research students should be encouraged and assisted to attend conferences and joint discussions, and in field work and study abroad.

As far as the participation of students in research was concerned, the first consideration should always be their mental training and the development of their own ideas, and a research 'school' should not be allowed to degenerate into a workshop manned by an ever-changing series of technical assistants carrying out operations planned by the director. The immensely accelerated war-time progress in the applied sciences showed what could be done in the rest if the men and the money were made available. Both the number and the size of the postgraduate awards were too small, and an adequate two-year maintenance grant should be made available for every postgraduate student recommended by a university. Finally, valuable research work was not confined to full-time students, workers in industry and other occupations should be encouraged to pursue part-time degree courses, and to this end those universities which still made the Ph.D. an internal degree should open it to part-time students.

The Report then applied these principles to the organization of research in the faculties of arts, science and social studies, and the contributions which each could make to the development of culture, the progress of man's control over his physical environment and over his own social and political organization and relationships, and to the usefulness of educated men and women in their subsequent careers and to society.

The section on the Relations of Academic and Industrial Science, the work of Dr. V. E. Cosslett of Oxford, emphasized the universities as the main source of fundamental research which, through subsequent development in the field of applied science, was one of the main determinants of industrial progress, and the special moral responsibility of the universities to take an active interest in the industrial application of their research and in the continued intellectual well-being of their graduates in industrial and other research laboratories. University applied science departments should aim at producing men not merely skilled in technical training and research but with the breadth of vision and balance of judgement to lead in the development of the industries in which they were to serve. Close contact should be maintained between university departments and Government and industrial research institutes, and students should be encouraged to take vacation jobs in appropriate industries. There should be closer links between universities and neighbouring technical colleges, perhaps on similar lines to those proposed in Part III for teachers' training colleges. One special field for co-operation was the professional training of laboratory assistants in the whole range of university sciences. The increased consultation during the War between industrial, Government and university laboratories, in both the physical and biological sciences, was to be welcomed, but it raised the whole question of the relation of university research to outside sources of finance and control. The growing tendency of industries and individual firms to subsidize *ad hoc* research in universities on their own particular problems ought to be resisted, since it might lead to a form of commercial domination alien to the true university spirit and to the advancement of science itself. Effective contact with the industrial world could be maintained in other ways, such as a separate Research Council for each industry composed mainly of scientists and technologists, under the general direction of a Government body such as the Department of Scientific and Industrial Research, which could funnel State and industrial funds not only to the universities but also to the research associations, technical colleges and individuals engaged in appropriate work. No restriction should be placed on consultancy work by university teachers, with the usual consent of the university, for private firms or research associations, since the intellectual resources of a university should be available to the whole community, but the question of payment raised complex and difficult considerations, and it was to be hoped that the scientists could come to an agreement on a code of professional conduct in such matters. The university had a special responsibility to maintain contact with its scientific graduates in industry, research laboratories, schools and colleges, and to offer them the opportunity through regional discussions, summer schools, refresher courses and the like to keep up to date in their subjects. Machinery for this work could be provided by the development of Extra-Mural Departments along the lines discussed in the following section. Other means, too, could be found for ministering to the intellectual needs of scientists working in the region served by the university, and of dispelling the all too prevalent idea that a graduate's professional education was finished when he left the university.

The section on the University as a Regional Focus was largely the work of R. S. T. Chorley, Professor of Commercial and Industrial Law at the London School of Economics, and later to be Laurie's successor as Honorary General Secretary of the A.U.T. It pointed out that the older universities had for centuries been a dominant influence in the life of the community, and that the newer ones were now beginning to exercise the same influence within their own regions. A stage had been reached when the influence, though largely and rightly indirect, should become more positive and dynamic. 'We are now a democracy in which political power is widely distributed, and our society has become so complex that knowledge and understanding are essential to its effective control. One of the fundamental problems of our time is to ensure that our citizens are effectively equipped for life in the modern democratic state.' The universities had two different functions or responsibilities in this connection: to provide university training for the youth of the region, and it was to be expected (wrongly, as it turned out) that in the earlier post-war years the newer universities would continue to draw most of their students from their own regions; and, secondly, to act as centres of ideas and information for their regions. This second function of adult education was institutionalized in their Extra-Mural Departments, but these had never received the encouragement and financial support they deserved. The first step should be to put the Extra-Mural Departments, possibly renamed as Departments of Adult Education, upon a sound and firm basis, and secure for them adequate recognition from university governing bodies. Persons of academic distinction should be appointed to their staffs. They should be equipped on the same scale as internal departments. Some internal appointments, especially in arts, law, science, education, music and theology, might carry some responsibility for extra-mural teaching, though a number of full-time extra-mural staff would always be necessary, and these should be taken fully into the university body and given their own Board of Studies. Distinct and dignified premises should be provided for them, and there should also be in every large centre of population 'a cultural centre, Institute of Arts and Sciences, People's College, or whatever it might be called', in which the university's service to the community could be inter-woven with all the chief cultural activities and major civic pre-occupations of the locality, under the auspices of the Workers' Educational Association and the Local Authority. In addition to these urban colleges there should be rural hostels, of two kinds: the short-period hostel for weekend courses and con-ferences and holiday courses of a week or a fortnight, which could also serve for university staff and student working parties; and the folk high school (on the Scandinavian model) or residen-tial college for adult students, an institution then much in public discussion.

Within the institutional framework thus provided, and especially on the premises of the university and the People's Colleges, the traditional forms of adult education could be substantially developed: the university tutorial class extending over two or three years for one evening a week; lectures and dis-cussions of a more popular type, along the lines of the W.E.A. tutorial; an intermediate type of class by which students could mount to the more advanced level; classes in vocational subjects, some of whose students might be encouraged by a system of scholarships or maintenance grants to go on to the university; refresher courses and conferences for professional men, including lawyers, doctors, teachers, accountants, architects and local government officers; and courses, in co-operation with Chambers of Commerce, for young business men aspiring to leadership in commerce or industry. Students as well as university staff should be drawn into the work of the People's Colleges and rural hostels. Extra-Mural Departments should collaborate with the Local Authorities in providing non-political discussion groups on current affairs, with the Training Colleges in interesting potential teachers in part-time adult education, and in the educational work of the university settlements. Greater use should be made of radio for adult education, and of the many excellent museums in the country. The universities should set up Joint Committees with other bodies in the field of adult education, along the lines of those already existing with the Workers' Educational Association, with which they should continue to work in the closest co-operation and harmony. International contacts were as important in extra-mural as in internal university education, and should be developed through exchange visits of adult students, short residential courses in foreign countries, and the like. Finally, in order to influence national policy in this important field, the universities should set up a Joint Committee to co-ordinate their policy and assist the Ministry of Education in its implementation.

Part III of the Report dealt with the Education of Teachers and with the International Functions of a University, and was adopted by the A.U.T. Council in May and published in November 1945. The first section was a response to the Report of the McNair Committee on the Supply, Recruitment and Training of Teachers and Youth Leaders (1944), which suggested two alternative schemes for training the teachers who would be needed in much larger numbers to carry out the 1944 Education Act. Scheme A would place the responsibility on the universities, Scheme B on the existing Joint Boards, strengthened by the addition of such persons 'as directors of education, teachers, parents and other representative citizens'. The A.U.T. naturally favoured Scheme A, in which the university in each region would take over responsibility for the training of teachers, in association with the local training colleges, on the grounds that the universities owed a duty to the local community and that the education of (graduate) teachers had long been one of their functions; that as the highest stage in the hierarchy of educational institutions they ought to do what they could to strengthen the whole system; that they had the prestige and ability to establish and maintain academic standards without the rigidity and uniformity of a centralized body; and that they alone were in a position to unify the training of the whole profession, graduate and non-graduate. The A.U.T. agreed with the McNair Committee that the 'pledge', by which intending teachers received L.E.A. maintenance grants in return for promising to teach for a specified period, should be abolished, and grants provided on the same terms as already recommended for university degree students.

The universities would of course require additional finance, preferably in the form of a 'block grant' to each. Organization might follow the lines of the 'University Schools of Education' suggested by the McNair Report, perhaps modelled on the London University Delegacy for Training Colleges, which replaced the Joint Board for the London area. The new General and Special degrees recommended earlier in the A.U.T. Report would be specially valuable for graduate teachers. Non-graduates should receive a three-year course of both educational and professional training in the colleges, which should be part of the university body responsible for them. The location of the colleges and the delimitation of the area of each university's responsibility was a matter for national planning in consultation with the universities.

The final section, on the International Functions of a University, was largely the work of Professor R. C. McLean, the A.U.T.'s leading internationalist. It started from the position that international co-operation in the intellectual field had never been more necessary than at present, with the subjection of science and learning to political ideology in many countries, and the need for the rehabilitation of the universities and of academic life in the devastated areas of Europe and Asia. The British universities should co-operate by providing experts and advisers with the Conference of Ministers of Education of the Allied Governments which since November 1942 had been considering the re-equipping of universities, libraries and similar institutions damaged by the war, and should provide facilities for study and research for those university teachers and students abroad who would be deprived of them for some time to come. The A.U.T. should give all support to the International Association of University Professors and Lecturers formed in September 1944, in order to counter nationalist and racialist distortions of research and to liberate science and learning from the control of governments and political groups, and to encourage and co-operate with free associations of university teachers in all lands. The universities should promote meetings and interchanges of teachers and students, by means of lecture tours, visiting professorships and fellowships, the pairing for exchange and other relationships of British and foreign universities, the provision of accommodation for foreign visitors in halls of residence, holiday courses and conferences, and the like. Since many foreign academics and students would find it difficult to obtain currency, a fund should be established to support them. The mutual recognition of entrance requirements, courses and degrees should also be explored and encouraged. Finally, an International University Institute should be established under the governance of I.A.U.P.L., to perform for the universities of the world the functions which the Universities Bureau of the British Empire provided for imperial ones: to be a world centre of up-to-date information on all phases of university life and organization, including methods of instruction, new educational movements, and student welfare; to arrange exchanges and other contacts; to organize international university conferences, and act as a focus for international student organizations; and to be a stronghold for the maintenance of academic freedom.

This great Report on every aspect of the role, functions, organization and responsibilities of the universities in the post-war world was the first conspectus of the university system and its place in society which the Association had ever attempted. It had taken a world war to evoke it, since it is only in great emergencies which bring to a halt the normal routine of life and business that those involved are forced to look at what they stand for and where they are going. The A.U.T. was rightly anxious that it should have the influence it deserved, and sent out hundreds of offprints to associations connected with education, members of the U.G.C., university M.P.s, heads and finance committees of university institutions, and the press. The Executive held a Joint Conference with representatives of nineteen university governing bodies in June 1944 on aspects of the Report, and seven members met a group of university M.P.s at the House of Commons on 25 October 1944 to discuss it and a 'Memorandum on University Needs' arising out of it drawn up by Professor Brodetsky.[1] A Joint Conference was held in February 1945 with representatives of the nine Associations of teachers in secondary schools to discuss the section on university entry, at which the teachers opposed the separate examinations at 17-plus for School Leaving and University Entrance; the A.U.T. members sympathized with their alternative of one examination with additional 'scholarship' papers as in the existing Higher School Certificate, and the Association's policy was subsequently modified.[2]

What effect the policy for university reconstruction had on post-war developments it is, as always with pressure-group politics, difficult to say. Most of the important objectives were indeed achieved, notably the opening of university education to all who could prove their fitness to the universities' satisfaction by being accepted; the provision of full maintenance grants for all who needed them (as judged by a test of parental income and commitments); an expansion of student numbers not of 50 but of 80 per cent within a decade; some experimentation with broadening specialist honours courses and introducing general honours degrees; a further trend towards non-professorial participation in university government; a step towards university co-ordination not quite so large as an Academic Council in the shape of the annual Home Universities Conference from 1946 onwards; after the immediate post-war crush an improved staff-student ratio; academic salaries eventually higher than the 1943 scale though rapidly overtaken by inflation and the scramble of income increases for other professions; a considerable improvement in student residence, Appointments Boards and Health services and in finance and facilities for student social and recreational activities; a very large expansion of university research and much closer contacts between Government agencies, industry and the universities; almost a revolution in the role and status of Extra-Mural Departments and the involvement of the universities in adult education in their regions; the assumption by the universities of academic though not financial responsibility for the teacher training colleges; a useful contribution by the British universities and the A.U.T. itself to the rehabilitation of German and other European universities, and the successful establishment

1 Council Minutes, 10 June and 20 December 1944.
2 *Ibid.*, 26 May 1945.

of the I.A.U.P.L. as a permanent international forum for the university teaching profession (though not, sad to say, of the International University Institute) and one of the few international bodies of any kind in the cold-war world to unite both sides of the Iron Curtain.

Not all these achievements, it goes without saying, were exclusively due to the A.U.T. The Government, the Local Education Authorities, the teachers' organizations, and public opinion generally which was in favour of better and more egalitarian education all played their complementary and more decisive parts. The University Grants Committee in particular began in April 1944 to press the Government to prepare for the post-war reconstruction of the universities by the early release from national service of staff and students, the restoration of requisitioned premises, and the provision of substantially increased capital and recurrent grants.[1] Nevertheless, the existence of a clear-sighted, comprehensive and visionary plan by the university teachers at least ensured that their interests in and contribution to the post-war expansion would not go by default.

3. THE POST-WAR EXPANSION

The end of the War was immediately followed by an unprecedented growth of student numbers. As the U.G.C. put it in 1953, 'The period since the war has seen an expansion in the universities of this country at a rate to which no past period of the same duration affords a parallel.' The full-time student population, which had been about 50,000 before and about 37,000 for the greater part of the War, rose from 37,839 in 1944–45 to a peak of 85,421 in 1949–50.[2] The immediate rise was due to the rapid and orderly release, many under the Class B priority scheme, of ex-servicemen and other war workers, and to the generous provision by the Ministry of Education of 'Further Education and Training Grants' under which many thousands of students whose education had been interrupted by the War, and some who had never before thought of seeking a university place, were given full maintenance and fees. When these came to an end in the early 1950's, numbers fell back, but only by $5\frac{1}{2}$ per cent to

1 *University Development, 1935–47*, pp. 23–5.
2 U.G.C., *University Development, 1947–52* (1953), p. 11.

131

80,602 in 1953–54, which proved to be the post-war trough.[1] The eagerness for higher education fostered by the atmosphere of social reconstruction, a series of manpower surveys like the Barlow Report of 1946 which recommended a doubling within ten years of the country's output of scientists,[2] and above all the more generous provision of State and Local Authority maintenance grants recommended by the Ministry of Education Working Party on University Awards in 1949, raised student numbers to a new plane at about 80 per cent above the pre-war level.

State support for universities also advanced to a new level. Exchequer recurrent grant rose tenfold, from some £2 million at the end of the War to £20 million in 1952–53, and the percentage of university income provided by the State from 31·4 per cent in 1938–39 to 66·5 per cent in 1951–52.[3] Capital grants, which had been negligible before the War, became substantial: the universities estimated in 1947 that, apart from expenditure on sites and equipment, they would need to spend some £80 million over the next ten years on renewal and extension of buildings, and in fact the U.G.C. provided some £44 million over that period.[4]

This dependence on public finance on an unprecedented scale was inevitably accompanied by a new pattern of relations between the Government and the universities. The machinery remained ostensibly the same, but the University Grants Committee acquired a more initiating and executive role, somewhat mutedly expressed in the extension of its terms of reference. The original terms of reference in 1919 had read:

To enquire into the financial needs of university education in the United Kingdom and to advise the Government as to the application of any grants that may be made by Parliament towards meeting them.

They were amended in 1946 as follows:

To enquire into the financial needs of university education in the United Kingdom; to advise the Government as to the application of any grants made by Parliament towards meeting them; to collect, examine and make available information on matters relating to univer-

1 U.G.C., *University Development, 1952–57* (1958), p. 15.
2 *Report of (Barlow) Committee on Scientific Manpower* (Cmd. 6824, 1946).
3 U.G.C., *University Development, 1947–52*, p. 11; *1952–57*, p. 68.
4 *Ibid., 1952–57*, pp. 60–1; *1957–62*, pp. 114–17.

sity education at home and abroad; and to assist, in consultation with the universities and other bodies concerned, the preparation and execution of such plans for the development of the universities as may from time to time be required in order to ensure that they are fully adequate to national needs.[1]

One symptom of the U.G.C.'s new role was the considerable, if temporary, development of the system of earmarked grants. These were additional grants specifically appropriated to particular fields of study and research, generally of a vocational kind, which were found by a series of sub-committees of the U.G.C. to be in need of special development, notably by the Goodenough Committee on Medical Schools, the Teviot Committee on Dentistry (Cmd. 6727), the Clapham Committee on the Provision for Social and Economic Research (Cmd. 6868), the Loveday Committee on Higher Agricultural Education in England and Wales (Cmd. 6728), the Alness Committee on Agricultural Education in Scotland (Cmd. 6704), the Loveday Committee on Veterinary Education in Great Britain (Cmd. 6517), the Scarborough Commission on Oriental, Slavonic, East European and African Studies, and the McNair Committee on Teachers and Youth Leaders already noticed. Earmarked grants for these subjects rose from £8·9 million in 1947–48 to £16·6 million in 1951–52 and from 26·6 to 30·7 per cent of total recurrent grant. They were much criticized at the time for diminishing the universities' autonomy and diverting their energies into unwanted directions, but the U.G.C. argued that no university had been obliged to accept such a grant against its will, that block grants were not affected by them, and that they were in any case temporary and would be absorbed into the general grants as soon as the subjects concerned were on their feet.[2] This promise was indeed kept, but in a situation in which, as we shall see in the next chapter, the U.G.C. came increasingly to give advice and 'guidance', which it was extremely unprofitable to ignore, over the whole range of university expenditure.

Another symptom of the U.G.C.'s new role was the much tighter control over university building. At first this was an inevitable consequence of the post-war shortage of building materials and the limited capacity of the construction industry.

1 *Ibid.*, 1935–47, p. 7.
2 *Ibid.*, 1947–52, pp. 51–3.

In response to the U.G.C.'s estimate that the universities would need £40 million for new buildings and £10 million for sites and equipment during the quinquennium 1947–52 Hugh Dalton, the Chancellor of the Exchequer, warned that it was not likely that more than £20 million of building work could be started, and even that proved to be too optimistic. The rationing of steel supplies and the system of Government licensing of all building projects inevitably affected the universities.[1] Yet when general rationing and licensing came to an end, Government control over university building remained. Not only did the Treasury fix the quantum of building starts (expressed as the total sum of the contract prices of the buildings to be started) which could be made in each year, but the U.G.C. came to scrutinize the plans and contracts for each building, from the first schedule of requirements to be met by the architect to the final specifications put out to tender, so as to 'ensure so far as is humanly possible that full value is obtained for this expenditure'.[2]

A third symptom of increasing U.G.C. control was the establishment for the first time of uniform salary scales for university teachers. This was an objective for which the A.U.T. had striven from its earliest years, but the manner of its achievement underlined the weakness of the Association and indeed of the universities in face of the growing domination of the State. The first move in this direction seemed harmless enough. In fixing the quinquennial grants for 1947–52 the U.G.C. recognized 'standard rates' for professors, of £1,450 a year in universities (£1,500 in London) and £1,350 for university colleges, and added for each institution a sum for paying higher salaries to certain professors, in scarce subjects or of eminence in any subject. The important change came in 1949. For once the A.U.T. was taken completely unawares by an impending salary increase. The Association had of course been agitating since the end of the War for a general improvement, and in 1946, partly as a result of its representations, the U.G.C. had recommended and the Treasury had agreed to an all-round cost-of-living increase of £100 on salary scales, together with a family allowance of £50 for each child of a member of staff.[3] This still did not at all

1 *Ibid.*, pp. 65–8.
2 *Ibid.*, *1952–57*, pp. 62–5.
3 *Ibid.*, *1935–47*, pp. 46–7; A.U.T., Council Minutes, 20–1 December 1946.

points meet the A.U.T.'s claim, based on the 1921 Agreed Scheme as adjusted to 1943 prices, and meanwhile prices were rising more steeply than during the War and incomes were rising faster in most other occupations. In 1948 the inauguration of the National Health Service and the Report of the Spens Committee on the remuneration of consultants and specialists, which recommended salary scales so far in excess of those of clinical university teachers that they threatened to lead to the depopulation of the medical schools, produced a crisis in the matter of university salaries generally. Clinical salaries had always been somewhat in excess of other academic salaries, and the gap which would have resulted from a rise to the Spens level without any increase for non-medical and pre-clinical staffs would have created friction throughout the universities.[1] The Vice-Chancellors were alarmed at the prospect, and early in 1949 the A.U.T., taking note also of a recent revision of the 1946 scales for civil servants, drew up a new Memorandum on Salaries which at last broke away from the 1921 basis. It proposed the following scales of non-medical salaries:

Professors	Within the range £2,000 to £2,500, with the possibility of a higher figure when warranted by special circumstances.
Readers	Within the range £1,300 to £1,800.
Senior Lecturers	£1,300, rising by annual increments of £50 to £1,600.
Lecturers	£700, rising by annual increments of £50 to £1,250.
Assistant Lecturers	£550–£600–£650, to be included in the Lecturers' establishment, and to receive the status and salary of lecturers on satisfactory completion of a period of probation not exceeding three years.

London salaries should be £100 higher throughout, and the child allowance should be increased from £50 to £60.[2]

Before the A.U.T. could press its claim, it was overtaken by events. In February and March the Chancellor of the Exchequer, Sir Stafford Cripps, announced revisions of medical

1 *University Development, 1947–52*, pp. 37–8.
2 Council Minutes, 20–1 May 1949.

and non-medical university salaries to operate from 1 April and 1 October 1949 respectively. The whole range of salaries was as follows:

Clinical posts
Revised salaries operating from a date not earlier than 1 April 1949.

Professors	Salaries ranging from £2,250 to £2,750 a year.
Readers	Salaries within the range of the maxima indicated below for lecturers.
Lecturers	Scales of salary rising from £600 a year to maxima ranging from £1,500 to £2,000 a year (or in the case of lecturers holding posts of special responsibility such as the headship of an independent department, £2,500 a year).

Pre-clinical posts
Revised salaries operating from a date not earlier than 1 October 1949.

Professors	Salaries ranging from £2,000 to £2,500 a year.
Readers	Salaries within the range of the maxima indicated below for lecturers.
Lecturers	Scales of salary rising from £600 a year to maxima ranging from £1,200 to £1,800 a year.

Non-medical posts
Revised salaries operating from 1 October 1949.

Professors	The grants will be related to basic salaries of £1,600 a year in universities and university colleges (in London £1,650), with increased provision for supplementation allowing for a wider range of salaries than hitherto.
Readers and Senior Lecturers.	A range of salaries with varying maxima up to £1,600 a year.
Lecturers	Scales rising generally from £500 to £1,100 a year.
Assistant Lecturers	Salaries ranging from £400 to £500.

Thus the 'standard rate' for non-medical professors in universities and university colleges, first introduced in 1947, was raised and the additional sum for each institution was reassessed to allow a wider range of professorial spread than before.[1]

In spite of some justifiable, if short-lived, satisfaction both at

1 *University Development, 1947–52*, pp. 38–9.

the level of the award and at its approach to uniformity between universities, the A.U.T. found two very disquieting features in it. The first and most obvious was the size and formalization of the medical differential. The Association had always recognized that clinical responsibility for the life and death of patients deserved some additional reward, but a difference of nearly 40 per cent in the basic salary of a professor, for example, was excessive; while the pre-clinical differential awarded for no difference in duties even in the same department but for the mere possession of the lowest medical over against the highest other academic qualification, could only be deemed a monstrous provocation, and a device for keeping down general university salaries by circumventing the pressure of external forces at the point where they threatened to be effective. The U.G.C. commented in its next Report:

We have received much evidence, in the course of our talks with representatives of staffs, of the unpopularity of this feature of university life, and the criticism does not come entirely from the non-medical side. We have much sympathy with this sentiment, but we are bound to recognize that this form of differentiation, while entirely lacking justification from the academic point of view, is an unavoidable necessity. There can be no question of levelling down the medicals, and levelling up the non-medicals is not going to be a practicable policy for some time.[1]

In fact, it took fifteen years and a National Incomes Commission report to get rid of the pre-clinical differential, and even then not completely or permanently.

The other and more disturbing feature of the award was 'the atmosphere of complete secrecy in which it was enshrouded. Neither the A.U.T. nor the University Governing Bodies . . . were permitted to know that anything at all was afoot until the Chancellor announced the new clinical and pre-clinical scales in February.'[2] Before the War the A.U.T. had been continually frustrated by its inability to bring to a confrontation the university teachers' ultimate paymaster, the Treasury, but in the inter-war deflation when salary increases were rare to the point of non-existence this was scarcely of burning practical significance.

1 *Ibid.*, p.39.
2 *The A.U.T. and Salaries* (pamphlet by Mr. W. A. Wightman), February 1955, p. 2.

In the post-war situation of spiralling prices and incomes, by contrast, the absence of any formal salary negotiating machinery was a handicap of the most serious kind, adding helplessness to frustration as the incomes of more fortunately placed professions raced ahead. This was particularly inflaming to the wave of new assistant lecturers and junior lecturers who came in in the expansion of staff numbers in the first post-war decade, at starting salaries much lower than those in schoolteaching, the civil service and most other professions, and the 1949 award did little or nothing for these. Indeed, the A.U.T. labelled the period 1949–1954 'the turbulent years',[1] in which staff discontent, especially at the junior level, rose to a crescendo, and in many universities assistant lecturers' or junior staff associations sprang up to challenge or put pressure on the A.U.T. – a near-repetition of the situation which had originally given birth to the Association.

Deprived of formal means of attacking the problem, the A.U.T. resorted to the traditional informal one of lobbying the Vice-Chancellors and the U.G.C. In 1952 the announcement of the quinquennial grant with no provision for increased salaries and a complacent speech by the Chancellor of the Exchequer that the ensuing five years would be a period of consolidation provoked the A.U.T. to issue a fresh memorandum on salaries and to press it upon the Vice-Chancellors' Committee at an interview on 13 May. The Vice-Chancellors were sympathetic, but could do little about it except offer to relieve the assistant lecturers if they were permitted to. In the event the Chancellor of the Exchequer did permit their maximum to be raised by £50, provided that the universities found the money from their own resources, and the U.G.C. gave recognition to weight-for-age schemes in some universities by which older-than-average assistant lecturers received from £50 to £150 more. Convinced that this was not enough to alleviate the hardship, the A.U.T. took the matter up at a meeting on 13 November with eighteen interested M.P.s chaired by Hilary Marquand, who undertook to discuss with the U.G.C. and the Chancellor of the Exchequer the question of how far the 1949 scale was binding on the universities and to what extent they might supplement it out of their own resources. The U.G.C. refused to see them, on the grounds that its responsibility was not to Parliament but to the Chancellor

1 *Ibid.*, p. 3.

of the Exchequer. Hilary Marquand, M.P., and Christopher Hollis, M.P., early in 1953 approached the Chancellor, who flatly stated that in the present state of the country he could not provide the additional grants to increase university salaries.[1]

Meanwhile, the cost of living had risen by no less than 25 per cent since the 1949 award and Local Associations were agitating for a general review of salaries. Professor R. G. D. Allen of the London School of Economics, with considerable experience in the field of civil service and other professional remuneration, pointed out that tribunals attached more importance to salary rates in analogous professions than to cost of living. The publication of the White Paper on National Income and the preliminary returns of the 1951 occupational Census enabled Mr. Wightman, who in 1949 had succeeded Professor Brodetsky as Convener of the Salaries and Grading Committee, to calculate the average rise in professional salaries between 1949 and 1953, which he found to be also 25 per cent. He also learned that the British Medical Association had claimed an increase for consultants and specialists in line with the Danckwertz award for general practitioners, which would, if conceded, have had the same repercussion on university medical salaries as the Spens Report of 1948. His sub-committee therefore drew up a Memorandum with a new scale, 25 per cent above that of 1949 (the one claimed, not the one awarded), and laid it before a joint meeting with representatives of the Vice-Chancellors on 25 September 1953. The meeting proved to be crucial. The Vice-Chancellors were not aware of the B.M.A.'s claim, and agreed that its success would involve the universities. They also expressed sympathy with the continued hardships of the junior staff, and undertook to give the matter further consideration. At a second meeting on 23 April 1954 they informed Mr. Wightman and his colleagues that they had decided to press for an immediate revision of salaries. Further pressure was brought to bear on local M.P.s and questions asked in the House of Commons in July and October. Finally, on 16 November 1954 the Chancellor, Mr. R. A. Butler, announced a special grant of £2¼ millions for the improvement of university salaries.[2]

1 *Ibid.*, pp. 3–4; Council Minutes, 16–17 December 1952, 22–3 May 1953.
2 *The A.U.T. and Salaries*, pp. 4–5; Council Minutes, 22–3 May 1953, 28–9 May, 15–16 December 1954.

The scales awarded in 1954 were much less than the A.U.T. asked for, but a substantial improvement on 1949:

Clinical posts

Professors	Range £2,500—£2,850.
	(May be increased to £3,000 in certain cases.)
Readers	Within range of maxima for lecturers.
Lecturers	£700 to maxima ranging from £1,750 to £2,400 (£2,750 for posts of special responsibility).

Pre-clinical posts

Professors	Range £2,250—£2,850.
Readers	Within range of maxima for lecturers.
Lecturers	£700 to maxima ranging from £1,450 to £2,050.

Non-medical posts

Professors	Basic salaries £1,900 with provision for supplementation up to £2,850.
Readers and Senior Lecturers	Range with varying maxima up to £1,850.
Lecturers	£650—£1,350.
Assistant Lecturers	£550—£650.[1]

These scales were received not unfavourably, until it was discovered that in their implementation lecturers would not be transferred to the corresponding point on the new scale but instead given a flat increase of £150 throughout, less anything they were already receiving under the weight-for-age scheme, and, since the annual increments remained at £50, would take longer to get to the top. In December the A.U.T. Council deprecated this, together with the continued pre-clinical differential and the still unsatisfactory position at the lower end of the profession.[2]

This, then, was the salary position when the first wave of university expansion after the War had spent itself. Considerable gains had been made, and the A.U.T. could claim in 1955 that since 1949 it had been the prime mover in action taken on salaries.[3] But every move made by the prime mover had to be a new initiative, since there was still no accepted machinery

1 *The A.U.T. and Salaries*, p. 5.
2 Council Minutes, 15–16 December 1954.
3 *The A.U.T. and Salaries*, p. 7.

through which the making and negotiation of salary claims could be routinized. The A.U.T. might be excused for thinking that those on the receiving end of this muffled chain of almost non-communication preferred it this way, since it was only after prolonged and exhausting shouting that the noise from without could reach them. Even then, the award, if any, was handed down by administrative fiat, through the device of a Parliamentary announcement by the Chancellor of the Exchequer, without any opportunity for objection or argument. By a silent revolution the State had taken over control of academic salary scales from the universities, while at the same time rejecting the responsibility for negotiating or even listening to arguments about them. The only argument which had any effect was the threat that university teachers might 'vote with their feet', and depart for other professions or for universities abroad. But unfortunately, as we shall see, the conditions of work were so attractive that there never was in this period a problem of recruitment.

The post-war expansion of student numbers naturally led to a large expansion of staff. The total number (excluding those of the rank of lecturer and below at Oxford and Cambridge) rose from 3,994 in 1938–39 to 8,952 in 1951–52, an increase of 124 per cent. This was considerably larger than the increase in student numbers, since a deliberate attempt was made to extend individual and small group teaching, and the staff–student ratio (outside Oxford and Cambridge) improved from 1:10 in 1938–39 to 1:8 in 1951–52.[1] The improvement was partly due to the large increase in postgraduate students, who naturally took up more staff time than undergraduates but, being nearer the frontiers of knowledge, repaid it in greater interest for the staff. Their presence, smaller group teaching to undergraduates and, in spite of an increased burden of administration in expanding institutions, more time for research and for keeping abreast of modern knowledge in their subjects, made the profession more attractive to newcomers, who were willing to accept the low initial salaries for the sake of the intellectual advantages. This 'substitution' of, as it were, payment in kind (time to do one's own work) for cash made the task of the A.U.T. more difficult since, except in the case of the doctors and some other professional men such as engineers and architects who could earn more

1 *University Development, 1947–52*, p. 35.

The War and Reconstruction, 1939–54

for doing the *same* work outside, very few university teachers felt so strongly about the low salaries as to resign from the profession. For the great majority it was a privilege to be a university teacher, and privileges have to be paid for.

The A.U.T. of course gained in other ways from the expansion. Membership much more than doubled, from 1,899 in 1938–39 and 2,167 in 1945–46 to 4,421 in 1951–52 and 4,949 in 1953–54.[1] Part of the increase was due to the affiliation of the Scottish A.U.T. in 1949. Much of the credit for the merger must go to Mr. W. A. Wightman, President of the southern Association in 1948–49, who toured all the branches of the Scottish Association and won them over. The Scottish Annual Meeting at Edinburgh in February 1949 voted to affiliate to the A.U.T. (U.K.) as the A.U.T. (Scotland), a separate Section with its own constitution, Officers and Executive Committee, electing two of its members and its Secretary to sit on the Executive of the United Kingdom body. The first Scottish representatives, ten of them, were welcomed to the A.U.T. Council in December 1949, and in 1953 the first President from the Scottish Section, Dr. G. R. Tudhope, was elected President of the British A.U.T.[2]

The united Association managed to maintain its pre-war percentage of the profession, approaching half the total including Oxbridge and the medicals, and over two-thirds of the non-medical university teachers outside Oxford and Cambridge.[3] Towards the end of the period membership was rising faster than staff members, and was to reach 56 per cent of the whole profession by 1955–56. One strongly marked feature of the expansion was the declining proportion of professors both in the profession and in the A.U.T. Between 1938–39 and 1951–52 the total number of professors increased by 45 per cent, that of lecturers by 190 per cent, and the ratio of professors to other ranks declined from 1:3·5 to 1:5·9. A.U.T. membership naturally reflected this change, and professorial members declined from 20 per cent of the total in 1935–36 to 14 per cent in 1953–54. This also affected the composition of the Executive, which before

1 Council Minutes, 1939–54, *passim*.
2 T. R. Bolam, 'The Scottish Association of University Teachers', *British Universities Annual*, *1964*, pp. 82–4; Council Minutes, 20–1 December 1949.
3 Council Minutes, 5–6 January 1949 (only 5¾ per cent of medical university teachers were members, compared with 68½ per cent of the non-medicals in 'Redbrick' universities).

the War had normally had a slight professorial majority and now normally had a slight non-professorial one, while from 1945 to 1954 there were five professorial and four non-professorial Presidents, compared with fifteen to five between the Wars.[1] As before, however, Officers and Executive were elected for their ability, personality and contribution to the work of the Association, without regard to their academic status, and there was no specific polarization between the two levels. The lynchpin of the administration was still that old work-horse Laurie, long now a professor emeritus, and the doyen of the convenors was Mr. W. A. Wightman, Senior Lecturer in Chemistry at Leeds, and Convenor of the two most time-consuming sub-committees, Salaries and Grading and Superannuation, and, as we shall see, an important *ad hoc* committee on technology in the universities.

A more important division was that between Oxbridge and the rest. Although both Oxford and Cambridge now had Local Associations, Oxford had only 103 and Cambridge only 18 members in 1947–48 out of staffs numbering over 800 and over 700 respectively.[2] Their few members were very keen, and some of them, such as Professor E. R. Dodds of Oxford and Dr. V. E. Cosslett of Cambridge, both sometime Presidents of the A.U.T., played a very active role in the national Association. Nevertheless, the old tension between the Oxbridge tradition of a community – or, rather, a group of collegiate communities – of gentlemen-scholars who did not need any other form of support, and the professional academics elsewhere with their natural penchant for professional organization, still polarized university teachers into Oxbridge sheep and Redbrick goats.[3] One of the gibes of the former against the latter was that the A.U.T. was really a trade union, and from time to time some members of the Association who are not automatically horrified by the notion have toyed with the idea of registering, or procuring a certificate, as a trade union in order to bring the universities and through them the U.G.C. and the Treasury to arbitration in salary matters. One such occasion was in 1953, when the A.U.T. sought the advice of the Registrar of Friendly Societies who, having

1 Council Minutes, 1919–54, *passim*.
2 Council Minutes, 5–6 January 1949.
3 Cf. 'Bruce Truscott', *Redbrick University* (1943).

looked at the Rules, 'felt some doubt' whether the Association was a trade union within the meaning of the 1913 Act.[1] For better or for worse the A.U.T. was driven back into its accustomed role as a professional association, concerned with all the interests, and not only the material ones, of its members.

The subscription was raised in 1946 for the first time since 1921, from fifteen shillings to one guinea. Together with the increased membership this considerably improved the income of the Association from about £1,400 a year before the War to about £5,000 in the early 1950's. Despite the rising prices, such an income together with the increased responsibilities of an expanding membership gradually turned the Executive's thoughts towards a more professional administration. Miss Davies, the Assistant Secretary, was allowed to engage a typist in 1948, and from 1952, with Laurie's impending retirement, the Executive began to look for a suitable house for a London headquarters to accommodate her and her exiguous staff. On the death of Laurie in 1953, a part-time Development Officer, Mr. R. L. Collett, M.B.E., M.A., F.R.I.C., was appointed at £400 a year to assist the new Honorary General Secretary, Lord Chorley, in the work of fostering and expanding the Local Associations, but the London headquarters was not finally acquired and converted until 1955, and belongs to the next chapter.[2] In 1954 the Association, in spite of its doubled size and trebled income, was still the same amateur professional body it had been before the War.

It was, nevertheless, even more active, both in its economic and educational functions. On the material side, we have already seen the new and more aggressive role it was forced to play in salary matters. It was also successful in its long-term policy of bringing the salaries of parallel professions employed by the universities into line with those of academics and of getting the Vice-Chancellors' Committee and the U.G.C. to accept the A.U.T.'s legitimate interest in them, notably the librarians, the extra-mural tutors and, in 1951, the staffs employed in the universities on the Ministry of Agriculture's Provincial Agricultural Economics Service. In 1949 a Committee on Sabbatical Leave convened by Professor R. B. Onians of Bedford College,

1 Council Minutes, 18-19 December 1953.
2 *Ibid.*, 5-6 January 1949, 22-3 May 1952, 18-19 December 1953.

London, urged that a regular system of study leave, such as existed in seventeen out of twenty-six countries surveyed by the International Association of University Professors and Lecturers, should be instituted in this country, on the basis of one term or year off in seven.

On superannuation, an enquiry in 1946 came to the conclusion that in most cases F.S.S.U. 'gives actually better yields than any scheme in which pension is based entirely on the retiring salary, even when a substantial death benefit is available as well'. Only where past salary scales had been very low or promotion to a high salary came very late in life did the civil service and local government schemes show an advantage, and even this tended to disappear if the large F.S.S.U. death benefit were sacrificed by taking out a deferred annuity policy. Besides providing better yields the F.S.S.U. scheme gave a variety and flexibility which no other could compass, and transfer in or out of the profession, at any stage of a man's career was extremely easy.[1] All this, however, related to a reasonably stable prices and incomes situation such as had existed between the Wars, and the Association found itself continually having to plead on behalf of 'hardship cases', men and women retiring currently whose pensions, based on 15 per cent contributions out of a lifetime of low salaries, were too small to live on. In 1947 the U.G.C. asked for definite evidence of hardship, and the sub-committee collected returns of the 115 university teachers who had retired in the previous eight years, and had no difficulty in convincing them and the university authorities that there was a case for augmentation. Some universities were already doing something to help, and others were persuaded to, but the level did not satisfy the A.U.T., which in 1950 adopted the principle that a retired man and wife ought to be able to count on a pension equal to two-thirds of the retiring salary. Some alleviation was achieved by a general scheme of supplementation which came into operation in 1953, but it was still below the A.U.T.'s standard. One difficulty was that the Treasury would not sanction supplementation greater than that allowed to civil servants under the Pensions (Increase) Acts, and this was particularly hard on university teachers who retired on pre-1954 salaries. However, steady

1 *Report on F.S.S.U. and other Superannuation Schemes* (adopted 21 December 1946), 1947.

pressure on the Vice-Chancellors' Committee and the U.G.C. led to the announcement by the latter in 1954 that funds would be provided for all universities to bring the simple annuity value (on the member's life only, not his wife's) of F.S.S.U. benefit up to £700 for a lecturer, £850 for a reader or senior lecturer, and £1,000 for a professor.[1] £700 was nearly two-thirds of the then non-medical lecturer's maximum of £1,100, but it was little more than half of the new maximum of £1,350 which came into operation in October. In short, F.S.S.U. continued to be the best pension scheme for those due to retire in the future but never, it seemed, at least in a period of inflation, for those retiring now.

The age of retirement exercised the A.U.T. during these years. Before the War, with high unemployment, there was a tendency to think in terms of earlier retirement, and amongst the salaried professions university teachers were amongst the few who retired at 65 (70 in Scotland) rather than at 60, and even they retained the option to do so under F.S.S.U. policies, which matured at 60 and accumulated at compound interest thereafter. After the War, with expansion, shortages of experienced staff, and a further increase in the average expectation of life, there was a move to increase the age of retirement in many universities to 67. The Association was divided on this, between those who wanted the right to continue to work as long as possible and those who wanted to retire early or, more to the point, wanted their senior colleagues to retire early to make room at the top for themselves. After long discussions in Council, Executive and an *ad hoc* committee, the Association failed to agree on any change from the usual retiring age of 65, with option to retire at any time after 60, but made no objection when universities such as Oxford and Manchester extended the age to 67.[2]

On the educational side, university expansion itself was the consuming interest. In 1947 a sub-committee was set up on the subject, divided into arts, science and technology, and social science sections, convened respectively by Professor Roy Pascal of Birmingham, Dr. V. E. Cosslett of Cambridge, and Professor

1 Council Minutes, 1947–54, *passim*; Note by Mr. Wightman supplied by Miss Davies.
2 Council Minutes, 22–3 May 1953, 28–9 May, 15–16 December 1954.

C. B. Fawcett of University College, London. After much deliberation and amendment in Council the Report was adopted by Council in May 1949. Its recommendations, apart from a doubling instead of a 50 per cent increase of student numbers over the pre-war level, added little to the Report on University Developments of 1944–45, on which indeed it drew heavily.[1]

More to the point was the A.U.T.'s involvement in these years in campaigns for the general expansion of opportunities for higher education, and for the particular expansion of technology in the universities. In 1949 the Sub-committee on the Selection and Maintenance of Students, under Professor R. B. Onians, instituted an enquiry into the methods of selection of students, and followed this up with a questionnaire on the number and adequacy of the maintenance grants received by new entrants in that year. From these it became clear that some Local Education Authorities were not carrying out the recommendations of the recent Working Party on University Awards (to which the A.U.T. had made representations), and a series of meetings was arranged with the main secondary school teachers' organizations, who co-operated by enquiring into the number of suitably qualified pupils who were unable to enter universities owing to lack of places or inadequate grants. The numbers proved not to be large, but the most serious wastage occurred amongst bright pupils leaving school for various reasons, including financial ones, at the age of 15 or 16. At that time limited numbers of awards were made by the State mainly in the form of State Scholarships (raised from 2,000–2,500 to 4,000 a year on the recommendation of the Working Party) and by Local Authorities (raised from 4,000 to 7,000 a year) on the results of the Higher School Certificate and the Advanced level of the General Certificate of Education which replaced it in 1951. In effect this meant that it was the Ministry of Education and the L.E.A.'s, not the universities, which determined who and how many should receive grants, and this had the doubly unfortunate result of taking the decision as to the candidate's suitability out of academic hands and of adding to the uncertainty of the pupil as to whether, even if he were accepted by a university, he would be able to find the money to go – an uncertainty which discouraged many from staying at school and making the attempt.

1 'Report on University Expansion', *Universities Review*, September 1949.

There ensued by 1953 a tug-of-war between the A.U.T. and the universities on one side and the L.E.A.'s on the other over who should be the ultimate arbiter of university entrance, with the A.U.T. considering a system of exclusively State awards and the Association of Education Committees attacking the universities for their high wastage rates in the first year (which an A.U.T. survey for 1949–53 showed to be only 4·9 per cent). However, partly as a result of the publicity given to the matter in the press, it appeared that the new Selection Panels for University Awards – chiefly sub-committees of the L.E.A.'s – were in fact making grants mainly on the basis of acceptance by the university and that the level of awards had generally been improved, and the A.U.T. Council in May 1954 came down in favour of the existing system.[1] The question was not finally resolved until the Anderson Report on Student Awards in 1960, but that belongs to the next chapter.

The A.U.T. also became involved in a controversy over the expansion of technology. In 1949 the Sub-committee on Professional Vocational Training under Mr. S. G. Richardson of Leeds had its attention diverted by a heated discussion in *The Times* and elsewhere on whether the country's increasing demand for technologists could be better met by the existing university departments or by new Institutes of Technology along the lines of the Dutch and Swiss Technisches Hochschulen or the Massachusetts Institute of Technology. The Association was naturally in no doubt, and the Council in December 1949 passed resolutions that technological education was a proper and desirable part of the work of a university, that technological progress in the United Kingdom could best be secured by the expansion of existing and the development of new university faculties and departments, that no branch of technology should be excluded from universities, and that if new Institutes of Technology were set up they should be sponsored by existing universities and come under the U.G.C. These were followed up by a Report by the indefatigable Mr. Wightman in 1950 on the Place of Technology in Universities which pointed out that universities from their medieval origins had contained such 'technologies' as law and medicine, that the modern ones were admirably equipped to teach the underlying scientific principles

1 Council Minutes, 1949–54, *passim*, and information from Miss Davies.

and the breadth of vision which technologists needed to advance the progress rather than merely service the existing needs of industry, and that the Continental Technisches Hochschulen and M.I.T. were really technological universities with a wider range of studies than the applied sciences.[1]

In the spring of 1951 it was learned that the Government was contemplating early action along lines unwelcome to the universities, and the A.U.T. arranged an all-party meeting on 5 March with twenty M.P.s and peers with the war-time scientific adviser, Lord Cherwell, in the chair, to press its views. Whether or not they had any effect, a Government White Paper shortly afterwards expressed interest in a Technological University (not an Institute of Technology), but postponed it because of the heavy capital cost. After the general election the new Conservative Government changed the policy, and in January 1953 the Financial Secretary to the Treasury, Mr. Boyd-Carpenter, announced that the Government proposed to finance a major expansion of Imperial College, London, from 1,650 to 3,000 students by 1957–62, as a co-ordinating centre for technological education, and that similar centres would be developed in other parts of the country.[2] In due course larger resources were put into the Glasgow Royal and the Manchester Colleges of Science and Technology, but the twists and turns of this policy, and especially the upgrading of the Colleges of Advanced Technology in 1956 and their transformation after the Robbins Report of 1963 into universities also belong to the next chapter.

The Association was also concerned to improve the quality and supply of university technicians in scientific and technological laboratories, and joined with the Association of Scientific Workers and the British Association of Chemists in calling a Conference on the training of laboratory technicians on 23 February 1946, which was attended by over 200 representatives of the three Associations, the universities, Government Departments, and both sides of industry. The scheme of training presented there was substantially that of the A.U.T., and Professor R. C. McLean of Cardiff was elected to the Committee to

1 *Ibid.*, 20–1 December 1949; *Report on the Place of Technology in the Universities*, 1950.
2 Council Minutes, 20–1 December 1949, 18–19 May 1950; *Laurie*, pp. 36–8.

draw up the Conference report on ways of putting it into practical effect. He reported to the A.U.T. Council in December 1947 that the Committee had surveyed the existing provision and drawn up a national scheme of part-time training, with a three-year course for the Certificate and a further two years for the Diploma. Detailed syllabuses had been prepared by the technicians themselves, and would be submitted to wide examination and discussion by interested parties before being brought before a further Conference. After a further Report, the Committee handed over the papers to the City and Guilds of London Institute, already providing a wide range of courses and examinations in technical education, which set up an Exploratory Committee on which the A.U.T. was again represented by McLean. Courses were instituted at various technical colleges, beginning with Paddington in 1950, and in 1951 the Institute set up a provisional national joint body on the recruitment and training of laboratory technicians (other than those in clinical medical laboratories), which did much to achieve the A.U.T.'s objective.[1]

In the field of library co-operation the figures of books requested through the Enquiry Office at the National Central Library took a leap to a new level of activity, from under 5,000 a year before and during the War to over 18,000 in 1953. The annual Joint Conferences were broken off by the War, but were resumed again in 1948, when Professor Onians of the A.U.T. was elected Chairman. Laurie resigned the Secretaryship in 1950, but remained as Treasurer to provide a link with the A.U.T. office. A new problem faced by university and indeed other libraries was the drain of historical materials and especially back sets of periodicals from the country, chiefly to wealthy American libraries. The Conference therefore launched a project in 1949 by which British university libraries divided the labour of purchasing such materials, each of them specializing in a short period of about ten years between 1600 and 1800, which has since been extended back to 1550 and forward to 1835.[2] By this means large masses of invaluable historical printed sources have been preserved in this country.

1 Council Minutes, 24–5 May 1946, 19–20 December 1947, 19–20 December 1950; information from Miss Davies.
2 *Laurie*, pp. 43–4; A. J. Hatley, 'The Role of the A.U.T. in Library Co-operation', *British Universities Annual*, 1964, pp. 75–6.

The Association pursued its interest in broadening the general education of students, expressed in its war-time Report on University Developments, through a series of discussions in Council from May 1947, and the May Council in 1948 was extended to allow for a fuller discussion on the methods adopted in other countries, led by Professor I. L. Kandel of Manchester, formerly Professor of the History of Education at Columbia University, New York. A sub-committee was later set up and collected information which it circulated to Local Associations, but the Council came to the conclusion in May 1951 that the more useful form of progress would be to invite interested individuals to publicize their views in the *Universities Review* and elsewhere. Such progress as has been made was the work of dedicated individuals, such as Professor Roy Pascal who played a large part in the establishment of the general honours degree in arts at Birmingham, and was a member of the Committee of Sponsoring Universities for the new University College of North Staffordshire which opened in 1950. The latter was the only major innovation in the field of general education uniting both sides of the arts-science divide in the first decade after the War. It was of course the brain-child of Lord Lindsay of Birker, Master of Balliol College, Oxford, and first Principal of the new University College, which through his influence with the Labour Government and the U.G.C. acquired the at that time unique right in a new university institution of granting its own first degrees, instead of the external degrees of London University. It cannot be said that the A.U.T. played any part in the founding of the only new university institution between Hull and Leicester in the 1920's and the New Universities of the 1960's, nor in the development of its revolutionary educational ideals, and the 1949 Report on University Expansion did not so much as mention it, although it was then being built. Only when the formation of a new Local Association was announced at the December Council in 1950 and it was found that all but one of the members of staff at Keele had joined, did the A.U.T. officially notice this new and significant development for the future expansion of the universities.[1]

The general education of students was one of the topics at

1 Council Minutes, 30–1 May 1947, 28–9 May 1948, 19–20 December 1950, 18–19 May 1951.

the Home Universities Conference in 1949. This annual meeting in the Senate House of London University of Vice-Chancellors, professorial and non-professorial academics, and lay members of governing bodies of universities, together with representatives of the U.G.C. and the A.U.T., was the only result of the Association's war-time campaign for an Academic Council which could speak for the universities as a whole, and which was recommended by a Joint Conference of Vice-Chancellors, Registrars, Chairmen of University Councils, members of the U.G.C., and university M.P.s called by the A.U.T. on 13 October 1945. The first Home Universities Conference, so-called because it is organized by the Association of Universities of the British Commonwealth who provide the office and secretariat for the Vice-Chancellors' Committee, was convened on 27-28 September 1946 to discuss in three sessions the relations of the home universities to colonial universities and colleges, the humanities and science, and the universities and the training of teachers. In 1947 the Conference discussed at the suggestion of the A.U.T. the expansion of the universities, and also the selection of students and the establishment of a representative Inter-University Council. From the last discussion there emerged a joint Organizing Committee of Vice-Chancellors and A.U.T. representatives to select topics and speakers for the annual Conference. In the next few years the subjects discussed included 'The Crisis in the Universities' (the title of the book by Sir Walter Moberly, ex-Chairman of the U.G.C., on the theme that scientific and technical knowledge had outrun cultural and spiritual values as the focus of a university education), university graduates in industry, the university as a regional focus, the universities and the fine arts, as well as a host of more domestic topics such as general education, student selection and awards, success and failure, halls of residence and amenities, student health, and the like.[1] The Conference proved to be a useful forum for airing views and sounding opinion, but with its custom of passing no resolutions or recommendations it did not become the co-ordinator of university policy for which the A.U.T. had hoped.

Student affairs which figured so prominently at the Home Universities Conference also occupied the attention of the A.U.T.

1 *Proceedings of Home Universities Conferences, 1946–54* (published by the Association of Universities of the British Commonwealth); *Laurie*, pp. 57–8.

One of the pre-occupations of the post-war period was national service and whether it should be served before or after university education. An enquiry set on foot in April 1947 showed that opinions amongst university teachers were divided, a small majority preferring the greater maturity, physical fitness and uninterrupted progression from undergraduate to postgraduate studies of post-service students, a considerable minority preferring the mental keenness and the potential usefulness to the Forces of pre-service undergraduates, while the rest thought it should be at the free option of the student.[1]

One of the side benefits of national service was the improved physical health of students, as of other teenagers. The problem of student health had given concern to the universities and the National Union of Students before the War and had been the subject of the Fourth International University Conference in Switzerland in 1938. In 1947 the A.U.T.'s Sub-committee on Student Health and Physical Education, convened by the Secretary of the International Conference, Professor R. C. McLean, produced a Report which urged the setting up of a student health service in every university, with a full-time medical officer, to examine all students on entry and to supervise throughout their career not only their medical care but also their mental health and their diet and physical environment in lodgings and halls of residence. It also recommended the appointment of a full-time director of physical education to take charge of all physical training and advise on facilities for games and athletics.[2] In 1948 the inauguration of the National Health Service made the provision of medical treatment by university medical officers less necessary, but most universities found it useful to have some provision for early medical advice and help for students, particularly in the sphere of mental health. Meanwhile, the scheme for an International Student Sanatorium launched at the Swiss Conference in 1938 was revived, and the A.U.T. became a founding member of the British Students Tuberculosis Foundation which opened a pilot centre at Pinewood in Berkshire in 1952, where treatment was accompanied by tutorials with university dons. Dr. R. E. Jennings, then of

1 *University Students and National Service*, February 1948.
2 'Report of Committee on Student Health and Physical Education', *Universities Review*, May 1948.

University College, London, who replaced Miss A. Woodward of Royal Holloway College as the A.U.T.'s representative on the Foundation in 1953, played a very active part in its affairs and its plans for other centres in Essex and Aberdeenshire, and later became its Chairman.[1]

In the international field the Association's first concern after the War was to make contact with university teachers in the lately occupied countries and to broaden the international association founded in 1944. In October 1945 it was approached by the Union Française Universitaire with a view to closer Anglo-French academic relations, and as a result a Joint Conference was held in Paris on 2 January 1946. This was attended not only by British and French delegates but by guest representatives from Belgium, China, Czechoslovakia, Greece, Holland, Poland, Rumania, Sweden, Switzerland, the U.S.A., the U.S.S.R. and Yugoslavia. The two main topics discussed were Anglo-French relations, and what to do about the German universities. After the Conference the A.U.T. Executive got in touch with representatives of universities in the Allied countries about the second matter, on which it was felt that the renewal of contacts with German academics should depend on their giving proof that they were no longer tainted by Nazi influence and outlook. Professor E. R. Dodds for the A.U.T. approached the British Control Commission in Germany with a view to sending a Commission of Enquiry representing the French association, the A.U.T. and the British Vice-Chancellors' Committee. The French and the Vice-Chancellors, however, declined to act, and the A.U.T., on the initiative of Lord Chorley who had paid a brief private visit to some of the German universities, determined, with the agreement of the Control Office, to send its own commission of enquiry.

The A.U.T. delegation which visited Germany from 3 to 17 January 1947 inclusive consisted of Lord Chorley (Professor of Commercial and Industrial Law, London School of Economics), Professors Dodds (Greek, Oxford), C. H. Browning (Bacteriology, Glasgow), J. A. Hawgood (Modern History and Government, Birmingham), R. C. McLean (Botany, Cardiff), T. H. Marshall (Social Institutions, London School of Economics), Roy Pascal (German, Birmingham) and Mr. D. M.

[1] *Laurie*, pp. 51–2.

Tombs (Electrical Engineering, Imperial College, London). It had two tasks: to give advice on university reconstruction in Germany; and to explore the possibility of re-establishing relations between British and German universities. In Germany it split into two groups, one party visiting the Universities of Göttingen, Hamburg and Kiel and the Technisches Hochschulen of Brunswick and Hanover, the other the Universities of Cologne, Bonn and Münster, and the Medical Academy at Düsseldorf and Wuppertal, before uniting again in Berlin to visit the Technische Universität in the British and the old University in the Soviet Sector. Nearly everywhere they held separate meetings with the Rektor and with individuals or groups representing the professoriate, the non-professorial staff, and the students. They also discussed the question of the universities with the German Länder Education Authorities and in some places with representatives of the political parties and the trade unions, as well as with the British Control Officers, military and civil, and some American and Soviet officials in charge of university affairs in Berlin.

Their Report was written in what the Russians would call a spirit of comradely frankness:

we feel that we should place in the forefront of our Report our strong and unanimous impression that no radical and lasting reform of the universities which we have visited is likely to come about on the sole initiative of the universities themselves.

This was because, quite apart from whether or not the process of denazification had been effective and from the proposed transfer of the universities from the Control Commissions to the new German State, they were firstly controlled by small groups of elderly professors whose academic ideals were formed in another age and whose capacity for responding to new circumstances was likely to be small; and, secondly, the social structure of the universities was bound up with that of the secondary schools, and both of them with the traditional structure of German society as a whole, so that reform of the educational system was unlikely to be brought about save in the context of a much wider movement for social reform. They recommended as the best hope for the future that British policy should encourage the right type of younger teacher, by quicker promotion, a better financial status, and a larger voice in university policy; the bringing of the universities into closer touch with public opinion, and with any movements outside their walls which tended to create a new and healthier social structure; and the creation of channels through which the influence of the best foreign opinion could be brought to bear on German university life. The delegation had much sympathy for the harsh material conditions of German staff and student life, and recommended that aid should be given, especially in the form of books and equipment. They were suspicious of the extent and processes of denazification, and recommended that the procedure should be speeded up so that the politically sound teachers could feel secure and build on a surer foundation. They made various recommendations for constitutional reform to increase the participation and self-respect of the ill-paid and underprivileged non-professorial staff, and for opening the doors to a much wider social selection of students. And they finally suggested an International Educational Commission, under the auspices of U.N.E.S.C.O., charged with examining the fundamental problems of the German university system and advising the Occupying Powers on a common policy for reform.[1]

The Report was favourably received by Lord Pakenham and Mr. Robert Birley for the British Control Commission, which made some attempt to urge its recommendations, and it was translated into German and circulated to the German universities.[2] The German universities, in spite of their complete financial dependence on the Länder Governments and the latter's direct control of academic appointments, have been freer since the War of ideological political influence. Indeed, they have reasserted the old Humboldt tradition of *Lehr und Lern-freiheit*, to an extent unheard of in this country. Unfortunately, academic freedom of this absolute kind means only freedom for the professors, whose long hard road to a chair is a conditioning in conservatism and a bulwark against reform and democratization. Even today, except in such rare innovations as the new University of Konstanz, the absolute power of the German professoriate means absolute weakness for every other section of the

---

1 'The Universities in the British Zone of Germany (Report of the Delegation of the A.U.T.)', *Universities Review*, May 1947.
2 Council Minutes, 19–20 December 1947.

German universities, and above all for the forces of reform.[1] The International Association of University Professors and Lecturers called its first post-war general congress at Brussels on 9–14 April 1947, where U.N.E.S.C.O. had been represented, definite statutes adopted, and a programme of work agreed on. The A.U.T. on amalgamating with the Scottish Association became the British National Group, and paid £120 a year (approximately a shilling a head) towards the expenses. Congresses were held in Paris (March–April 1948), Basle (April 1949), Florence (April 1950), Nice (September 1951), Amsterdam (April 1953), and Vienna (September 1954), on a variety of topics ranging from the idea of an international university to access for the different social classes to the university. Laurie remained Secretary General until his death in 1953, when he was succeeded by Professor F. T. H. Fletcher of Liverpool University.[2]

It was at the Amsterdam Conference on 7 April 1953 that Douglas Laurie, still in harness as Secretary General of the I.A.U.P.L. and General Secretary of the A.U.T., died at the age of 78. To this selfless and dedicated man the Association of University Teachers owes a debt of greater magnitude than to anyone else in its fifty years of existence. He was its founder, its first President, and its General Secretary for over thirty-two years, during which times he was absent from the Council meetings only twice, and then only in old age and through illness. His home for two-thirds of the Association's life was its only office and headquarters, and its tintinabulating name, Tyn-y-Gongl, Caradoc Road, Aberystwyth, became known to thousands of British university teachers, and to thousands more in foreign lands who knew it as the unexpected place of publication of some remarkable international reports. In spite of his enormously time-consuming service to the national and international profession, he was a dedicated zoologist with a keen interest both in nature study in the field and the social implications of his subject in such studies as that of eugenics, and he had the reputation of being an inspiring teacher and of taking a permanent

1 Cf. E. Böning and K. Roeloffs, *Innovations in Two New Universities in Germany* (Report for the Directorate for Scientific Affairs, Organisation for Economic Co-operation and Development, Paris, 1969).
2 Council Minutes, 1947–54, *passim*.

interest in his students and their postgraduate careers. The secret of his unresented domination of the A.U.T. for a third of a century could be found not merely in his devotion to its service and determination in pursuit of its objectives, but to a personal charm which sprang from a modesty and a tolerance for others' opinions unfortunately rare in the academic man. It is best described by R. C. McLean, who worked closely with him for many years, especially in the international field, and was with him when he died:

Douglas Laurie was one of the kindest-hearted of men. He never made a disparaging remark, never showed irritation, never lost his patience, even when people were tiresome, but would simply comment on their behaviour with a little laugh, as if he found human peculiarities interesting and amusing. This feature of his character was one of his greatest assets, for it was impossible not to feel friendly to so amiable a man. Thus people softened towards him as they got to know him well, and were the more easily moved to fulfil his purposes. In his purposes he was formidable. He saw clearly what was needed and he recognized in other men the qualities which would help to reach the ends in view, and in pursuit of those ends he had the tenacity and single-mindedness of a child, united to a deep wisdom. One of those present in Amsterdam referred to him as 'the old leader', and a leader and creator he undoubtedly was, as the present position of the Association of University Teachers and the International Association of University Professors and Lecturers bears witness. They were his life-work and few men leave a better memorial behind them when they go. Yet in all his work he was selfless, without a mean thought or a base motive in his character. He lived for others and truly he had his reward, for of no man could it be said with greater truth that those who knew him best loved him most.[1]

Laurie's death left a hole in the organization of the Association which it took a whole team of people to fill. It is not too much to say that the demise of this greatest of the amateurs made inevitable the professionalization of the A.U.T.

---

1 Quoted by Rev. W. Neil, 'An Address delivered at the Memorial Service at St. George's Church, Sheffield, 22 May 1953'; *q.v.*, and Obituary, *Universities Review*, October 1953, pp. 36, 39–40.

Chapter 5

A Professional Professional Body
1954–69

The death of Laurie would in any case have forced the A.U.T. to reorganize its administration, but the next fifteen years were to see an expansion of the university teaching profession, of public concern with its role in the national life and hopes of development, and of its relations with Parliament and Government, on such a scale that the Association would be compelled to abandon its traditionally amateur organization and become as professional as the organs of government, industry and the trade unions with which it was called upon increasingly to deal on equal terms, of argument and expertise if not of power. These years witnessed an unprecedented growth in the number of university institutions, from twenty-five (including three university colleges and two colleges of science and technology of university status) in 1954 to no less than forty-eight in 1969. This near-doubling of the University Grants Committee's grant list (plus the Northern Irish Government's list of Belfast and the New University of Ulster at Coleraine, included in the figures) is less dramatic than it appears, since the twenty-five institutions of 1954 included the federal universities of Wales, with four self-governing colleges and the Welsh National School of Medicine, and London, with thirty-three self-governing schools and ten university postgraduate institutes, so that there were over sixty institutions to which students could apply for an internal degree course. Moreover, by no means all the new universities of 1969 were new institutions. Newcastle and Dundee were previously constituents of the Universities of Durham and St. Andrews, ten more were previously colleges of technology (and from 1956 colleges of advanced technology able to award a Diploma in

Technology equivalent to a degree), Heriot-Watt University was previously their Scottish equivalent, while the sole university college of 1969, St. David's, Lampeter, admitted to the U.G.C.'s list only in 1961 under an arrangement by which it received grant through its sponsoring institution, the University College of South Wales and Monmouthshire at Cardiff, had been granting its own degrees since 1852. Only the nine 'New Universities' opened between Sussex in 1961 and Coleraine in 1968 were strictly new institutions in every sense of the world. Nevertheless, since they were nearly all new to university teaching, the number of Local Associations with which A.U.T. headquarters had to keep in touch rose from thirty-nine in 1950 to seventy in 1967.[1]

Meanwhile the expansion of the universities, old and new, was real enough. Student numbers in Great Britain rose from their post-war trough of 80,600 in 1953–54 to 184,500 in 1966–67 and to over 200,000 in 1968–69.[2] The numbers of full-time academic staff (excluding Oxford, Cambridge and Northern Ireland) rose from 9,249 in 1953–54 to 16,774 in 1964–65 and to 25,353 in 1967–68.[3] The A.U.T.'s role in this expansion will be dealt with in Section 4, but in the meantime it could only benefit from it. Its membership (excluding life members, mainly non-paying retired, who numbered between 50 and 100) increased from 4,949 in 1953–54 to 15,508 in 1966–67 and to 16,550 in 1967–68. The Association's income, with the subscription raised from one guinea to two in 1956 and to three in 1962 (though remaining at one guinea for assistant lecturers throughout) rose even faster, from £5,495 in 1953–54 to £43,423 in 1965–66 and to £49,014 in 1966–67.[4] The increased numbers as well as the problems of expansion and increasing responsibility to the State provided the need, while the money provided the means, for a larger and more professional organization.

Used to their magnificent tradition of voluntary service, it

1 For the growth in the number of universities since the War, see my *Innovation in the New Universities of the United Kingdom* (O.E.C.D., Paris, 1969), Introduction; for the numbers of Local Associations, see A.U.T. Council Minutes, 1954–67.
2 U.G.C., *University Development, 1952–57*, p. 15; *The Times*, 13 September 1967; *Robbins Report*, p. 161.
3 U.G.C., *Returns . . . 1953–54* and *1964–65*, and information from Mr. R. C. Griffiths, Deputy Secretary of U.G.C.
4 Council Minutes, 1954–68, and information from the Assistant General Secretary.

took the university teachers a long time to recognize the need for paid, full-time expertise, and they took each step in the inevitable direction reluctantly. Laurie, that giant amongst amateurs, was replaced by a team, but with one or possibly two partial exceptions it was a team of amateurs. He was to have retired in any event at the end of the session, and would have been elected Honorary President. As his successor as Honorary General Secretary the Association was fortunate to be able to elect Lord Chorley, Professor of Commercial and Industrial Law at the London School of Economics and Political Science, 1930–46, and subsequently a part-time lecturer there.[1] He was an old member of the A.U.T., had been attending Council meetings since 1937, and since 1943 a member of the Executive, where he had done sterling service as a member and convener of various sub-committees and, as we have seen, took a special interest in the international field and was instrumental in bringing about the visit of the delegation to the Universities of the British Zone of Germany in January 1947. After the usual two years as Junior and Senior Vice-President he was elected President for the session 1947–48. He was admirably qualified for the post of Honorary General Secretary. His legal training and expertise were especially useful in advising members on difficult cases arising out of their contracts of employment – a field of activity which was to expand even faster than the profession – and his political flair and contacts, especially with the Labour Party, were to be invaluable to the Association in its dealings with Parliament and the Government. Not the least of his qualifications, of course, was that he had been raised to the peerage by the Labour Government in 1945. This not only gave the A.U.T. the entrée to Government offices and access to up-to-the-minute information on policy, but was quite as useful in providing a Parliamentary platform as a seat in the Commons – perhaps more so, since it is easier to intervene in a Lords debate and, as I have heard him say many times, you can ask a question just as easily there as in the Commons, and you are more likely to get it answered by a Minister in person. Unlike many peers, he was an assiduous attender at debates, especially those which concerned his chief interests in life, education, the National Trust and the Council for the Preservation of Rural England, and the liberty of the

1 *Ibid.*, 22–3 May 1953.

subject in this and other countries. The A.U.T. could scarcely have found another academic with such a combination of useful qualities and qualifications.

So busy a public figure on the London scene could not be expected to do all that Laurie had done in his years of retirement as a professor emeritus, and it was decided to appoint a part-time Development Officer whose main duty was to assist the Local Associations in their efforts to recruit new members, and to try to develop new ones in those institutions without them. This was Mr. R. L. Collett, M.A., F.R.I.C., formerly Registrar of the Institute of Chemistry. Apart from Laurie himself he was the first male professional employee of the Association. Through his visits to the Local Associations he was becoming a familiar figure until his death in office in 1955. He was succeeded as part-time Development Officer from 1956 by a man almost as well known in the A.U.T. as Laurie himself, his friend Professor R. C. McLean, the pioneer of the International Conferences and of I.A.U.P.L., who had now retired from the Chair of Botany at Cardiff and was willing to do the job as one last labour of love for the Association. At the same time a part-time Press Officer, Mr. R. L. Buckley, previously of the *Times Educational Supplement*, was appointed.[1]

As Secretary-General of I.A.U.P.L. Laurie was succeeded by F. T. H. Fletcher, Professor of French at Liverpool, who had been a member of the A.U.T. since 1924 and was President in 1951–52. He had long taken an interest in international affairs, was at Amsterdam with Laurie when he died, and was elected his successor at the same Conference. He was to play an outstanding role in organizing the 8th, 9th and 10th I.A.U.P.L. Congresses at Vienna in 1954, Munich in 1956 and Brussels in 1958.[2] As representative on the Joint Standing Committee on Library Co-operation Laurie was succeeded by Mr. A. J. Hatley of Imperial College, London, Convener of the A.U.T.'s Library Sub-committee, who eventually took his place as Honorary Treasurer.[3] Including the Press Officer appointed in 1956, then, it took five people to fill the gap left by Laurie. All of them, of

1 *Ibid.*, 22–3 May 1953, 15–16 December 1955, 25–6 May 1956.
2 *Ibid.*, 22–3 May 1953; *Communication* (I.A.U.P.L., Ghent, Belgium), No. 56, January 1968, p. 69.
3 Council Minutes, 22–3 May 1953; A. J. Hatley, 'The Role of the A.U.T. in Library Co-operation', *British Universities Annual*, 1964, pp. 74–6.

course, were part-timers – but then so, in theory, was Laurie – three of them, or four if we count McLean, were amateurs in the sense of doing the job for love. The only full-time paid staff were still the indefatigable Assistant Secretary, Miss Davies, and her hard-working assistant typist.

Even so small a staff had to be housed, and an Aberystwyth headquarters made no sense once Laurie was gone. As we have seen, the Executive had already begun to look for a suitable London Office in 1952 and, after some abortive attempts, bought in 1954 the freehold of a Bayswater house, 21 Dawson Place, W.2, for £5,000. It was a Georgian-type house which had seen better days and was remarkable only for the somewhat grandiose glass arcade over the stone staircase leading up to the front door. One could imagine carriages and pairs depositing Edwardian *grandes dames* who would ascend, protected from the inclement weather, to leave their visiting cards. Most of the A.U.T. Executive members who met at Laurie House, as it came to be named, over the years from 1955 to 1964 arrived and departed on foot. The house was to have cost £2,500 to convert into offices and two flats, one for Miss Davies and one to let, plus a further £1,500—£2,000 for furnishing. In the event it cost some £7,500, including central heating and a fire escape, which led to a first-class row in the Council from some of the thriftier members, who were not assuaged when it was pointed out that the house, having cost a total of £12,500, was valued in 1957 at £11,000! However, the rising property market came to the rescue, and it was sold, in 1964, at a handsome profit, for £17,000.[1]

The move to Laurie House took place on 12 December 1955, and it was officially opened on 16 December by the Chairman of the Committee of Vice-Chancellors and Principals, Sir Philip Morris. It was a very plain and business-like place, the only adornment being the portrait of Laurie by M. de Saumarez commissioned as a memorial out of funds contributed by members. Its one spacious room could just accommodate the whole Executive Committee, and in between quarterly meetings of this and the sub-committees served for collating the enormous and still growing bundles of documents distributed to members

1 Council Minutes, 15–16 December 1954, 18–19 December 1956, 17–18 December 1957, 19–20 December 1963.

before each Council and Executive meeting. Yet Laurie House served its turn, for it was here that the A.U.T. was transformed from a two-woman-power enterprise into a full-blown professional organization.

Within a few years it became clear that the amateur organization was creaking and could not cope with the increasing volume and complexity of the work. The initiative for reconstruction came from the Birmingham Local Association, which at this time acquired its reputation for being one jump ahead of the Executive in thinking about questions of organizational efficiency. At the December Council in 1957 their representative, Mr. Henry Maddick, a stern critic of the Executive, presented a list of grievances and proposals for reform, including the appointment of a full-time Executive Secretary, and carried a resolution to set up a sub-committee, some of whose members were to be drawn from outside the Executive, on the future policy and organization of the Association. The sub-committee agreed with Birmingham on the need to appoint an Executive Secretary, and spent most of its time discussing his terms of appointment, recommending to the 1958 May Council a salary within the range £1,750–£2,500, then the senior lecturer-reader scale. The post was widely advertised, the appointment committee, including two representatives of Council, interviewed six candidates, and finally selected the President of the Association, Dr. Kenneth Urwin, M.A., D.U.P., D.U.C., Barrister-at-Law, Senior Lecturer in French and Romance Philology at the University College, Cardiff. He was to complete his year of office as President, and take up his new post on 1 October 1959.[1]

After the usual criticisms of 'an internal appointment', it began to be seen that this was a most fortunate one. As a university teacher of considerable standing Dr. Urwin knew the mores and the problems of the profession from the inside; as an old A.U.T. hand who had been through the arduous mill of being Local President, Council representative since 1948 and member of the Executive since 1954, where he had quickly won sufficient respect and confidence to be elected to the presidential ladder, he 'knew the ropes' and especially how to handle critical Council meetings and hypercritical individual members; and as a practising barrister he had an unusual

1 *Ibid.*, 17–18 December 1957, 19–20 December 1958.

second string to his bow which he was able to use to much effect and great benefit to the Association in a multitude of political issues and legal cases. Above all, he had an easy-going amiability which enabled him to get on with a wide range of people, from smooth, unyielding Vice-Chancellors and irritable Conveners to individual members with personal problems and typists with too much to do, and he had a self-deprecating wit which took the sting out of his sharp and penetrating comments. After some initial difficulties over staffing, he was soon able to build up a remarkably efficient, if always overworked, headquarters administration.

On his appointment it was decided that the post of Development Officer was no longer necessary, and accordingly Professor McLean laid down the office at the end of September 1959. The Press Officer, Mr. Buckley, also shortly resigned and was not replaced, leaving behind him a useful memorandum on the A.U.T.'s dealings with the Press, and especially some advice on how to make Council meetings more newsworthy, which the Council characteristically rejected.[1] It would not be long before something very like them would be needed again, on a full-time basis.

The next part of the machinery to come under strain was the Treasurer's department. By 1961 there were over 8,000 members and an income and expenditure of over £17,000. Professor H. V. A. Briscoe of Imperial College, London, the Association's second Treasurer, who had carried the burden with the help of a part-time clerical assistant, Miss C. J. Tooley, for fifteen years, was coming up to retirement, and the attempt to find a replacement for him revealed how large the task had become. Dr. T. G. Halsall of Oxford, a longstanding member of the Executive who was elected in his place, had a flair for financial organization, as well as a keen interest in the stock market which was to stand the Association's investments – a luxury, or necessity, unheard of before the War – in good stead. A new sub-committee, the Finance and House Committee, was set up, with the new Treasurer as Convener, and all work connected with the collection of subscriptions from Local Treasurers and with expenditure of every kind centralized at Laurie House. A part-time Finance Clerk, a retired bank official, Mr. R. W. Harborow, was appointed from September 1961, and an office provided for him

1 *Ibid.*, 22–3 May 1959.

... .he cellar of Laurie House, where pressure on accommodation was causing concern.[1]

At the same time the headquarters woman-power was increased to five, but this soon proved inadequate, and in the spring of 1962 Miss Jean A. Whitt, B.A., Dr. Urwin's personal secretary, was appointed Assistant Secretary, Miss Davies promoted to Chief Assistant Secretary, Miss Jean Farquhar, B.A., was appointed to deal chiefly with the affairs of the Colleges of Advanced Technology which now, as we shall see, came within the purview of the A.U.T. In the same year the Association launched a publicity campaign to draw attention both to the need for university expansion and to the anger and frustration of the university teachers over their salaries, and it was decided to appoint a full-time Personal Assistant (Information Officer) to deal mainly with the press and the Local Associations (in short, a combined Press and Development Officer), at £1,500—£1,750 (the upper part of the lecturer scale), a Research Officer to collect statistical and other data on comparative salaries and related questions, at £1,000 a year (in the junior lecturer range), and an additional typist. The Information Officer was to be a short-term post for the duration of the publicity campaign, probably two years, but the research post was thought likely to be permanent. An experienced journalist, Mr. A. L. Colston Jones, was appointed Information Officer, and a young graduate in social studies, Mr. S. R. Hatch, Research Officer. Both did good work for the publicity campaign and contributed to its successful outcomes in the Robbins Report of 1963 and the National Incomes Commission salary award to university teachers in April 1964, but this combination did not prove to be the answer to the Association's permanent publicity and information problems, and both were terminated early in 1964, when Mr. M. J. Crook, B.A., was appointed Personal Assistant to the Executive Secretary and made chiefly responsible for research.[2]

Miss Davies had retired at the end of August 1963, after serving the Association, first as Laurie's secretary and later as Assistant and Chief Assistant Secretary, for no less than 42 years. At the last Council meeting she attended officially, in May 1963, Lord Chorley paid a warm tribute to her lifetime's work and

1 *Ibid.*, 26–7 May, 20–1 December 1961.
2 *Ibid.*, 25–6 May, 19–20 December 1962, 29–30 May 1964.

devotion to the Association and, noting that the A.U.T. had already decided to supplement her small pension from the scheme which had been in existence for only a small part of her career, presented her with a cheque for £140. Miss Whitt succeeded her as Chief Assistant Secretary, and was eventually succeeded as Assistant Secretary by Miss R. M. Jones, B.A.

By May 1964 the office staff, apart from the Executive Secretary, consisted of nine persons: the Chief Assistant and two Assistant Secretaries, four other secretarial staff, the part-time Finance Clerk and the Personal Assistant. The total salary bill, including the Executive Secretary who was now on the professorial scale, was £11,500, and regular scales were in operation for the various grades. Having become a multiple employer, if not a large-scale one, the Association had felt obliged as a staff defence organization to be a good one, and had introduced its own staff pension scheme, sick pay scheme (three months on full pay, three months on half), generous holidays, and luncheon vouchers for all except the Executive Secretary.[1]

Laurie House had never been intended to accommodate a staff of this size, and indeed was in a residential zone where the Planning Department of the London County Council refused to sanction further office conversions. Temporary permission had been granted for the use as offices of extra rooms, and this was extended for a further and final three years early in 1962, but by then it was obvious that Laurie House would soon have to be sold and other accommodation found. After a considerable search, in which expert help was called in from a member of the College of Estate Management which had recently formed a local Association, the Association took over on 6 July 1964 the first floor of Bremar House, a two-year-old office block near Paddington Station; 2,400 square feet on the remaining twelve years of the lease at £3,350 per annum plus about £1,000 in rates and a service charge of £400 a year – a total of £4,750 a year, or more than the whole income of the A.U.T. before the 1950's. The office was, and is, modern and functional, and just adequate to the purpose. Its only drawbacks were that it contained no room large enough for the Executive and the larger sub-committees to meet, and they took to meeting, between Councils at least, in the Great Western Royal Hotel

1 *Ibid.*, 24–5 May 1963, 29–30 May 1964.

at Paddington Station; and since the office block already had a name it was no longer possible to perpetuate Laurie's in the address. A third drawback, as far as some members were concerned, was that the Association was no longer a property owner at a time when property, especially in London, was the fastest growing investment, and just as some Council representatives opposed the original purchase of Laurie House there were now some who opposed its sale, and agreed to it only on the understanding that the Executive would look out for suitable office accommodation to buy.[1]

For, by the standards of its former penury, the Association was now comparatively rich. The subscription had been raised to three guineas in 1962 not out of dire necessity but partly to build up the reserve fund, then standing at £15,000, so as to safeguard the Association against all contingencies, such as expensive legal cases, and in the meantime to guarantee a substantial income from investments. At 22 April 1968 the total investments, as a result of the shrewd judgement of Dr. Halsall and his Committee, stood at £76,990, against a purchase price of £62,704, and yielded an annual dividend of £3,692. In addition a sophisticated system of short-term investment had been developed, by which incoming subscriptions were invested in short-term loans and securities, yielding an extra income until the money was needed for current expenditure. The staff pension fund, under separate trustees, was eventually also invested to yield the highest returns, and so was the separate Benevolent Fund which was set up in 1965 to receive voluntary donations from members plus £500 a year from the Association for the benefit of hardship cases amongst the membership and their families, such as young widows of members with children and inadequate F.S.S.U. benefits.[2]

The final stage in the professionalization of the office came with the impending resignation of Lord Chorley as Honorary General Secretary in 1965. This produced a division in the Executive and in the Council between those who thought that, once separated from the unique qualities and connections of Lord Chorley, the office would become redundant, and those

1 *Ibid.*, 25–6 May, 19–20 December 1962, 29–30 May, 17–18 December 1964.
2 *Ibid.*, 25–6 May, 19–20 December 1962, 17–18 December 1964, 28–9 May 1965, 31 May–1 June 1968.

who wished to see it filled by some public figure approaching his eminence. The Officers' report recommending the former course was opposed by Lord Chorley at the December Council meeting in 1964 and, amid somewhat emotional scenes, was rejected by 62 votes to 60. However, Lord Chorley made it clear that he in no way opposed the other principal recommendation, that the Executive Secretary be renamed the General Secretary, and in May 1965 Dr. Urwin was duly given the title. A committee, including two Council members, was set up to try to fill the post of Honorary General Secretary, and the majority reported in December that they had been unable to fill it, and that the post should be abolished. The two Council members, however, signed a minority report to the effect that the post should be kept open, so that in the event of Dr. Urwin's retirement or resignation, if it were found impossible to replace him by someone with his experience of academic life, the former arrangement of an Honorary General Secretary and an Executive Secretary could be revived. In the event, Council accepted the majority report, including a recommendation to appoint an Assistant General Secretary at a salary overlapping the lecturer and senior lecturer scales. Once again the Association was fortunate in its search, and was able to appoint from September 1966 Mr. Fred Garside, M.A. (Oxon), headmaster of St. Clements Dane's Grammar School in the City of London, a man of considerable ability and a most equable temperament.[1]

With the appointment of a professional General Secretary and an equally professional deputy the professionalization of the A.U.T. was complete, at least on the administrative side. But that is only half the story, and the rest of it is concerned with the increasingly exacting demands upon the Association's skill and expertise, especially from the University Grants Committee, the Vice-Chancellors' Committee and the Government, as well as from the members themselves, which compelled an increasingly professional response, as we shall see in the next three sections.

2. PROFESSIONAL SALARY NEGOTIATION

A professional response to the demands of the outside world

1 *Ibid.*, 17–18 December 1964, 28–9 May, 21–2 December 1965, 26–7 May, 21–22 December 1966.

was most obvious in the field of salary negotiation, where the A.U.T. was increasingly involved in exchanges, inquiries and discussions with official bodies, of such complexity and technicality that only acknowledged experts in industrial relations and the economics of remuneration could understand them or sustain credibility as negotiators. In a field increasingly dominated by specialists, where the Government which, whatever the theory, was the ultimate employer of university teachers, could not only ensure to itself the services of specialists but could set up the expert tribunals before which the discussions were to be held and also determine the rules of the debate to the extent of ruling certain types of argument out of court, the A.U.T. was forced to find in its ranks and finally to employ specialists as expert as those on the other side.

It was only in this period, indeed, that the Association achieved its lifelong ambition of establishing formal negotiating machinery for university salaries. At the meeting with the Vice-Chancellors' Committee on 23 April 1954 at which the decision to press for an immediate salary revision had been taken, 'a firm undertaking had been given by the Chairman that in future no decision would be taken by them on salaries or cognate matters and no representations made to higher authority, without full prior discussion with the A.U.T. Such discussions could be initiated by either body whenever it was felt that they were needed, and the A.U.T. would preserve its right to make its own representations to the U.G.C. as hitherto.' This was a promising step forward, but it was not the same thing as formally constituted negotiating machinery, since the A.U.T. could only make its views known to the Vice-Chancellors, was not allowed to see their submission to the U.G.C. or the latter's advice to the Chancellor of the Exchequer, and certainly could not negotiate directly with their real paymasters in the Treasury. Accordingly the Executive set up a special sub-committee on salary negotiating machinery, to press its establishment upon the Vice-Chancellors and the U.G.C. In September Lord Chorley had an interview in which he put the problem to the Chief Industrial Commissioner of the Ministry of Labour, who regarded the situation as unique and could suggest no immediate solution, and a further interview, attended also by Mr. Wightman, the Convener of the Salaries and Grading Committee, in November was no more fruitful.

The manner of the award, through an announcement by the Chancellor of the Exchequer in the House of Commons on 16 November 1954, with no opportunity for the recipients to say yea or nay, showed that nothing had changed, and this was further confirmed by Mr. Butler's answers to M.P.'s questions, expressing 'satisfaction with the present arrangements'.[1]

Frustrated at this level, the A.U.T. determined to call a joint meeting on 29 April 1955 with representatives of university governing bodies to thresh out the whole matter, and preliminary letters were sent before other events contrived to render it redundant. Meetings with the Vice-Chancellors on 25 March and 20 April showed that they were just as satisfied with the present arrangements as the Chancellor of the Exchequer:

> The V.C.s' Committee were of opinion that the present procedure was the most satisfactory way of conducting negotiations in view of all the considerations involved, but suggested the holding of regular, informal meetings (say once a year) with representatives of the A.U.T. to exchange views, both sides to retain liberty of action in any direction.

Between the meetings Lord Chorley suggested in a letter to the Vice-Chancellors' Committee the establishment of a joint committee to study the whole question of procedure, but this they rejected. The most they would accept was that, if agreement could be reached at their informal consultations with the A.U.T., they would forward these to the U.G.C. with their comments, and the A.U.T., in view of the urgency of the discussions affecting the next quinquennium, reluctantly agreed to go forward on this basis, without prejudice to any further action it might wish to take or to the general question of the need for an adequate basic framework for salary negotiation.[2]

Further action included a meeting on 9 May between Lord Chorley, Mr. Wightman and the President, Professor Robert Niklaus of Exeter, for the A.U.T., and the Chairman, Sir Keith Murray, and two senior officials of the U.G.C., at which Sir Keith made certain tentative suggestions, unauthorized as yet by his Committee, for supplementing the present procedure, the most important of which were that the Association should be

1 *Ibid.*, 28–9 May, 15–16 December 1954.
2 *Ibid.*, 20–1 May 1955; 'Report on Salaries Negotiation' [by W. A. Wightman], *Universities Review*, October 1955, pp. 36–42.

granted the same right as the Committee of Vice-Chancellors and Principals to make representations to the Grants Committee in respect to salary matters, and to have their representations considered and, if necessary, elucidated by further discussion in the same manner as was done with the Vice-Chancellors. The A.U.T. Executive promptly agreed to this, subject to the general authorization of Council, which it obtained at the May meeting and communicated to the Chairman of the U.G.C., who obtained the agreement of his Committee. The result came to light in a written reply by the Chancellor, Mr. Butler, on 20 July 1955 to a prompted question from Mr. Kenneth Robinson, M.P., asking whether he would make a statement about future arrangements for determining the salaries of the academic staffs of universities:

Yes. Those who are responsible for these matters in the universities have been giving very careful consideration to this matter since it was raised by Hon. Members after my Statement on Academic Salaries on 16 November 1954. I must emphasize that the relationship between the governing bodies and the academic staffs of the universities is in important respects different from that between employers and employees. This relationship is unique and I should be sorry to see any attempt to change it. Its effect is to make inappropriate the development of negotiating machinery of the normal type. Nevertheless, it has been helpful to review the machinery of consultation.

The University Grants Committee will be ready to receive representations any time as to changes in the basic salary framework for the academic staffs of universities from the Committee of Vice-Chancellors and Principals or from the Association of University Teachers. Thus the Association as well as the Committee of Vice-Chancellors and Principals will have a formal right of approach to the University Grants Committee on this subject. It will be the duty of the Committee after examining these representations, and if necessary elucidating them by discussion, to give a considered reply. Before replying the Committee would, if necessary, make a submission to me. The Committee of Vice-Chancellors and Principals will also have full discussions with the Association of University Teachers as occasion demands on general salary questions. These arrangements seem to me to be the best which can be devised in view of the great complexities of this question, and I have every hope that they will work satisfactorily.[1]

Thus it was that the A.U.T. at last achieved the establishment

1 Council Minutes, 20-1 May, 15-16 December 1955; 'Report on Salaries Negotiation', *loc. cit.*

of a formal procedure for determining salaries, and recognition of itself as having a role in that procedure. The credit for this achievement must go as much to Sir Keith Murray, Chairman of the U.G.C., as to the A.U.T. negotiators who pressed him to it. Whether it was even yet worthy of the name negotiating rather than consultation machinery was open to doubt, since the A.U.T. could make representations and even elucidate and discuss but could not actually negotiate the terms of an award with the body, the Treasury, which actually made the decision. It was, however, well worth a trial, and at the December Council meeting in 1955 a prescient motion, 'that Council notes that the present negotiating machinery makes no provision for the referring of disagreements between the parties to an independent adjudicating body', was defeated, 'the general feeling being that the new arrangements were a sufficient advance to be tested by experience over a period.'[1]

The Association hastened to take advantage of the new procedure. The same Council meeting instructed the Executive

to ensure through the new consultation machinery a further revision of basic salary scales to come into operation not later than the beginning of the next quinquennium (October 1957); such revision should eliminate the existing differential between pre-clinical and non-medical salaries and should take into account all aspects of the rise in the cost of living and the current remuneration in other professions involving broadly comparable work.[2]

The last clause implied expert information and advice, and here the Association was once again fortunate to find on its Executive, since 1954, and Junior Vice-President for 1955–56, one of the leading experts in the field, R. G. D. (later Sir Roy) Allen of the London School of Economics, Professor of Statistics in the University of London. He had already drawn up a memorandum on the general principles on which salary scales could be based, and this had been discussed at a meeting with the Vice-Chancellors' Committee on 15 November. In the ensuing consultations with the Vice-Chancellors' Committee Professor Allen acted as adviser and consultant to both sides – a remarkable tribute to his standing, impartiality and the confidence placed in him –

1 Council Minutes, 15–16 December 1955.
2 *Ibid.*

and after the announcement in 1956 of the Priestley Commission's recommendations on Civil Service salaries and of new Burnham scales for lecturers in Technical Colleges and in the newly scheduled Colleges of Advanced Technology he drew up a 'reasoned statement of revised salaries which an interested party could justifiably put forward and support', which was endorsed by the A.U.T. and the Vice-Chancellors' Committee and forwarded to the U.G.C. The result, after further discussions with the U.G.C., was the announcement by the Chancellor of the Exchequer on 12 March 1957 of new salary scales to operate from 1 August. Mr. Wightman reported to the May Council meeting that the substantial increases gained were largely due to the unity of the A.U.T. and the Vice-Chancellors behind the scales and the arguments underlying them, and that the Vice-Chancellors 'had freely acknowledged the part played by the A.U.T. and particularly by Professor Allen'.[1]

The award provided for the following salary scales:

Non-medical posts

Professors (range, not scale)	£2,300—£3,000
Reader and Senior Lecturers	Range with varying maxima up to £2,150—£2,250
Lecturers	£900—£1,650
Assistant Lecturers	£700—£850

Medical posts

	Pre-clinical	Clinical
Professors (range)	£2,300—£3,000	£2,500—£3,000
in certain cases to:	—	£3,250
Readers, Senior Lecturers and Lecturers	From £900 to varying maxima from £1,650—£2,250	£1,750—£2,550
in certain cases to:	—	£2,900

The A.U.T. Council welcomed these scales and the co-operative spirit in which the new procedure was operated both by the U.G.C. and the Committee of Vice-Chancellors, but it regretted the lowness of the lecturer's maximum, the manner of the transfer to the new scale which meant it took longer for lecturers

1 *Ibid.*, 15–16 December 1955, 25–6 May, 18–19 December 1956, 24–5 May 1957.

to reach the top, and above all the postponement until August which inordinately spun out the delay in catching up with other professions.[1]

Over the next few years Professor Allen kept an eagle eye on the course of prices and other professional incomes, and a series of increases in 1959 for school teachers, lecturers in training and further education colleges, senior civil servants and National Health Service doctors touched off a new claim for the revision of university scales in November, U.G.C. proposals to the Chancellor, Mr. Heathcoat Amory, in March 1960, and announcements of new scales of non-medical and pre-clinical salaries in May and of clinical salaries in September, both back-dated to 1 January 1960:

Non-medical posts

Professors (range)	£2,600—£3,600
Readers and Senior Lecturers	Range with varying maxima up to £2,425
in certain cases to:	£2,525
Lecturers	£1,050—£1,850
in certain cases to:	£2,000
Assistant Lecturers	£800—£950

Medical posts

	Pre-clinical	Clinical
Professors (range)	£2,600—£3,600	£2,800—£3,900
Readers, Senior Lecturers and Lecturers	From £1,050 to varying maxima from £1,850—£2,525	£2,200—£3,200
in certain cases to:	—	£3,500[2]

The most striking feature of this award was the 'flexibility' allowed to university institutions especially at the top and bottom of the lecturer's scale, a 'disguised differential' such that teachers in scarce subjects could be appointed above the basic rate and could even be allowed to proceed, without promotion, beyond the usual maximum. This and other unsatisfactory features of the award shook the Association's faith in the consultation machinery to the point of demanding an entirely new

1 U.G.C., *University Development, 1957–62*, p. 212; Council Minutes, 24–5 May 1957.
2 U.G.C., *loc. cit.*

negotiating procedure in the form of an independent review body such as the Priestley Commission for the National Health Service or the Franks Committee for senior civil servants. But their dissatisfaction with the award itself was as nothing to their anger when they discovered that the Treasury, which had based its award on comparisons with other professions including the Civil Service, immediately announced (in June) a 4 per cent increase for Principals in the Administrative grade which it must have known was in the offing when the announcement of university scales was made. The implicit charge of bad faith even shines through the factual prose of the subsequent U.G.C. report.[1] The inevitable response was an A.U.T. demand, backed by the Vice-Chancellors, for a 'rectification claim' in July 1960. The U.G.C. preferred to wait for further ammunition from an expected round of Burnham increases for teachers and lecturers in State-maintained colleges, but in April 1961 at a joint meeting of A.U.T. representatives with the full U.G.C. gave support for a major revision forthwith. Meanwhile, the A.U.T. was pursuaded to accept the consultation machinery for a further experimental period.[2]

Unfortunately, the U.G.C.'s recommendations reached the Treasury on the eve of Mr. Selwyn Lloyd's six months' 'pay pause' of 25 July 1961, and although the U.G.C. argued that university teachers should be treated on the same lines as other teachers, who had just been awarded an increase in Burnham Committee sessions which had held up the U.G.C.'s own discussions with the Treasury, the Government held that since there was no prior commitment on university salaries they could not escape the pay pause.[3] Rightly or wrongly, many members of the A.U.T. saw in this rebuff a retaliation to previous criticism of the Treasury's sharp practice over the 1960 award.

After considerable agitation and further awards to other professions which were allowed to operate from the end of the pay pause on 1 January 1962, totalling, since the January 1960 award to university teachers, 17 per cent for lecturers in teacher training colleges and C.A.T.s, 21 per cent for the Scientific Civil Service and 24 per cent for Civil Service Principals, the

1 *Ibid.*, p. 37.
2 Council Minutes, 20-1 May, 15-16 December 1960, 26-7 May 1961.
3 U.G.C., *op. cit.*, p. 38.

Treasury announced on 14 March 1962 an increased grant for university salaries of no more than 3 per cent, sweetened by a promise of a fresh review next year. The extra £1 million sufficed only to raise the salaries of lecturers and assistant lecturers by £100 a year. The U.G.C. was 'gravely disturbed'. The Vice-Chancellors considered it 'entirely unrealistic . . . the increase, no matter how distributed, will not enable universities to retain and recruit the academic staff required for the proposed expansion: nor can it be supposed that the promise of a review next year will enable lost ground to be recovered.' The A.U.T. called an emergency Council meeting on 9 April which described the award as 'completely unacceptable' and urged its rejection, affirmed its conviction that the promised expansion of student numbers could not now take place and recorded its sympathy with disappointed candidates, and re-opened the question of negotiating machinery.[1]

At this nadir in its fortunes the A.U.T. could no longer call on the full services of Professor Allen. He had been adviser and consultant to both the A.U.T. and the Vice-Chancellors for the previous seven years, and had been President of the Association in 1957–58, but latterly his other commitments had increased and he was no longer able to provide the background information on parallel salary movements. Moreover, a recent Government White Paper had ruled out from the evaluation of pay claims the factors of cost of living and comparability between salaries on which he was expert. It became imperative therefore to find someone capable of replacing him.

In the professionalization process Professor Allen was a transitional figure, an amateur in the traditional A.U.T. mould, elected to office in the normal way and freely devoting his services for the good of the profession, yet accidentally, as it were, possessed of expertise from his main occupation as professional as anyone in the country. How difficult were the problems he had to face can be seen from a comment of the U.G.C. itself made soon after the 1957 award:

We doubt whether there is any field of employment in which the settlement of rates of salary raises issues more difficult and far-reaching than those which arise over the remuneration of academic staffs. Any organization faced with a claim from highly qualified personnel for

1 *Ibid.*, pp. 39–40; Emergency Council Minutes, 9 April 1962.

improvements in salary has to ask itself what salaries the qualifications it requires will command elsewhere, and what salaries must therefore be paid to obtain those qualifications. Universities have to ask those questions no less than other organizations, but the difficulties which they meet in finding answers to them and in applying those answers are exceptionally great. This is because the qualifications with which universities are concerned cover the whole range of knowledge, a wider range than that with which any other organization has to deal. Moreover – and this is the heart of the difficulty – they include both qualifications of a high economic value for which there is a keen demand outside, and also qualifications of which the value is hardly economic at all and for which the outside demand, in the economic sense, is small or even non-existent.[1]

These arguments led up to a justification for the exceptional differential for medically qualified university teachers (accepted as permanent for clinicians but declining and then expected gradually to disappear for pre-clinical staff), the use of the 'professorial spread' for paying more to specialists of high economic value, and the possibility of temporary adjustments in the application of the lecturer's scale to 'buy in' or retain teachers in scarce subjects – as in fact occurred in the 1960 award less than two years later.[2] Indeed, when the 1962 White Paper ruled cost of living and comparability of salaries out of the evaluation of pay claims, what else was there left but the determination of salaries by naked market forces? To try and find an answer to this question or, if no answer could be found, to squeeze the best result out of the market, the A.U.T. turned to a panel of outside experts.

The Advisory Panel appointed early in 1962 consisted of M. P. Fogarty, Professor of Industrial Relations at Cardiff, as chairman, and Professors H. C. Edey and B. C. Roberts of the London School of Economics and D. J. Robertson of Glasgow, and Mr. J. E. G. Utting of Cambridge. It prepared a draft report on the proper bases on which future salary claims could be based which was presented to the May Council meeting by Professor Fogarty. The main principles were: (1) a once-for-all structural adjustment of university salaries to bring them generally into line (for recruiting and retention purposes rather

1 U.G.C., *op. cit.*, p. 32.
2 *Ibid.*, p. 33.

than mere comparability) with other relevant occupations, together with backdating of such part of the adjustment as was required for 'rectification' of the 1960 award; (2) agreement on clear principles for the making of future settlements; and (3) some procedure to permit salaries to be brought up to date annually, with a general review of the whole structure every five years. In view of the concentration of the whole 3 per cent award in 1961 on the junior grades, the claim should be weighted more towards the senior. The Panel was also asked to review the existing negotiating machinery, and reported, to the surprise of many, that taking into account that no machinery could bind the hands of a government unwilling to pay, it was relatively efficient, that good working arrangements had been established and that only minor improvements were necessary. It later confirmed that the machinery worked well up to the point at which all procedures would break down, i.e. where the Government had to accept or vary or reject a U.G.C. recommendation.[1]

The claim on the Panel's basis was submitted in October, but it soon became clear that the normal procedures were not being allowed to operate. The Government had recently set up the National Incomes Commission, and it was rumoured that the university teachers' claim would be referred to it. The A.U.T. Council in December expressed grave disquiet at the delay, objected to the apparent discrimination in the N.I.C.'s terms of reference between the private sector of the economy where its awards were not binding and the public sector where they were, but wisely, as it turned out, declared that it would not necessarily refuse co-operation if the claim were referred to the N.I.C.[2]

The claim was so referred by the Government in January 1963, accompanied by an announcement that meanwhile the university teachers would receive from 1 April an interim award of 10 per cent. The reference stated:

The Government consider that a full review of the remuneration of the academic staff of Universities and Colleges of Advanced Technology is called for, in the light of the following factors:

a the need to provide for the expansion of higher education;

1 Council Minutes, 25–6 May, 19–20 December 1962.
2 *Ibid.*, 19–20 December 1962.

b the requirements of the Universities and the Colleges of Advanced Technology in relation to other types of employment drawing on persons with similar qualifications;

and in the light of the general considerations set forth in the White Paper 'The National Incomes Commission' (Cmnd. 1844).[1]

The hearings by the N.I.C. turned out to be the nearest thing to real salary negotiation ever achieved by the A.U.T. For the first time, its negotiators were able to confront, before an independent tribunal, not only their immediate employers in the shape of the Vice-Chancellors and their immediate paymasters, the U.G.C., but the ultimate controllers of the purse strings, the Treasury officials, who found themselves in the unprecedented situation *vis-à-vis* the A.U.T. of having to provide specific answers to specific arguments and of having their recommendations rejected. It was an opportunity to be exploited, but it could only be exploited by professionals who knew the ropes, had done their homework thoroughly, and were ready for every twist and turn of the debate.

The team included the General Secretary, Dr. Urwin, who explored informally with the N.I.C. secretariat the form which the hearings would take and the kind of evidence which would be required, and besides taking part in the A.U.T. delegation sat through three rounds of evidence by the other interested parties, taking notes on arguments to be answered and points to be followed up. It also included Dr. Andrew Young, the A.U.T.'s statistical expert, and his Committee, which prepared a large part of the evidence, including the surveys of salaries and promotion prospects of university teachers and of lecturers in Colleges of Advanced Technology, the estimates of future demand and supply of university teachers, and, at short notice when the N.I.C. raised the question, the first supplementary earnings survey.[2] The last showed that 59 per cent of all university teachers earned less than £100 in outside earnings additional to their salaries, 75 per cent earned less than £300, 92 per cent less than £500, and only 8 per cent over £500 a year.

1 National Incomes Commission, *Remuneration of Academic Staff in Universities and Colleges of Advanced Technology* (Cmnd. 2317, 1964), p. vii.
2 A.U.T., *The Remuneration of University Teachers, 1961–62* (1962); *Colleges of Advanced Technology: Salary Survey, 1 April 1963* (1963); *Memorandum on Salaries in Universities and C.A.T.s submitted to the N.I.C., 22 May 1963* (1963), Appendix IX, 'The Outside Earnings of University Teachers'.

The team was led by Professor Fogarty, who by now had been elected to the Executive and replaced the veteran Mr. Wightman as Convener of the Salaries and Grading Committee (though the latter continued to attend and give his experienced advice). Fogarty drafted the various submissions and dealt with the technical questions of comparability of competitive salaries, and the like.

The main submission started from the 'crisis of confidence between university teachers and the Government', arising from doubts about the adequacy of the Government's programme for university expansion and from the way in which the Government had dealt with academic salaries and their negotiation since 1956. The central issue was the career prospects of first-class academic staff, who differed from other teachers in being required to do original research and advance the frontiers of knowledge. The universities and C.A.T.'s faced stiff and, in the coming expansion, increasing competition for such staff from industry, the Civil Service and Government research establishments, and since 1956 had fallen a long way behind in the competitiveness of their salary scales, as was documented by the comparison of salary and wage movements in Appendix I. Detailed arguments were mounted about the comparability in qualifications, duties, responsibilities, hours, conditions of service, promotion prospects and miscellaneous earnings of university and C.A.T. teachers, leading up to a 'fair comparison' justifying a major structural adjustment in their salary scales. Further submissions dealt with supplementary earnings, the university family allowance of £50 a child which came under the N.I.C.'s fire, and the case for an independent review body for academic salaries on the lines recommended by the Report of the Robbins Committee on Higher Education.[1]

After hearings lasting, with a break, from 17 September to 12 December 1963, and some delay to digest the implications of the Robbins Report published in October, the N.I.C. published its findings in March 1964. It concluded that over the years there had been a decline in the relative position of university salaries which was having an effect on the welfare of the universities, that in terms of an incomes policy a long-term change in relativities was desirable in the national interest in order to restore the

1 *Memorandum . . . to N.I.C.*; *Robbins Report*, p. 245.

universities to a position from which they could compete effectively for staff of the requisite quality, and that, although the expansion of the universities did not require them to be put in a dominant competitive position, 'they should be enabled to face the strains and difficulties of the next few years with a feeling of confidence that they stand on a competitive footing with other services and occupations seeking the best academic talent.' It recommended that substantially revised rates of remuneration should come into operation with effect from 1 April 1964, which took account of all the relevant considerations so that a further review would not be necessary for some time, though to maintain the universities' competitive position annual adjustments in line with the 'standard rate of advance' in other occupations would be necessary. It endorsed the existing grading system and opposed differentials in principle, though it reluctantly accepted that the medical teachers' differentials could not yet be eliminated, but it made great play with the principle of 'flexibility' under which the universities could overcome temporary shortages of specialist staff by appointments higher up the existing scales. It avoided beating university teachers with the stick of outside earnings, since the great majority received so little, but advised the university authorities not to allow the fortunate few to neglect their academic duties. It recommended that family allowances should be abolished for all new appointments (later clarified to include promotions), so that they would gradually disappear. It rejected any increase in or extension of the London allowance except to the London C.A.T.s. It recommended that C.A.T. salaries should be assimilated to university scales along suggested lines. And, with the proviso that collegiate earnings should be controlled and limited by the university authorities in the same way as other supplementary earnings, it accepted that, allowing for the differences in grading structure, Oxford and Cambridge salary ranges were not anomalous or unjustified. Finally, it rejected the Robbins Report's recommendation of an independent review body for university salaries, on the ground that this would add one more to the long list of independent bodies advising the Government on salaries in the public sector.[1]

The N.I.C. Report was a triumphant vindication of the A.U.T.'s case on salaries and of its expertise in negotiation. The

1 N.I.C., *Remuneration of Academic Staff*, esp. pp. 90–5.

A.U.T. naturally welcomed the award with acclamation, while expressing reservations on the principle of flexibility without adequate safeguards against its abuse at the local level, and deploring the rejection of an independent review body and the exaggerated dependence on its own subjective judgement of what salary levels should be instead of on the objective principle of fair comparison, the N.I.C.'s view of which the A.U.T. considered historically inaccurate. Other reservations included the low and uncompetitive level of assistant lecturers' salaries, which assumed that they were appointed at 24 instead of 27 as they actually were on average, the overlong scale for lecturers, the abolition of family allowances which the Association refused to consider final, the refusal to admit back-dating, and the lack of firm review dates for the 'standard rate of advance'.[1] The award, which was accepted by the Government and implemented from 1 April 1964, nevertheless represented a substantial advance:

Non-medical staff

Assistant Lecturers	£1,050 × £75 (3 steps) to £1,275
Lecturers	£1,400 × £85 (13 steps) to £2,505
Readers and Senior Lecturers	Range of salaries with varying maxima up to £3,250
Professors	Minimum £3,400; all universities without distinction of size to be free to determine additions to the minimum, subject to the total sum distributed by way of additions to non-medical and pre-clinical Professors together not exceeding £800 multiplied by the number of such Professors and to no salary exceeding £4,750 in any individual case.

Pre-clinical staff

For Professors, Readers and Senior Lecturers the same provisions as for non-medical staff in these grades. For Lecturers a scale with a minimum of £1,400 to maxima ranging from £2,505 to £3,250; universities to determine individually the scales and annual increments.

1 Council Minutes, 29–30 May 1964.

Clinical staff

No change in present rates except the minimum for Lecturers which should be £1,400.[1]

The A.U.T.'s response was to use the N.I.C.'s Report as a firm base from which to go forward. One line of advance was to strengthen still more the objective principles on which salary negotiation rested, and here the professional expertise of the Conveners of the Salaries and Statistics Committee were brought to bear. Professor Fogarty launched a study of 'job evaluation' in the universities on the lines advocated by Elliott Jacques in his study of Glacier Metal Ltd., and operating in organizations like the B.B.C., I.C.I., Standard Telephones, and Unilever. This meant applying such unfamiliar concepts as multi-factoral analysis, the 'timespan of responsibility', and the like, to university teaching and research, and comparing them with other professional and managerial occupations. Andrew Young, by now Professor of Numerical Analysis at Liverpool, continued the sequence of remuneration surveys with a further study of university and C.A.T. salaries in 1964–65, for which purpose the A.U.T. appointed a full-time computer assistant, Miss Dinah Sowry, to work with him on the Liverpool University computer. His Committee also conducted surveys of 'fringe benefits' – the financial provisions made for university teachers for travel for research purposes, secretarial assistance, teaching aids and study leave – which had been questioned by the N.I.C.; of the age distribution of the profession and its effect on promotion prospects on the basis of which they evolved a fairer, more sophisticated and flexible formula for calculating the quota of senior non-professorial posts which they pressed, unsuccessfully, upon the U.G.C.; of the staffing position and expansion prospects in the sample departments of physics, economics and French; of the 'brain drain' from the universities to other occupations in this country and to universities abroad; and, in co-operation with the Secretariat of the U.G.C., of the whole problem of obtaining and processing university statistics.[2]

Another line of advance was to press, despite the adverse

1 N.I.C., *op. cit.*, p. 93.
2 Minutes and papers of Salaries and Grading and Statistics Committees, and Appendices to *Memorandum on Salaries in Universities submitted to the National Board on Prices and Incomes*, 1967.

comments of the N.I.C., for a revised system of salary negotiating machinery. Professor Fogarty drew up an outline of such a system, under which the U.G.C. would appoint a Remuneration and Conditions of Service Panel from amongst its own members, together with additional members specially experienced in the field, which would decide which aspects of academic remuneration and conditions of employment would be determined nationally, collect the factual data necessary for a proper review of these and make it available to the Department of Education and Science (to which the U.G.C. in 1964 became responsible), the Committee of Vice-Chancellors and the A.U.T., accept a case from any of the interested parties and transmit it to the rest, and arrange full discussions with written evidence and oral hearings before drafting proposals and submitting them for approval by all three bodies, with an automatic and binding reference in case of disagreement to the Industrial Court. This outline scheme did not arouse the enthusiasm of the U.G.C. or of the Vice-Chancellors, nor, at a meeting in 1965 with Mr. C. A. R. Crosland, the Secretary of State for Education and Science, of the Government, which also categorically rejected the separate, independent review body recommended by the Robbins Committee. Mr. Crosland offered to look into the possibility of a choice between a confrontation machinery of the Burnham type with the Minister on one side and the staff on the other, and a general review body for all the public services. The A.U.T. opted for the first – though once again agreeing to go forward with the existing machinery for their current claim for a 'standard rate of advance' – but in the event both alternatives were withdrawn and the question determined by the Government's standing reference of university salaries to the Prices and Incomes Board in October 1967, to which we shall return.[1]

The third line of progress was, naturally, to seize on the 'standard rate of advance' and submit an annual claim for an adjustment to maintain the universities' competitive position. The A.U.T. claimed to be in a unique position as the only profession which had been right through the whole process of an incomes policy reference, and to have been judged by the very criteria which the Government laid down in its White Paper

[1] Council Minutes, 28–9 May 1965, 21–2 December 1966, 21–2 December 1967.

Uſwin

on Prices and Incomes in 1965. By July 1965 other salaries in general were running at 6½–7 per cent above the N.I.C. level of April 1964, and wages 8–9 per cent above. The A.U.T., foreseeing the usual long-drawn-out negotiations, had submitted a claim in January 1965. Dr. Urwin now wrote to Mr. George Brown, First Secretary for Economic Affairs, pointing out that the maintenance of the relativities established by the N.I.C. was a test of the Government's own incomes policy, and asked for a reference to the Prices and Incomes Board which had replaced the N.I.C. This suggestion was ignored for the time being, but on 16 February 1966 an award of 5 per cent was announced from 1 April. Since by that time university salaries were running at 15–20 per cent behind the competitive levels established by the N.I.C., the A.U.T. asked the U.G.C. for the 'considered reply' to which it was entitled under the existing procedure, when it came rejected it as inadequate, and once again demanded negotiating machinery which would truly provide for negotiation.[1]

Further advance was blocked in July 1966 by the announcement by Mr. James Callaghan, Chancellor of the Exchequer, of the Government's 'pay freeze', which also caught the readjustment of clinical salaries which the U.G.C. was recommending, and this was followed by the period of 'severe restraint' which lasted until 30 June 1967. During this twelve months of 'zero norm' in all pay claims the question of a 'standard rate of advance' was lost sight of and hope shifted to the Prices and Incomes Board, which the A.U.T. hoped to convince as it had convinced the N.I.C. The main problem was to obtain the reference to the Board which the Government had promised as long ago as 16 November 1966. The reference was eventually made on 30 October 1967, and when it came took the form of a standing reference, which meant that the P.I.B. became a general and permanent review body for university salaries. Even that, which was not unwelcome to the A.U.T., did not unblock the channels of advance, since the reference included the appointment to the Board of two independent members with special knowledge of university salaries. These soon proved almost impossible to find, since the Act setting up the P.I.B. required that the two special members should serve as full members of the Board for all other references as well as for university

1 21–2 December 1965, 26–7 May 1966

salaries, and that they should not be themselves academics able to benefit from the decision. Nor would they allow their own academic members, Mr. W. B. Reddaway, Professor H. A. Turner and Miss Joan Woodward join in the decisions on university salaries. In July 1968 the two special members had still not been found, and discussions of an informal kind began without them.[1]

Meanwhile, the A.U.T. in preparing its submission had suddenly been faced with the loss of its chief negotiator. In 1966 Professor Fogarty, now Senior Vice-President and in line for the Presidency in 1966–67, resigned from university service to take a full-time research post with Political and Economic Planning, and felt obliged therefore to resign the Convenership of the Salaries and Grading Committee. It proved impossible to find a new Convener with his intimate knowledge of salary movements and career earnings and the technicalities of job evaluation and comparability, and Mr. D. E. Varley, an economist at Nottingham and Junior Vice-President for 1966–67, stepped into the breach as Chairman of the Committee, on the understanding that he would not have to draft and present salary claims. The original notion was that the General Secretary should do this part of the work, but it was decided by the Executive that, since incomes policy had changed radically and future claims would have to be based on job evaluation, 'it was impossible for anyone but a technocrat to prepare a claim so based.' Dr. Fogarty was therefore invited to become a part-time, paid consultant to the Association and to prepare the submission to the P.I.B. and lead the team at the hearings.[2]

This was the final – or perhaps the penultimate – step in the professionalization of the A.U.T.'s salary negotiating system. M. P. Fogarty was even more a transitional figure in the process than R. G. D. Allen. He had begun as an expert from outside the Executive who, as a member of the Association, had freely given his professional services, and had gone on to stand for election to the Executive and the presidential ladder in the normal way. Then his resignation from university service had precipitated a crisis which could be resolved only by the employment

1 *Ibid.*, 21–2 December 1967, 31 May–1 June 1968, and papers of Salaries and Grading Committee.
2 *Ibid.*, 21–2 December 1966.

of a part-time professional consultant, namely himself. In this reluctant and hesitating way the A.U.T. was forced to accept the logic of professionalization. The only remaining step, still not yet taken, would be to appoint a full-time salary negotiator, either a Fogarty – if the Association could afford him – or the General Secretary himself, who by now has considerable expertise in the field.

Dr. Fogarty prepared the Memorandum with the help of the team and a new Working Party on Productivity including himself, Professor Young and Dr. G. C. Routh, the wages and salaries economist from Sussex university. Approved by the Council, it was submitted to the P.I.B. on 30 May 1967. It claimed:

1 A general increase of salaries to restore the competitive equivalence between salaries and prospects in the universities and in other occupations drawing on the same pool of recruits which the N.I.C., in the light of criteria similar to those laid down in Schedule 2 of the Prices and Incomes Act, 1966, judged to be in the national interest. This was estimated at 10 per cent up to the time of submission, raised at the May Council in 1968 to 15 per cent.

2 An additional increase – making at its highest point a total of 16 per cent – at the bottom of the lecturer scale; raised to 24 per cent in May 1968.

3 To allow for the fact that prospects of promotion beyond lecturer were deteriorating sharply, *either* the opening of the senior grades to promotion by merit on the A.U.T.'s formula for adjusting the quota of senior posts to the age distribution of the profession, *or* an increase beyond the 10 (later 15) per cent claimed at the top of the lecturer grade.

These claims were underpinned by twelve pages of closely reasoned argument, covering the academic labour market, the principle of fair comparison and the impossibility of finding a satisfactory alternative to it, the irrelevance of 'fringe benefits' which were merely necessary aids to efficiency and of outside earnings which for the great majority were no greater than overtime and bonus payments in industry, the extreme lowness of post-probationary salaries in the universities compared with colleges of technology and the administrative civil service, the sharp deterioration in promotion prospects owing to the lull in university expansion (to which we shall return in Section 4), and the contribution which the university teachers in general and the Association in particular, through its studies of teaching methods, university organization and method, and the like, were making towards increasing productivity.[1] The main Memorandum was accompanied by a supplementary one on clinical salaries, which accepted that university clinical teachers should be paid salaries equivalent to those in the National Health Service, but proposed to abolish the differential without loss to the academic clinicians by a system of dual source payment such as already operated in Northern Ireland, the university paying the basic salary and the hospital the clinical supplement (though in a single pay cheque). It was also accompanied by a series of appendices, giving an exact description of the salaries and duties of the various grades of university teacher; the rank order of outside sources of competition for intellectual manpower in different faculties (other U.K. and overseas universities, technical colleges, other teaching, government service, industry and commerce, professional or private practice, etc.); independent estimates of general salary movements, 1964-66; comparisons of university salaries with 'average career' and 'minimum efficiency' salaries in industry and commerce and the civil service; the A.U.T.'s 'sophisticated formula for senior posts'; levels of work and responsibility of university clinical teachers; the operation of dual source payment of clinical teachers in Northern Ireland and in the University of Otago, New Zealand; and the clinical salary scales currently in force in the universities and in the National Health Service.[2]

Whether or not the submission to the P.I.B. represents the ultimate in professional salary negotiation, it can be argued that the A.U.T. is now working at the frontier of current knowledge and expertise in this field. Its level of argument and marshalling of evidence set the pace for the negotiators on the other side, who must answer with equally effective and well-founded arguments and evidence or lose the debate. The only fear is that, as with the previous Government's White Paper on Incomes Policy in 1962 or the National Incomes Commission in 1964, the arguments will not be answered but evaded by ruling them out of court or preferring subjective judgements to objective principles – the

1 *Memorandum . . . to P.I.B.*, pp. 2-13.
2 *Ibid.*, pp. 14-18, and Appendices A-J.

ultimate refuge of authoritarian paymasters and their apologists when outflanked by rational argument. In the outcome, this fear, expressed before the P.I.B. reported, proved to be only too well founded, as will appear in the following three paragraphs, written since that unhappy event.

The Report of the Prices and Incomes Board published in December 1968[1] was greeted with astonishment and derision by most university teachers. It was an extraordinary document, confused and confusing, which bandied about the terms 'teaching' and 'research' without any attempt at defining them, in such a way as to suggest an utter ignorance of what university teachers do and how they do it. It rejected, without attempting to refute, the detailed arguments of the A.U.T. submission, on the grounds, first, that 'a claim based on a movement in salaries which has been inflationary would, if conceded, add further to that inflation,' and that 'the endless chain of increases' must be broken somewhere; and, secondly, that an 'overall' increase, proportionately the same for everyone, was not justified by any problem of recruitment and retention, as was shown (*mirabile dictu!*) by the maintenance over a decade of the same staff-student ratio – though it immediately gave away the case by admitting that there might have been some deterioration in the quality of recruits to university life. These extraordinary arguments, that the chain of inflationary increases could somehow be broken, and the equilibrium of the national economy restored, by attacking not only the smallest and weakest but the *last* link in the chain, a tiny profession whose salary increases always came too late to effect anyone else's, and that the morale, efficiency, and competitive position of a profession can be gauged by the maintenance of an abstract staffing ratio based on an expectation that the profession would in the long term be treated fairly in comparison with competing professions, would have been labelled specious and callous if they had been put forward by an ordinary employer. They led on to a claim that 'the present salary and career structure is biased towards research and that steps need to be taken to encourage and reward excellence in teaching'. It may, indeed, be so, but the P.I.B. adduced no evidence whatsoever to support it, and showed no sign of comprehending the many activities which go under the name of research, and how many of them directly affect, and are in fact a necessary preparation for, teaching at the

1 National Board for Prices and Incomes, *Report No. 98, Standing Reference on the Pay of University Teachers in Great Britain. First Report* (Cmnd. 3866, December 1968).

frontiers of knowledge. It would be very easy to double the number of staff-student contact hours without any significant increase in learning by the student, and at a cost in quality of total education due to the decline of 'research' which would be prohibitive. The sum total of the P.I.B.'s jejune contribution to this difficult and delicate subject was a suggestion that the quality of an individual's teaching, and so part of his salary, might be assessed partly on the basis of students' answers to question-naires and of their performance in examinations – without the least inkling of the difference between students' immediate im-pressions and the long-term effect on them of a particular teacher's work, or the lack of correlation in students of differing ability between quality of teaching received and examination performance.

Nevertheless, upon these ill-conceived and half-digested arguments the P.I.B. based its main recommendations: a basic award of about 5 per cent, backdated to October 1968, and shared unequally between the various grades, so that professors received an average increase of 2 per cent, readers and senior lecturers an average of 3 per cent, lecturers a minimum of 4 per cent rising at some points on the ladder to 8–10 per cent, and assistant lecturers 10–17 per cent; and a supplementary award equal to 4 per cent of the salary bill to be devoted in the case of the non-professorial staff to discretionary payments' to individuals as a reward for heavier teaching loads, better quality teaching, or in some cases additional administrative work, and in the case of professors to 'distinction awards' for special merit or effort, to be assessed by committees drawn from outside the universities. In addition, the P.I.B. recommended the abolition of the assistant lecturer grade and its amalgamation with a shortened lecturer grade (fourteen steps instead of the four plus fourteen of the two grades it replaced) – both points for which the A.U.T. had long pressed – but exacted as the price of them a lengthy probationary period of four or five years, plus a rigorously operated efficiency bar between the eighth and ninth rungs. It also recommended the fading-out of the London allowance, on the curious ground not that Londoners had access to better academic facilities but that they had greater opportunities for outside earnings – true of a few but by no means of all. Other recommendations included the abolition of the minimum and maximum for the 'professorial spread', the payment by the Research Councils of part of the salaries of teaching staff engaged on their research projects, the payment of clinical university teachers of consultant status on the same scale as National Health Service consultants, and, rather than a differential for pre-clinical teachers, the placing of them on the non-medical scales at appropriate (presumably higher) points.

The Secretary of State for Education and Science, Mr Edward Short, accepted the main recommendations, though not the recommendation on student assessment of teaching ability which had caused a minor *furore*, and the salary scale for non-clinical university teachers as from October 1968 became as follows:

Professor	Average salary at each institution not to exceed: £4,500 (no minimum or maximum)
Reader and Senior Lecturer	Range with varying maxima up to: £3,520
Lecturer (including old Assistant Lecturer)	£1,240 × £115 (13 increments) to £2,735
Discretionary payments	Available for payment annually to up to half those eligible – i.e. readers, senior lecturers and lecturers – within 4 per cent of the annual salary bill for these grades.
Distinction awards	Available for payment annually to professors within 4 per cent of the annual professorial bill.

3. AN ÉQUIPE OF EXPERTS

The professionalization of the A.U.T. has followed a parallel course in other fields than salary negotiation but, under less urgent pressure, has not gone so far. The next most urgent pressure was in the field of superannuation, where two official committees in the space of eight years have recommended major revisions of the system. The first was a sub-committee of the U.G.C. under the chairmanship of its Secretary, Sir Edward Hale, which reported in February 1960. It put forward two alternatives: a completely new terminal salary scheme on the lines of those in the Civil Service, school teaching and most of the public services, under which pension would be calculated as a fraction of the average salary of the member in the last three years before retirement, multiplied by the number of years of service; and a continuation of the insurance-based F.S.S.U. now to be safeguarded against inflation by guaranteed supplementation calculated as under the terminal salary scheme but at a slightly lower level, though still equal to about two-thirds of final salary after a full career of forty years' service.[1] The differences between the two schemes were many and highly technical, but the most important were that F.S.S.U. offered the opportunity of a much larger benefit in case of death in service; because of peculiarities in taxation law (which would probably not be allowed to continue in operation if F.S.S.U. were to be substantially altered so as to require retesting by the Inland Revenue), its option to take the proceeds of the maturing insurance policies as a lump sum and to purchase an annuity offered the chance in certain cases, at existing interest and taxation rates, of a much higher post-tax income than the terminal salary scheme; and transferability of pension rights into and out of university service was remarkably easy. Not surprisingly, therefore, the A.U.T. on Mr. Wightman's advice opted for F.S.S.U. with supplementation, and in this they were followed by the majority of university institutions represented at a preliminary conference at the Senate House, University of London, on 18 March 1960 and reporting back to its steering committee under Sir Francis Hill. The Hale Committee scheme of F.S.S.U. with supplementation therefore came into operation on 1 April 1960.[2]

There were, however, three drawbacks to the scheme. The first was that it still provided no safeguard against inflation after retirement, so that old retirants, however adequate their pensions had once been, could still suffer hardship after a few years of rising prices. We have seen in the last chapter how much effort Mr. Wightman and his Committee had devoted since the War to redressing this injustice, and how they had finally managed to get the principle accepted in 1953 that the (Government service) Pensions (Increase) Acts, 1944–53, could be applied by analogy to university teachers, though as of right only to those retiring since 1 August 1953. Most universities in fact supplemented by

1 *Report of the (Hale) Committee on the Superannuation of University Teachers* (H.M.S.O., 1960).
2 Council Minutes, 20–1 May 1960; Conference of University Representatives at Senate House, University of London, 18 March 1960, and *Hale Report*, pp. 7–8; cf. U.G.C. *University Development*, 1957–62, pp. 40–2.

ex gratia payments the pensions of those who retired before then, and those retiring later continued to benefit by the analogous Pensions (Increase) Acts, including that of 1960, so that although the A.U.T. continued to press for it the lack of an automatic readjustment of old retirants' pensions was not keenly felt.[1]

The second drawback only came to light when the Manchester representatives to the A.U.T. Council, who had been awakened to the point by their Bursar, Mr. R. A. Rainford, a member of the Hale Committee, raised the question whether a member retiring at 60, as he was entitled to do under F.S.S.U., would be eligible for automatic supplementation. The notion that he might not be was laughed aside at the time, but on enquiry it transpired that many universities took the view that leaving university service before the official age of retirement (70 in Scotland, mostly 65 or 67 elsewhere) was resignation not retirement, and that supplementation was at the discretion of the university. This view was upheld by the U.G.C., and in spite of A.U.T. opposition, based on Leading Counsel's Opinion, still continues in force.[2]

The third drawback was the unsatisfactory premium rates which many of the F.S.S.U. panel companies offered to members, a grievance which the A.U.T. had long aired, and which was one reason why it continued to seek representation on the F.S.S.U. Council. That there was still room for improvement is shown by the striking increases which actually took place between 1960 and 1966 in the sums assured on without-profits endowments (15 per cent on a policy taken out at age 30, 5 per cent at age 50) and in the bonus rates on with-profit endowments (simple bonuses rising from 51s. to 71s. per cent, compound bonuses from 52s. to 62s. per cent). Other improvements included the waiver of medical examinations for endowment policies maturing at 60 (an improvement shared by F.S.S.U. members with other beneficiaries of policies taken out by institutions in Great Britain), better rates of accumulation between 60 and actual retirement on the proceeds of policies (which from 1965 could, still better, be encashed and invested for the member's benefit in trustee securities), certain retrospective improvements to the cash

---

1 Council Minutes, 16–17 December 1960, 26–7 May, 20–1 December 1961, 19–20 December 1962; U.G.C., *op. cit.*, p. 42.
2 Council Minutes, 20–1 May 1960.

value at maturity of existing policies, and an improvement of the order of 9s. per cent in annuity rates guaranteed under F.S.S.U. policies.[1] These improvements came partly under persistent A.U.T. pressure, mounted with the aid of the professional services of its consultant actuaries, Messrs. Bacon and Woodrow; partly through the efforts of a new and vigorous Secretary to the Council of the F.S.S.U., Mr. J. Fleming; partly through an unusually favourable combination of economic circumstances, including inflation, high interest rates and exceptional capital gains, due mainly to take-over bids, in the panel companies' investments; and partly, according to the A.U.T.'s expert advisers, to the sword of Damocles left hanging over the companies' heads by the universities' decision in 1960 to reconsider the whole question of superannuation 'after a lapse of not more than five years'.[2]

Because of the accelerated expansion of the universities, the raising of the C.A.T.s to university status and the projected transfer of their staff to F.S.S.U. on 1 April 1965, and the Robbins Report's recommendation that superannuation be looked at again from the point of view of transferability between all sectors of higher education, the question was re-opened in four years rather than five.[3] A Working Party on University Teachers' Superannuation under the chairmanship of Sir George Maddex was set up jointly by the U.G.C., the F.S.S.U. Central Council, the Government Departments concerned, the Committee of Vice-Chancellors, the Committee of Principals of C.A.T.s, the Association of Teachers in Technical Institutes (then acting on behalf of the non-university level teachers in the C.A.T.s), and the A.U.T. By this time Andrew Young, the A.U.T.'s statistical expert, had replaced Mr. Wightman (in 1962) as Convener of the Superannuation Committee, and he was the natural choice for the A.U.T.'s representative on the Working Party. He was – and is – a formidable expert on the technicalities of superannuation, an implacable critic of the shortcomings of F.S.S.U. and the record of the panel companies, and an exponent of 'dynamic pensions', by which he means pensions which are

1 Department of Education and Science, *University Teachers' Superannuation*: *Report of a Working Party* (Chairman, Sir George Maddex, H.M.S.O., 1968), pp. 31–2.
2 U.G.C., *op. cit.*, p. 42; *Maddex Report*, p. 8.
3 *Robbins Report*, p. 179; *Maddex Report*, pp. 8–9.

automatically adjusted *after* retirement to keep up with the increase in current salaries. Although against Treasury opposition he was unsuccessful in getting his colleagues on the Working Party to accept the last, many of his ideas inform the Maddex Report, and especially the two variant terminal salary schemes which, although no clear recommendation is made between the three, it offers as alternatives to the F.S.S.U. scheme as supplemented since 1960. He was also asked by the Joint Consultative Committee of the Vice-Chancellors and the A.U.T. to write, in collaboration with Sir Douglas Logan, Principal of London University, a simplified version of the report, *A Guide to the Choice of Pension Schemes for University Teachers* (February 1968).

The two terminal salary schemes, which the *Guide* called T.S.S.1 and T.S.S.2, differed chiefly in their provision of death and dependants' benefits. T.S.S.1 offered a benefit on death in service of two years' pensionable salary plus, for married men only, widows' and orphans' pension, paid for by an additional 2 per cent of salary by men. T.S.S.2 offered no dependants' pensions but a death in service benefit of four years' pensionable salary. Both offered ill-health retirement benefits varying from the return of contributions with interest for under five years' service to a pension equal to one eightieth of pensionable salary for each year of service plus a lump sum equal to three years' pension for a career of over twenty years (the same as for retirement). Both offered transferability of pension rights to new recruits to and resigners from university service, except that there was no right, as under F.S.S.U., to take away the cash value of the employers' contributions as well as the member's own. They differed in cost from F.S.S.U., at current rates of tax, as follows:

	Members' Contribution	
	Before Tax	*After Tax*
	% of salary	
F.S.S.U.	5	4·18
T.S.S.1 (women)	5	3·40
T.S.S.1 (men)	5+2=7	3·40+1·18=4·58
T.S.S.2	6	4·08

The university's contribution was 8 per cent under T.S.S., but to cover the £20 million deficit incurred in setting it up the institution would pay an extra 2 per cent a year (making 10 per cent in all, the same as under F.S.S.U.) for the first twenty years, and might have to pay more if the fund proved insufficient. The pensions under the two T.S.S. schemes were the same: one eightieth of terminable salary (the average of the last three years') for each year of service, plus a lump sum equal to three years' pension (compared with an F.S.S.U. pension requiring supplementation of one-seventy-fifth for each year of service and no lump sum).

The balance of advantages and disadvantages between the three schemes was impossible to calculate, since so many factors affected the benefits in any individual case. Under F.S.S.U. not only the length of career and the terminal salary affected the size of the pension, but the timing and size of every promotion and other increase in salary experienced, the rates of interest and capital gains controlling the bonus rates, etc., throughout the career, the accumulation rate between 60 and actual retirement and the going rate for annuities at point of retirement, and, above all, the rates of tax and the special tax concession by which annuities are partially untaxed as periodic part-repayments of capital. If all these factors remained favourable F.S.S.U. could be much more profitable than T.S.S. but if F.S.S.U. required supplementation at all – and 80 per cent of those retiring during 1966 required supplementation – then T.S.S. was the more profitable scheme. In short, the choice between F.S.S.U. and T.S.S. was perfectly rational, but the factors on which rational choice could be based were multiple and, being in the future of both the individual's career and the national economy, were all unknown. Since the scheme to be chosen would be compulsory only on new entrants to the profession, existing members could keep their options open by voting for a T.S.S. scheme and then deciding whether it or F.S.S.U. would better meet their individual needs. Beyond that, however, the choice was a matter of personal predilection and inclination, between the safety and near-certainty of T.S.S. (with or without dependants' benefits) and the gamble, with built-in safety net, of F.S.S.U.

The choice was to be made by the new Joint Consultative Committee of the Vice-Chancellors and the A.U.T., after seeking the views of their staffs and members. After a series of regional university seminars addressed by Professor Young in various parts of the country, the A.U.T. Council at its May meeting in 1968 provisionally opted for the T.S.S., on the grounds that for new entrants to the profession certainty of pension and comparability with other superannuation schemes in the public sector were more important than the chance of exceptional windfall gains in the most fortunate combination of circumstances under F.S.S.U.; and for T.S.S.2 because it was simpler to operate in not distinguishing between men and women and (for benefits) between married and unmarried men, because it was for men cheaper than T.S.S.1, and because, in addition to the double life cover (four years' pensionable salary instead of two), extra cover for dependants could be arranged quite cheaply under private policies. Acceptance, however, was subject to certain points of clarification and negotiation:

(1) the right to aggregate pension rights for broken service, especially overseas, explained in the Maddex Report but omitted from the outline of T.S.S.;

(2) no medical examination on entry (none was required since 1965 under F.S.S.U.); and none should be required, as the Maddex Report suggested it should, before a retirant could convert part of his pension in favour of his wife if she survived him;

(3) the need for arrangements for contracting out of the Government graduated pension scheme;

(4) the need to ensure that members' contributions would not be increased to meet possible actuarial deficiencies;

(5) skilled drafting of the rules to ensure that the benefits were not subject to estate duty.

Above all, a very large number of A.U.T. members set great store by the right under F.S.S.U. to retire at any age from 60 until the institution's age of retirement, in practice (though at the discretion of the institution) with full supplementation, and it was essential to maintain this right under the T.S.S., which allowed it only at the expense of a substantial reduction in pension.[1]

These views and reservations the A.U.T. representatives took with them to the Joint Consultative Committee with the Vice-Chancellors. The Vice-Chancellors were, of course, bound

1 Council Minutes, 31 May–1 June 1968.

by their institutions. The universities themselves, however, and their Senates and Councils, having held lengthy discussions on the matter, could not agree on the choice between one of the two terminal salary schemes and the continuation of F.S.S.U. The issues were too complicated, and the possible variation of pension in the case of any particular individual too great, for any swift decision to be agreed on by all the many interested parties. The major obstacle to agreement, as expected, proved to be the right of university teachers to retire, like school teachers and civil servants, at 60 years of age without substantial loss of pension, a right which some members of university staffs thought vital and others considered as being of little consequence compared with the other advantages of a terminal salary scheme, notably the certainty of the scale of pension and the more adequate defence against inflation, at least up to the point of retirement. If one of the chief characteristics of the academic profession – some would say their major fault – is that as individuals they see too many sides of a question, collectively they see them all, and are so adept at mounting arguments for each of them that they run the risk of arguing each other to a standstill. On a question like superannuation, which affects every individual differently, and even the same individual differently at different stages of his career, the sides were more numerous and the arguments more complicated and strongly held than on most. In 1960, it is true, at the time of the Hale Committee's Report, a decision had been reached with surprising speed, but then the universities had seemed to be offered the best of both worlds, the flexibility, high death-in-service cover and tax advantages of F.S.S.U. plus the hedge against inflation of the novel supplementation scheme, while the right to retire at age 60 without loss of pension did not arise until after the decision had been made. In 1968–69 the case was different: supplementation was no longer novel, and every side of the question was exposed and seen to be open-ended. It was not surprising, therefore, that the Joint Consultative Committee failed to arrive at a swift decision, and was still discussing the matter at the time of going to press.

The Joint Consultative Committee with representatives of the Committee of Vice-Chancellors which was to make the decision on superannuation came into existence only in 1967. It was the final, happy outcome of the A.U.T.'s continuous effort since the War to establish some kind of co-ordinating body to represent opinion not only of the university authorities but in the universities as a whole. We have seen in the last chapter how the Home Universities Conference failed to become that co-ordinating body. For long the A.U.T. sub-committee on University Co-ordination under Mr. D. W. Reece of Aberdeen and later Professor I. Gowan and Mr. D. E. Varley of Nottingham endeavoured to construct some more permanent and effective body than the H.U.C., to be called the British Council of Universities, but it always foundered on the obstacle which the size of such a body, if it were to be truly representative of all the various interests, would present to the effective discussion and expression of a 'university view' on matters of public interest. An attempt was made to make the Home Universities Conference more effective and in touch with the outside world by replacing it by a joint conference with industrialists in 1965,[1] but it gradually became clear that progress did not lie in this direction. Mr. Varley whittled down the choice to two alternatives: a large body of about 200 representatives elected by the different interests in the universities, with an executive committee of about 12–20 members, a machinery in which the A.U.T. would naturally have no direct role; and a small body consisting of representatives of the A.U.T. and the Vice-Chancellors. The latter would not only be more amenable to the A.U.T.'s influence but would be a more efficient and effective body. It was under his successor as Convener, Mr. A. M. Prichard, Reader in law at Nottingham, that the Vice-Chancellors agreed to the setting up of the Joint Consultative Committee, consisting of about four representatives on each side plus the Secretaries, which would meet once a term to discuss specific topics, excluding salaries and other matters of negotiation. Additional specialists could be called in for particular topics. The first meeting, to discuss the terms of reference, took place on 4 July 1967.[2] Since then the topics discussed have included the selection of students,

1 Association of Commonwealth Universities, *Industry and the Universities – Aspects of Interdependence*: *Report of Proceedings of a Conference convened by the Committee of Vice-Chancellors and Principals of the Universities of the U.K. and the Confederation of British Industry*, 1965.
2 Council Minutes, esp. 26–7 May, 21–2 December 1967, 31 May–1 June 1968.

the central collection of data on staff and students, the training of all kinds of staff including academic staff, and the U.G.C.'s memorandum of 'guidance' to the universities for the quinquennium 1967–72 (to which we shall return). It has also organized the Universities Spring Conference, 1968, on Universities and Productivity, in which quite revolutionary ideas for the measurement of productivity in teaching, research and the use of buildings and resources were presented and discussed.[1] The Joint Consultative Committee is one more step in the direction of the integration of the academic profession for the purposes of self-knowledge, self-expression, self-criticism and, regrettably perhaps in what often seems an increasingly hostile environment, self-defence.

One of the major criticisms made inside as well as outside the profession is that it is not professional enough, in that it gives its recruits no training in that part of its duties of most immediate concern to its clients, the students and the public, and most relevant to questions of their own productivity, namely teaching. University teaching is the most difficult kind to professionalize, since the methods of imparting to the student the capacity to think for himself differ markedly with the subject, the ability of the student and, not least, the personality of the teacher. No doubt a certain amount of elementary classroom technique, of voice projection, 'chalk and talk', pedagogic repetition, the use of visual aids, and so on, is relevant and useful, but hardly gets to the heart of the problem, which is to inculcate a love of the subject, an intense concern for truth however unpalatable it may be, a critical refusal to take anything on trust without rigorously tested supporting evidence, and, above all, an independence of mind and an inner self-propulsion which eventually make the teacher himself redundant. No ordinary teacher training course can enable a university teacher to do all this, which is why many academics, and not necessarily the worst teachers, believe that no formal training is or can be relevant, and that the only way to learn is to observe others doing it, which all university teachers have done through several years of undergraduate and graduate study.

1 *Universities Spring Conference, 1968*: *Universities and Productivity*: *Background papers* (Joint Consultative Committee of the Vice-Chancellors' Committee and the A.U.T., 1968).

Nevertheless, with the expansion of the universities and the recruitment of a wider range of ability and personality this purist view of university teaching as an art self-taught or craft passed on informally from master to apprentice is no longer quite so tenable, and the A.U.T., which has always maintained an interest in the question – it raised it with the Vice-Chancellors in 1945 and 1954 – has intensified its concern and sought to bring the expertise of its specialist members to bear on it. In 1963 it decided to set up a Panel on Teaching Techniques consisting of a wide range of experts in every kind of educational method and audio-visual aid, under the convenership of an amateur, the Convener of the University Development Committee, as a link with the Executive. No sooner had it done so than the U.G.C. established a Sub-committee on Audio-Visual Aids in Higher Scientific Education under the chairmanship of Dr. (now Sir) Brynmor Jones, Vice-Chancellor of Hull University, which immediately asked the A.U.T. to submit its views within one month. There was not enough time to set up the Panel and call it together for lengthy consultations, so the Convener, a social historian who fortunately had some experience with educational television, including a large variety of visual aids, collected the members' views by post and prepared a submission which was finally discussed with them only when they met for the first time to give oral evidence to the Brynmor Jones Committee on 26 September 1963. The Committee was critical of the Panel's warning that audio-visual aids were no easy road to teaching productivity but simply a means to better and more effective teaching through a greater investment of effort, but nevertheless it drew heavily on the A.U.T. submission in its Report.[1]

In later meetings the Panel went on to collect information on the small amount of in-service training of university teachers given to new recruits in some universities and to recommend that such courses be established in all of them; to urge that more research should be done on teaching methods and especially their evaluation, and to take part in the original conference on 16

1 Council Minutes, 24–5 May, 19–20 December 1963; Minutes and papers of the Teaching Techniques Panel; U.G.C., *Audio-Visual Aids in Higher Scientific Education: Report of the (Brynmor Jones) Committee* (H.M.S.O., 1965).

A Professional Professional Body, 1954–69

December 1964 which founded the Society for Research into Higher Education; to press the need for more audio-visual aids and a national centre for organizing and encouraging their use in universities and other colleges of higher education; to suggest that improved secretarial and technical assistance was just as important as hardware in the preparation of effective teaching; to explore the question of teaching assistance by graduate students and others; to recommend better abstracting and bibliographical services as aids to both teaching and research; and to insist that to raise the prestige of teaching especially for the purposes of appointment and promotion was an essential prerequisite of ensuring it the serious attention it deserved. The A.U.T. went into the business of higher education research for itself in 1966, when it set up an Educational Trust Fund, covenanting to pay into it £500 a year (worth about £850 on recovery of income tax) for the support of research into university education.[1]

Meanwhile, the U.G.C. had appointed another sub-committee under Sir Edward Hale to enquire into university teaching methods. The joint questionnaires to university staff and students circulated by this and the Robbins Committee on Higher Education are well-remembered for some of their curious assumptions on the nature and organization of university teaching. The Report, published in November 1964, was nonetheless a useful document which contained essential factual data on everything connected with university teaching from students' hours of work, types of class and examinations to students' opinions on the value of different types of class and staff opinions on the need for training in teaching methods. Its recommendations were couched in rather general terms, and included the need for greater flexibility in courses so that students could more easily change from one to another, the need for more experiment in teaching methods including 'programmed learning' and audio-visual aids, for training courses or other help for newly appointed staff, and for more research into higher education generally including the more productive use of buildings and equipment. The Convener of the Panel prepared a summary and critique of the Report for the December Council meeting in 1964, and shortly handed over his responsibility to a new and more expert Convener, Dr. Wolf

[1] Minutes and papers of the Panel; Council Minutes, 26–7 May, 21–2 December 1966.

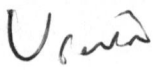

Mays of Manchester University, a philosopher who has made a special study of the problems of pedagogic communication. Since then it has continued to hammer away at similar themes, welcoming and holding joint meetings with the staff of the National Council for Educational Technology set up as a result of the Brynmor Jones Report – though as a second best to the National Centre favoured by the A.U.T. – conducting a questionnaire on the provision of in-service training, and, arising out of one of the topics referred by the A.U.T. to the Joint Consultative Committee with the Vice-Chancellors, helping to set up in February 1968 a Working Party on In-Service Training under the convenership of Mr. W. Martyn of Strathclyde.[1] Whether or not these endeavours will be any more successful than those of the past, they show a continuing concern with the professionalism of the profession.

In common with a number of other professional bodies the A.U.T. took part in 1962 in the formation of a Confederation of Professional and Public Service Organizations. Dr. Urwin represented the A.U.T. on its Liaison Committee. It could perhaps have become the T.U.C. of the professions but, lacking the economic solidarity and common political outlook of the trade unions, it failed to make any impact on the public or the Government, or to obtain the representation it sought on the National Economic Development Council, and the A.U.T. in 1964 decided to withdraw from membership.[2] The episode illustrates one of the fundamental, if unfortunate, characteristics of professional organizations, that although they exist for similar purposes and adopt parallel methods of publicity and pressure-group activities, their various professional interests are so diverse that they find it extremely difficult if not impossible to work together, except on limited common fronts as in the case of the A.U.T. and the B.M.A., the Librarians' Association or the Association of Teachers in Colleges and Departments of Education over the salaries of overlapping members.

Another failure in this period was the Commonwealth Association of University Teachers formed in 1959. This was the brain-child of Professor J. L. Montrose, a teacher of law at Queen's University, Belfast, who persuaded the corresponding Associa-

1 *Ibid.*, 31 May–1 June 1968.
2 *Ibid.*, 25–6 May 1962, 29–30 May 1964.

tions in Australia, Canada and New Zealand to come together, along with individual associations in the universities of Aligarh (Muslim), Cape Town, Ghana, Kuala Lumpur, Malaysia, Natal, and the West Indies, and was elected its first Chairman/ Secretary. It was always very much a one-man concern, without any clear idea of its function beyond keeping the Associations in touch with each other, which they did in any case by the exchange of their publications and the like, and after Montrose's death in 1966 it was wound up and its small remaining funds handed over to the larger international association, I.A.U.P.L.[1]

I.A.U.P.L. continued to function usefully under the secretary-generalship of Professor F. T. H. Fletcher until 1960 and his successor, Professor Armand Hacquaert of the University of Ghent, Belgium. Professor Robert Niklaus, ex-President of the A.U.T., was elected President for 1962–64, and Dr. Urwin was elected in 1962 to its Executive Committee. It continued to hold its International Congresses, in London in 1961, Istanbul in 1963, Vienna in 1965, Jerusalem and Haifa in 1967, and in Yugoslavia in 1969, to publish its journal, *Communication*, and issue periodical studies of university topics, including Dr. V. E. Cosslett's report on *The Relations between Scientific Research in the Universities and Industrial Research* (published with the assistance of UNESCO, London 1955) and symposia on *The Status of University Teachers* and *The Recruitment and Training of University Teachers* in sixteen countries (Ghent, Belgium, 1961 and 1967). In all these and many other activities, it worked closely with UNESCO, whose Director-General described I.A.U.P.L. in 1954 as 'one of UNESCO's oldest friends and supporters'. A special committee in 1966 recommended the professionalization of I.A.U.P.L. by the appointment of a full-time secretary and staff, but this was shelved for the time being for lack of funds.[2]

It would take too long to chronicle all the other varied activities of the A.U.T. in the last fifteen years. Expert sub-committees have studied and reported on university government and

1 *Ibid.*, 16–17 December 1959, 19–20 May 1967, *passim.*
2 *Ibid.*, 20–1 May 1960,–31 May–1 June 1968, *passim.*; *Communication* (I.A.U.P.L., Ghent, Belgium), esp. No. 49, October 1966 (special no, devoted to the history of I.A.U.P.L. and its relation with UNESCO, on the occasion of the 20th anniversary of the latter).

jrganization, recommending greater non-professorial participation and consultation of students; on conditions of service for academic staff, including the consideration of employment safeguards in new University Charters and Statutes and model clauses in individual contracts; on the financing of research in science and technology, coming to much the same conclusions as Dr. Cosslett in 1955 on the need for basic financial independence in the choice of research subjects and approaches; on technical assistance to university staffs, including the need for more technical and secretarial help, the backing of pay claims for technicians, the growth of new intermediate grades, part-way between technicians and academics, of Experimental Officer and Senior Experimental Officer and the need to determine their status and conditions of service; and the detailed, exacting and immensely fruitful Committee on the Selection and Maintenance of Students, under the convenership of Mr. Maurice Hookham of Leicester, who has done more than anyone to maintain good relations with the National Union of Students. Expert submissions have been made to a wide range of public enquiry bodies, including the Anderson Committee on Student Awards, whose Report in 1960 rejected the A.U.T. – N.U.S. recommendation to abolish university fees and the means test for students' maintenance grants but established the present system of automatic awards on acceptance by a university and on proof of need; the Royal Commissions on Trade Unions and on Medical Education; the Franks Commission on the University of Oxford; the Parry Committee appointed by the U.G.C. on university libraries and the Dainton Committee on national libraries; and, above all, as we shall see in the next section, to the Robbins Committee on higher education. The General Secretary and the Honorary Legal Adviser (Professor L. C. B. Gower until his migration to Nigeria in 1962, then Professor Dennis Lloyd, made a life peer in 1965) have dealt with an increasing number of legal cases, some of  them involving major questions of academic freedom, particularly in clashes with foreign and ex-colonial governments. Dr. Urwin and, until his retirement, Lord Chorley were given the task of vetting new university Charters and Statutes and, where they conflicted with A.U.T. policy, of making counter-submissions to the Privy Council, many of which have been successful in achieving improvements such as greater safeguards of academic tenure or larger non-professorial representation on governing bodies.[1] Much the most important activity of the A.U.T., however, has been its role in the recent expansion of the universities and of higher education generally. This was so vital a part of the development of the profession and of the Association that it deserves a section to itself.

4. THE ROBBINS ERA

Since the mid-1950's there has been a world-wide explosive growth in higher education. Between 1955 and 1965 student numbers more than doubled in most European countries: Albania, Austria, Belgium, Czechoslovakia, Denmark, Finland, France, West Germany, Greece, Italy, the Netherlands, Norway, Spain, Sweden, Turkey, the U.S.S.R. and Yugoslavia. The United Kingdom, with a rise from 131,400 to 312,200 full-time students of all kinds, in universities and other higher education colleges, has been no exception to this general expansion, nor has it been amongst the leaders of it.[2] We have had to do a great deal of running to keep up with the rest. In the end it was only the transformation of public opinion and Government policy brought about by the Report of the Robbins Committee on Higher Education, 1961–63, surprisingly the first major review ever made in this country of the whole field of full-time higher education and itself a product of the expansion crisis, which enabled us to keep up as well as we did. As far as Britain is concerned we may aptly call this age of expansion the Robbins era.

The reasons for a universal expansion were not peculiar to Britain, nor were they so parochial as much of the discussion by British politicians and the British press would have us believe. The first was the demographic increase in births after the Second World War in this and most other countries, which reached a peak in 1947 and was therefore bound to produce an

1 Minutes and papers of the Committees concerned; W. B. Palmer, *University Government and Organization* (A.U.T., 1963); E. W. Hughes, *The Internal Government of Universities* (A.U.T., 1964).

2 UNESCO, *Conference of Ministers of Education of European Member States on Access to Higher Education, Vienna, 20–5 November 1967, Factual background document No. 3*, p. 366.

'age-group bulge' of university and other college entrants in the years around 1965. This was well enough known, and would not in itself have produced more than a temporary over-crowding of the universities and colleges. The U.G.C. in their 1953 Report forecast that to accommodate the bulge as it emerged from the schools 'a marked increase in student numbers will be required from about 1960 onwards if the proportion of each age group which reaches the university is to be maintained'. They were also aware of the second reason, the need to keep up with other countries in the provision of university places both for the purposes of economic competitiveness and of intellectual development for its own sake. Pointing out that 'it is a matter of common knowledge that in certain overseas countries (both in Europe and America) university students form a far higher proportion of the total population than in this country', they asked whether, in the national interest, we ought not to be giving a university education to a substantially higher proportion of our young men and women, and quoted the fear expressed by the Zuckerman Committee on Scientific Manpower 'that if our institutions of higher education fail to grow they will not be able to keep pace with the growth in the demand for scientists necessary to promote increased industrial efficiency and productivity.' Finally, they were even aware, contrary to popular belief, of the *possibility* at least of the 'trend', that is, the growing demand on the part of the young and their parents for higher education expressed in the tendency to stay on at school beyond the statutory leaving age in order to qualify for university and other college entrance. Since in England and Wales in 1952 only 6·6 per cent of the age group were still at school at the age of 17, those who had left 'must include a considerable number who leave for reasons other than lack of academic promise, and who would be worthy university students if means could be found to retain them at school.'[1]

Yet to be aware of the need for short-term expansion and the factors making for it is not necessarily to be prepared either for the size of the crisis when it comes or the factors making for the long-term rather than temporary growth. What the U.G.C. did not, and could not in 1953, foresee was that the post-1947 decline in the birth-rate would be succeeded by a further up-

1 U.G.C., *University Development, 1947–52*, pp. 20–2.

turn, rising to a higher and more permanent 'plateau' from about 1960 onwards, to produce a long-term high-level demand for university places in the later 1970's and 1980's; and that the trend to stay on at school and qualify for university entrance would from the mid-1950's begin to accelerate so as to pile up the short-term bulge of university entrants in the mid-1960's even higher than had been forecast. The proportion of 17-year-olds remaining at school, 6·6 per cent in 1952, rose from 7·9 per cent in 1954 to 12·0 per cent in 1962, when the Robbins Committee estimated that it was likely to reach 18 per cent by 1973 and 22 per cent by 1980.[1]

The significance of these figures, visible in the mid-1950's only as the beginnings of curves which might or might not continue to rise, was that there was room for considerable disagreement not over the need for expansion, on which all were agreed, but over the precise size of the expansion required. The role of the A.U.T., along with other expansionist critics of Government complacency, was to press in season and out of season for reconsideration of the estimates on which planning was based, and to produce alternative estimates of their own, both before and after the Robbins Report, which proved in the event to be nearer to reality than the Government's own. The expertise which went into these estimates and into the demonstration that their fulfilment would require the founding of new university institutions was a further example of that professionalism which was forced upon the A.U.T. by the exigencies of the time. To what extent correct forecasts by an outside body actually influence rather than merely anticipate the course of official Government policy is always open to dispute. The U.G.C., for example, was privately convinced of the need for accelerated expansion before the A.U.T. or the Vice-Chancellors' Committee thought about it.[2] But there can be no doubt that A.U.T. pressure contributed to the general change in the climate of public and official thought in the late 1950's which produced both the Robbins Committee and the major revision of higher educational planning.

The turning point in public opinion on university expansion can be dated to the Home Universities Conference in December

1 *Robbins Report, Appendix One*, pp. 102–3.
2 Letter from Lord Murray of Newhaven to the author, 9 October 1968.

1955, at which one of the three sessions was devoted to 'the age-group bulge and its possible effects on university policy'. The opening speakers were Mr. Guy Chilver of the Queen's College, Oxford, chosen by the Vice-Chancellors' Committee, and Professor R. G. D. Allen for the A.U.T. They considered, like most other people at that time, that the bulge could easily be accommodated, except for the four years of its peak from 1964 to 1967, by a small permanent increase of 10,000 places to a stable long-term target of 90,000, plus a further temporary rise of 15,000 places, to about 105,000, during 1964–67. The short-term pressure could be met by temporarily stretching staff–student ratios, sharing university facilities, rearranging national service to spread the university entrants of the peak over the years before and after, and by a temporary raising of entrance requirements 'to keep out some, but by no means all, of the additional applicants'. The 'trend' was discounted by questioning whether an increase in sixth-form pupils would produce an effective increase in qualified applicants, and by a somewhat cold-blooded assumption that neither the schools nor the parents could afford to keep larger numbers in sixth forms during the four years of greatest stress.[1]

The reaction of the Conference to this complacency was explosive. It was headed by Lord Simon of Wythenshawe, Chairman of the Council of Manchester University, who declared that the proposed student numbers were 'totally and almost fantastically inadequate', that Britain had both the smallest proportion of the relevant age group at university of any civilized country and a desperate shortage of scientists and technologists, and that the trend to stay on at school was increasing at the rate of 5 per cent a year which would mean a doubling of student numbers within fifteen years, or, given the age-group bulge, more than double the existing total by 1965. There was a serious and increasing emergency and, he concluded:

I do hope that as a condition of the strength and welfare of the country, and almost of its survival as a great power, we shall immediately set to work on a great building programme for the universities and on achieving a steady and rapid increase both in total students and, more especially, in technologists.[2]

1 *Home Universities Conference, 1955: Report of Proceedings*, pp. 81–95.
2 *Ibid.*, pp. 95–104.

A Professional Professional Body, 1954–69

Lord Simon was followed by speaker after speaker supporting him and demanding action to expand the universities. The A.U.T. representatives were somewhat torn between their loyalty to Professor Allen, a Vice-President of the Association, and their natural inclination towards an expansionist policy, from which the profession could only benefit. As for the seven members of the U.G.C. who were present, not one of them spoke. Nearly a year later the Treasury announced capital grants for university buildings which assumed a target of 106,000 students in the mid-1960's, almost exactly the same as Professor Allen's, though now a permanent rather than a temporary figure.

When the A.U.T. representatives reported back to the Council in May 1956, a Leicester resolution asked the Executive to report on the implications of the discussion at the Home Universities Conference, and Mr. Maurice Hookham of Leicester successfully urged the setting up of a working party 'to consider forthwith A.U.T. policy on the expansion of the universities'. The working party, convened by Dr. D. A. Bell, an electronics engineer at Birmingham University, eventually produced the *Report on a Policy for University Expansion*, approved at the December Council in 1957 and published in May 1958. The Report considered the social, political and economic arguments for an expansion of university education, calculated the statistical contribution to future student numbers of the demographic rise in the 18-year-old population, the 'social trend' to stay on at school and qualify for university entrance, the distribution of intelligence in the population at large (which showed that at least twice as many were suitable for university entrance at present standards as were actually admitted), and the possible consequences of changes in the rest of the higher education system on university intake, and constructed a table of required university places in Britain up to 1975. This showed a progressive rise in potential student numbers from an actual 89,000 in 1956 to 145,000 from 1965 onwards (the 'social trend' thereafter compensating for the demographic decline after the 'bulge').[1] To meet this target the Report suggested that all existing universities which had less than 4,500 students, which it considered

---

1 In fact, the figures rose to a peak of potential student demand of 176,000 in 1966, but as this was a temporary bulge the working party accepted the long-term figure of 145,000.

the maximum number for a unitary, non-collegiate university compatible with the close social and educational relations traditional in British universities, should be encouraged to rise to that size, but that this would still leave a shortfall of 23,000 places to be provided. It was therefore essential to found, as soon as possible so that they could make a significant contribution to the expansion of 1961 onwards, some new universities (presumably at least five of them) in addition to the university college already mooted at Brighton. These, like the University College of North Staffordshire founded in 1949, should be allowed to award their own degrees, so as to be able to experiment from the beginning with their curricula and examinations. The Report also argued that new buildings elsewhere would have to be started immediately to prepare for the expansion, that more halls of residence would be essential in all universities to maintain the proportion of residential students, and that when the pressure eased in the years after the bulge the lull should be used to extend university courses to four years. Finally, it argued that the limiting factor in the expansion was almost certain to be the availability of staff of the requisite intellectual standard, and suggested various ways of alleviating the shortage, including the expansion of postgraduate studies, the extension of the retiring age from 65 to 67, the raising of university teachers' salaries, and increased prospects of promotion to senior posts and additional chairs.[1]

To some extent the Report was partially overtaken by events. In February 1958 the Chancellor of the Exchequer announced new building grants of £60 million (an increase of £15 million) for the universities in the years 1960–63 (including £1½ million for the new University College of Sussex), based on a new long-term target of 124,000 student places, with a temporary rise during the period of the bulge and after, 1965–70, to 135,000. The gap between this and the A.U.T. estimate was not great, but (taking the two long-term targets) it was critical, since it was exactly the size of the 'surplus' beyond the expansion of existing universities which the A.U.T. Report suggested should be catered for by the foundation of new universities. The Association therefore switched its main attention to the latter, and set up a Committee on New University Institutions, convened by

1 *Report on a Policy for University Expansion* (May, 1958).

A Professional Professional Body, 1954-69

Mr. Henry Maddick of Birmingham University, which began the very practical work of offering advice to and holding discussions with the Academic Advisory Committee for the University College of Sussex, and with the Local Authorities of Coventry, Norwich, York, Canterbury, Colchester and other towns seeking new universities. It soon found, however, that the question could not be divorced from that of expansion in general, and so it was amalgamated with that on University Expansion to form the University Development Committee, which since 1959 has dealt with a vast range of problems connected with every aspect of expansion, from the declining popularity of science and technology to the 'Open University' or 'University of the Air'.[1]

At almost the same time the U.G.C. set up, in April 1959, a Sub-committee 'to examine and report on proposals received by the University Grants Committee for new university institutions.'[2] The story of why and how the New Universities of the 1960's, Sussex, York, East Anglia, Essex, Kent, Warwick, Lancaster, Stirling and Ulster, were founded I have told elsewhere.[3] All of them except Stirling and Ulster were approved by the U.G.C. and the Treasury before the Robbins Committee reported, and owed their foundation to the general pressure for university expansion which developed in the late 1950's in the localities and in the public at large, and to the conviction on the part of Sir Keith Murray and the U.G.C. that, although new institutions might not contribute significantly to student numbers before the 1970's, they were needed immediately not merely to prepare themselves for later growth but to give the rest of the system a 'shake-up' by experimenting with new curricula, teaching methods and organizations. As Lord Murray of Newhaven, as he had become, put it when I asked him why they were created, 'It was one-third numbers and two-thirds new ideas.' The role of the A.U.T. in their foundation, as in university expansion in general, was to seize the opportunity of a favourable climate to press the case, and to support it with precise statistical argument. The University Development Committee under Mr. Maddick revised once again the estimate of the future demand

1 Council Minutes, 22-3 May 1958-31 May-1 June 1968, *passim.*
2 U.G.C., *University Development, 1957-62,* p. 96.
3 *Innovation in the New Universities of the U.K.,* Part I, chapter 3.

213

for student places, and at a meeting with the U.G.C. Sub-committee on the Need for New University Institutions in December 1959 argued the need for at least 170,000 places by the early 1970's, an excess of 35,000 over existing targets which, on the assumption that 4,500 was the accepted maximum size for a non-collegiate university, implied a need for at least six new universities, in addition to Sussex, to be started by 1963, and planned to grow swiftly to between 3,000 and 3,500 students. These arguments were spelled out in a Report, *Some Problems of University Development*, published in May 1960. Whether or not the A.U.T.'s views influenced the decision or merely reinforced its own convictions, the U.G.C. between March and July 1960 advised the Treasury that new institutions should be founded at York, Norwich and three or four other places to be chosen from the long list, 28 in all, of applications from different areas, and by November 1961 approval had been given, in addition to Sussex, York and Norwich, for new universities at Colchester, Canterbury, Coventry and Lancaster.[1]

Meanwhile, new universities of another sort were developing by the time-honoured method by which colleges of non-university status sought recognition as degree-granting institutions. In 1956, as a result of the drive for increasing the output of technologists which we noticed in the last chapter, ten of the larger technical colleges were scheduled for expansion as Colleges of Advanced Technology and encouraged to concentrate on advanced work for full-time students, including ones on 'sandwich courses' between spells of training in industrial firms, all of them working for a new qualification, the Diploma in Technology (Dip.Tech.) of the Hives National Council for Technological Awards, intended to be of degree standard. In retrospect this can now be seen as one more attempt in the long-standing campaign by the Ministry of Education (now the Department of Education and Science) and the Local Education Authorities to raise the status of their colleges and to break the universities' monopoly of granting degrees, which culminated in the present 'binary system' and the degrees of the Council for National Academic Awards. If so, it misfired, since the logic of the situation was that the C.A.T.s should seek to complete their upgrading by seeking recognition as universities, as indeed was

1 U.G.C., *op. cit.*, pp. 96, 100–1.

to be recommended successfully by the Robbins Report. Before that, however, the staffs themselves took the initiative and decided to hold a national referendum on whether to seek membership of the A.U.T. At three of them, Chelsea, Loughborough and Northampton (in the City of London), they did not wait for the referendum but formed Local Associations and approached the A.U.T. Executive for recognition. At the December Council at Keele in 1961 their representatives waited in the lobby while the Executive argued the case for their admission under Rule 4 (a) (ii), which allowed the recognition of institutions engaged substantially in work of university standard. After much discussion and criticism of the Executive's attempt at a *fait accompli*, the C.A.T. representatives were admitted, a development which more effectively raised the practical status of the C.A.T.s in the eyes of the profession than even the recommendation of the Robbins Report.

At the same Council meeting the Executive was criticized for another *fait accompli*, the presentation on 5 July 1961, before it had been discussed by the Local Associations, of the written Submission to the Robbins Committee, appointed in February, which asked for evidence much earlier than had been expected. The Robbins Committee's timetable precluded the delay entailed by local discussion, and the Submission made it clear that it was subject to modification by the Council in oral evidence to be given not earlier than January 1962. The Submission, drawn up by a working party and largely written by Dr. Dennis Chapman, the well-known broadcaster and a social scientist at Liverpool University, was, reflecting the Robbins Committee itself, the first attempt by the A.U.T. to produce a policy for the whole field of higher education. It started from the position that the increasing demand for higher education, due to the rise in the birthrate, the popularity of education for its own sake and for the status it conferred, the needs of industry and the growth of the professions, had faced the universities with a problem to which there were three broad solutions. They could take the élitist course of concentrating on the best and brightest honours students and restrict entry accordingly; but this, however attractive to specialist academics, would be a failure to recognize their responsibilities to society. They could take the egalitarian course and recognize the right of all colleges of higher education to grant degrees in any subject, whether or not it had an intellectual content; but this would merely debase the currency of the degree without making any practical contribution to the demand for genuine higher education. Or they could frankly accept that higher education was a hierarchy, in which the universities had the special role of teaching and studying those disciplines which had a body of knowledge demanding continuous development and reassessment, with an element of abstract thought and intellectual training, and the ultimate objective of comprehending its underlying principles, so that a graduate even when trained for a particular vocation was generally educated, in the sense of possessing a trained mind capable of applying itself to more than one profession. This third solution was the one favoured by the A.U.T., and, in the event, broadly accepted by the Robbins Committee.

Within the university sector the Submission expected the student population, even at present entrance standards (which it hoped would be the subject of research and experiment to admit more candidates of mature or unorthodox education), to rise to 200,000 by 1980. (For once this was a substantial underestimate, even allowing for the addition of the C.A.T.s: the Robbins estimate was 346,000.[1]) These should be catered for in more rather than in larger universities, since this would avoid the loss of quality in academic life in mass institutions and have the additional advantage of allowing for variety and experiment. Oxford and Cambridge, which were already too big and attracted too large a share of the best arts students, should not be allowed to expand further, or to develop into postgraduate universities. The current unbalanced expansion of science and engineering was to be deplored, since only a small proportion of such graduates used their training in industry, where in fact they found that they needed the management skills of accountancy, economics, social psychology and social administration which they did not have. There was a greater need for applied economists, statisticians, accountants, and specialists in the sciences of communication – sociology, social psychology, and languages – and of social control – public, industrial and social administration, criminology and law. Industrial design, structural engineering and architecture were also underdeveloped, as were the

1 *Robbins Report*, p. 152.

biological and especially the 'food producing' sciences, while 'in a prosperous society there is surely a case for a great expansion of general degrees to provide a higher level of literacy, numeracy and humanity, and the possibility of intellectual satisfaction both to the student who will get his vocational training elsewhere and to those with whom he lives.' First-year courses should in any case be more general, so as to give the student a better opportunity of selecting his course and to delay admission to specialized honours courses until more was known of his abilities and inclinations. The restoration of the four-year course which had been normal earlier in this century would provide room both for more general education and for a high level of specialization. Finally, on the side of university organization, there should be more academic representation on Councils and more non-professorial representation on Senates.

In the non-university sector, the Submission considered the then fashionable suggestion of liberal arts colleges of the American type, giving an education wider in scope and lower in standard than the university, but rejected it in favour of liberal arts faculties giving general degrees in existing universities. It welcomed the current trend to liberalize and professionalize the courses in the teacher training colleges since they had become associated with the universities, and suggested a still closer relationship, including the participation of university teachers in their courses and the possible award to selected students of a university degree (an anticipation of the B.Ed.). The Colleges of Advanced Technology should be free to develop individually along their own lines, but with university status, some in association with a nearby university, others as technological universities or as colleges of a federal technological university.

Finally, the Submission addressed itself to the difficult problem of the relation between the universities and the State: how best to reconcile the conflicting claims of the universities' legitimate desire for autonomy with the State's equally legitimate demand for the supervision of the expenditure of public funds. It considered that, in spite of certain difficulties particularly over salary negotiation, the existing machinery of the University Grants Committee was a reasonable compromise, and it was unlikely that any other machinery would achieve a better balance between the interests of the universities and of the community. At the same time, it ought to be strengthened by the addition of other full-time members besides the Chairman, with special responsibilities for such matters as the collection of data, planning and buildings, new universities, and new disciplines, and by expanding its secretariat. In conclusion, 'we fully accept the need for a greater degree of co-ordination of the various forms of higher education. Such co-ordination should, however, stop short of State control and direction.'[1]

There was a good deal of criticism of the Submission at the 1961 December Council meeting, but in the outcome the oral evidence was little modified. The delegates merely demanded a clearer call for the upgrading of the C.A.T.s and any other college of technology likely to be classified as one, by means of the appointment of an Academic Advisory Committee cognate with those for the New Universities; the consideration of arguments for large universities (upwards of 4,500 students) in addition to those for small ones; the replacing of the paragraphs critical of Oxford and Cambridge by a statement drawing attention to the need to examine the relationship between them and the rest of the universities; and the substitution for Dr. Chapman's personal (but later justified) views on the overproduction of scientists and technologists of a more neutral criticism of the lack of supporting evidence for the U.G.C.'s policy of encouraging the expansion by two science and technology students for every additional student in all other faculties.[2]

In the ensuing two years 'waiting for Robbins' became a kind of national game. Apart from the planning and building of the seven New Universities already scheduled, nothing could be done to prepare for the coming expansion crisis until the Committee had reported. At last, in October 1963, the Report was published. Its recommendations included a massive increase in the provision for higher education, from 216,000 student places in 1962–63 to about 392,000 in 1973–74 and about 558,000 in 1980–81 (including a rise from 130,000 university places in 1962–63 to 219,000 in 1973–74 and 346,000 in 1980–81); a reduction in the relative attraction of Oxford and Cambridge by making specially generous capital grants to improve residential and other amenities at other universities; the founding of six

1 *Submission to the Committee on Higher Education* (July 1961).
2 Council Minutes, 20–1 December 1961.

more New Universities, including at least one in Scotland, to provide about 30,000 places by 1980–81; the creation from amongst new and existing universities of five Special Institutions for Scientific and Technological Education and Research (the famous, and abortive, SISTERS); the upgrading of the C.A.T.s as technological universities, and the raising of the most advanced of the similar Scottish Central Institutions to university status; the transfer to the universities of financial and administrative as well as academic responsibility for the teacher training colleges, to be renamed Colleges of Education, and the institution for selected students of the four-year B.Ed. degree (the Scottish Colleges of Education to remain separate, but the universities to be represented on their boards); and all the foregoing, the university sector, to be financed through an enlarged and reorganized University Grants Commission, responsible along with the Research Councils to a Minister of Arts and Science, separate from the Minister of Education and the Secretary of State for Scotland. A recommendation near to the A.U.T.'s heart was that there should be an independent body to advise the Government on academic salaries in the autonomous institutions of higher education.

The rest of the higher education system, the further education sector with a small minority of full-time students (31,000 in 1962–63, rising to 51,000 in 1973–74 and 66,000 in 1980–81), though much larger numbers of part-time students, should remain under the Minister of Education for England and Wales and the Secretary of State for Scotland and the Local Education Authorities. Yet the ladder to university status should be kept open, in two ways: there should be opportunities for some Regional Colleges of Technology to become in due course parts of universities or universities in their own right; and, the most revolutionary proposal of the whole Report, all the further education colleges with a nucleus of full-time work should be eligible to apply for approval in specific subjects to grant the degrees of a new Council for National Academic Awards, to replace the Hives Council for Technological Awards. This would be the first time in Britain that degrees were awarded by a body other than a duly chartered university. Yet the Robbins Committee, it is clear, did not envisage this as in any sense a challenge or a competing alternative to the universities, but merely as a stepping stone or halfway house to university status.

There were many other recommendations in this large and fundamental Report, concerning the transition from school to higher education; the teaching of first degrees, including more general courses and the postponement of specialization, as recommended by the A.U.T.; an increase in the proportion of postgraduate students, and the introduction of taught postgraduate courses; a large increase in technological research; the maintenance or improvement of the staff-student ratio; academic salaries, facilities and conditions of work good enough to attract staff of the necessary calibre; a proper balance between teaching and research; closer staff–student relations both socially and in small-group teaching; consultation about examination methods and the reduction of wastage rates; the use of vacations for academic work, with student grants assessed accordingly; greater participation by non-professorial staff in university government and of academics in the government of other colleges; the reconstitution of the Vice-Chancellors' Committee to include representatives of the academic staff (like the Academic Council long sought by the A.U.T.); and the three Ministers should appoint a small Consultative Council representative of various educational and other interests to co-ordinate the whole field of higher education and consider major questions of policy relating to it (a sort of permanent Robbins Committee). Finally, to meet the immediate short-term emergency there should be a crash programme of capital grants for new buildings and recurrent grants to enable them to be used and to recruit the academic and ancillary staff needed for the expansion.[1]

The A.U.T. naturally acclaimed the Report since it triumphantly vindicated all their past endeavours in favour of university expansion. The Executive had reservations about certain points, notably the SISTERS and the C.N.A.A., and these were put to Messrs. Boyd-Carpenter, Secretary to the Treasury, and Quintin Hogg, Lord President of the Council and responsible for higher education and science, by an A.U.T. deputation on 29 November 1963. Most of the discussion was devoted to supporting the Robbins Committee's recommendations for a separate ministry for the universities and research, for more postgraduate work, and for the crash programme of expansion.

1 *Robbins Report*, esp. pp. 277–91.

The A.U.T.'s opposition to the SISTERS surprised the Ministers, who could not grasp the difference between scheduling 'centres of excellence' for the whole range of science and technology and letting excellence emerge competitively in any institution and any department which had the ability to produce it. In the event, of course, the SISTERS faded from view with the next change of government in 1964. Not so the C.N.A.A.: here the A.U.T.'s concern was not, as some wilfully misleading educational journalists would have it, to preserve the monopoly of degrees by existing universities and to prevent competition from non-university colleges, but to ensure that the currency should not be debased, that students should not be fobbed off with so-called degrees of less than university standard, that the teachers should not be exploited and undermined by being denied sufficient time and facilities for study and research to keep abreast of developments in their subject, and that the policy should not become a device for improving the statistics of so-called graduates by granting degrees 'on the cheap'. The A.U.T. would have preferred, and would still prefer, degrees to be granted only by universities, but that university status should be open to any institution which can prove its right to it by the standard of its work. If the C.N.A.A. had become a means of doing this, well and good, though the A.U.T. considered that an academic degree-awarding body ought to have a majority of academics. The Association does not oppose the C.N.A.A. in principle, and admits that, since the external examiners for the actual courses are all *bona fide* academics, it has done a good and necessary job. But in so far as it has become a means of denying the colleges the right to university status rather than of achieving it, many university teachers believe that it has become the innocent instrument of a bad political policy.

That policy was, of course, that of the 'binary system' as developed by Mr. Anthony Crosland, the Secretary of State for Education and Science, and his Department, which in 1964 became responsible for the whole field of education and research. This was a sort of educational apartheid, by which in the name of a spurious egalitarianism the Government attempted to enforce 'separate but equal development' of what Mr. Crosland, in a famous speech at Woolwich in 1965, misleadingly called the public and private sectors of higher education. Whether the first, which contained many sectarian Colleges of Education, is in fact entirely public, and whether the second, in which the universities are now so closely controlled by the State, is in any meaningful sense private, may well be doubted. But there can be no doubt that the policy was not for the benefit of the staffs of the further education colleges, who did not want their aspirations to academic autonomy and university status denied, but for the sake of the Department of Education and Science and the Local Education Authorities, who were determined to maintain their direct control over them. The latter were in fact successful in defeating the Robbins proposal to transfer financial and administrative responsibility for the Colleges of Education to the universities. As Mr. Crosland cynically remarked to the A.U.T. representatives who asked him why the Government had yielded to the pressure of the L.E.A.s, 'How many votes have the university teachers?'

Separate but equal development has come to mean an unequal policy of on the one hand deliberately raising the starting salaries in the State colleges above those of university teachers – in 1968 teachers of similar age and qualifications started in universities at £1,105 a year and in the Colleges of Education at £1,480 – and on the other of making the college lecturers pay for their initial financial advantage in heavier teaching loads, less time for research, and much less say in the government of their institutions. Some have even had to pay in greater insecurity of tenure, subject to the political prejudices of local politicians, as has been shown by the dismissal in 1968 of staff in certain art colleges who publicly sympathized with demonstrating students. Fortunately for the cause of academic standards and academic freedom, the professional bodies representing the staffs, the Association of Teachers in Technical Institutions and the Association of Teachers in Colleges and Departments of Education, are demanding academic conditions of service, security of tenure, more time for research, a share for their members in the government of the colleges, and emancipation from the direct control of politically biased local Councils. It is to be hoped that, for the sake of learning and the cause of truth and freedom, they achieve their aims. If and when they do so the self-defeating policy of trying to buy degree education on the cheap will have failed, as it was bound to do.

A Professional Professional Body, 1954–69

The Robbins Report, accepted in principle by both the Conservative and Labour Governments before and after the 1964 Election, had a major influence on the expansion of higher education, but it was not carried out to the letter, and its forecast of future demand for student places soon proved to be an underestimate. Quite apart from the retention of the Colleges of Education by the L.E.A.s and the departure from the spirit of the Report represented by the 'binary system' and the scheduling in 1967–68 of thirty 'Polytechnics' to concentrate on advanced work of degree standard but to be rigidly denied the right of aspiring to university status, several of its key recommendations were in practice rejected. All education was brought under one Ministry, the Department of Education and Science, instead of two, including one for the universities and research; the Grants Commission failed to materialize, and the U.G.C., admittedly with two full-time Deputy Chairmen and an enlarged secretariat, became imperceptibly the agent of the D.E.S. rather than the neutral mediator between the universities and the Government; and the independent review body for salaries was, as we have seen, evaded by the standing reference to the Prices and Incomes Board. Only one more New University, instead of six, was founded, at Stirling in Scotland in 1967, though another, recommended by the Lockwood Committee on Higher Education in Northern Ireland, was founded at Coleraine in 1968. The A.U.T. kept a close watch on the implementation of the other recommendations, and became increasingly concerned at the inadequacy of the Robbins projections of student numbers. In April 1967 the Assistant General Secretary drew up a document on the prospects for higher education which suggested that what evidence there was seemed to show that instead of a lull in the demand for places during the quinquennium 1967–72 there would be an increase of 20 per cent over and above the Robbins figures. This was later confirmed by the published statistics of the D.E.S., which showed that already in 1966–67 the total number of full-time students in higher education was 339,000 instead of the estimated 312,000, an increase of 20 per cent.[1] In November the Government recognized the need for a revision of the figures, and announced provision for an additional 20,000–25,000 university places by 1971–72. Meanwhile, the

1 *The Times*, 13 September 1967.

A.U.T. Executive decided, in the now well-established tradition, to have yet another independent look at the long-term need for university expansion, and set up a working party on a Policy for the Universities for the 1970s, under the convenership of Mr. A. M. Prichard of Nottingham. Its findings are likely to revise still further the Robbins estimates and Government targets for the next decade.

The post-Robbins expansion has inevitably increased still more the dependence of the universities on Government finance and with it the demand for Parliamentary supervision of their expenditure. In 1966 the Public Accounts Committee (P.A.C.) of the House of Commons renewed once again its longstanding demand for access to the books of the U.G.C. and the universities, and this time called for evidence from the parties involved, including the A.U.T. The latter called an Emergency Council Meeting on 12 November to discuss the questions put by the P.A.C. to the Officers at a hearing on the 3rd, and to consider what evidence should be given in reply. The Association was not opposed in principle to public accountability, some form of which over a university expenditure of public money totalling over £200 million a year was both reasonable and inevitable, but was naturally concerned to preserve freedom from State control of academic matters and in particular from the interference of the Government itself in the internal affairs of the universities. The danger was not from the P.A.C. and its agent, the Comptroller and Auditor General (C.A.G.) but from the Accounting Officer who would be responsible to him for any discrepancies or misspending, and who would therefore have to have prior access to the universities' accounts and a right to regulate their expenditure. If this were to be an official of the D.E.S. rather than of the U.G.C. or the individual universities, and the rules seemed to say that it must, then direct control of the universities by the D.E.S. would be a long step nearer. Because of this both Council and Executive resisted access to the accounts by the P.A.C. as a threat to academic freedom, while wishing to see the U.G.C. reformed and strengthened in order to satisfy the legitimate requests for improved accountability.[1] The University Development Committee and the Executive subsequently considered various schemes by which the U.G.C. or its Chairman

1 Emergency Council Minutes, 12 November 1966.

might become the Accounting Officer responsible to the C.A.G., by transforming it into a chartered body like the Research Councils or a public corporation like the B.B.C. But it was all in vain. In January 1967 the P.A.C. reported in favour of direct access by the C.A.G. to the books and records of the U.G.C. and the universities from the beginning of the next quinquennium (1 August), and that in the meantime steps should be taken to work out suitable conventions on the conduct of his scrutiny and the handling of his queries and to ensure that the universities were fully informed about the nature and purposes of the scrutiny and what would in practice be involved. In July the Government accepted the report, and Sir Herbert Andrew, the Permanent Under-Secretary of the D.E.S., as the Accounting Officer, and from 1 January 1968 the universities for the first time in their history became directly accountable to Parliament and, more significantly, in the event of complaint or difficulty to the Permanent Secretary of the D.E.S.

This was the end of an epoch in the relations between the universities and the State, so long held up as a unique and very British compromise by which the Government provided the funds but let an independent body, the U.G.C., allocate them without any mandatory control of how they were spent. It was also the beginning of a new epoch in which the difference between the 'private' or 'autonomous' sector of higher education, financed to the extent of over 70 per cent of its recurrent and over 90 per cent of its capital expenditure and subject to the scrutiny of *all* its expenditure by the State, and the 'public' or Local Authority sector, equally subject to the D.E.S. and the same Accounting Officer, is so abstruse as to demand the casuistry of a Jesuit. It is true that the present C.A.G., Sir Bruce Fraser, has been the most discreet and considerate of inquisitors, holding informal discussions with the General Secretary of the A.U.T. and even addressing a special session of the Council at Hull in December 1967 to explain the methods of his scrutiny, and that the first visits of his officials in the spring of 1968 to the universities were exploratory and amicable in the extreme.[1] But there can be no doubt that the State now possesses, whether or not it

1 Council Minutes, 21–2 December 1967; Assistant General Secretary 'Report on a Visit to Sussex University to examine the Impact of the Recent Visit of the C.A.G.'s Team' (Report to Executive, March 1968).

wishes to use it, a degree of control over the universities in Britain comparable with that of most other countries of the Western world.

This is confirmed by the change in the role of the U.G.C. from an independent body advising the Treasury on the allocation of its grants into a specialized agency of the D.E.S., with a large expert secretariat which very properly scrutinizes and costs every new development in each university, and every new building from the architect's first outline sketch to the final tenders and contracts. It is even beginning to question old-established activities, and in 1966 under the name of rationalization recommended the winding-up of undergraduate teaching in one university department, that of Agriculture at Leeds, and is thought to be considering the redundancy of others, much to the alarm of the A.U.T., which has demanded prior consultation and public discussion of the reasons for such closures, together with safeguards for the employment of the staff. Finally, the U.G.C.'s letters of 'guidance' to the universities at the start of the 1967–72 quinquennium suggest a new threat of positive direction which subsequent assurances and discussions with the A.U.T. have done little to allay.[1] The A.U.T. could, with at least as much justification, paraphrase Dunning's famous House of Commons motion of 1772: 'the influence of the State has increased, is increasing, and ought to be diminished.' Whether or not one agrees with the last clause of that forlorn declension, there is no doubt whatever that with the increasing monopoly of higher education by the State there is no effective defence of the individual university teacher or of the academic profession as a whole save in the mutual aid of a well-organized pressure group able to unite the interests of its members and galvanize the support of public opinion. If the A.U.T. did not exist in 1969, and was not the efficient, expert, *professional* professional body which it has become in the last fifteen years, it would have to be invented.

---

1 Council Minutes, 21–2 December 1966, 19–20 May 1667, 31 May–1 June 1968.

Chapter 6

The Academic Profession in Professional Society

During the half-century since the foundation of the A.U.T. the academic profession has changed profoundly in its character and functions, but then so too has the society which it exists to serve. To understand and prepare for the most appropriate and effective role of the Association in the next fifty years it is necessary to analyse the ways in which both the profession and society have changed, are changing and are likely to change, so that the A.U.T. can either swim with the tide or, if it chooses to oppose it, will know the strength of the currents it will have to negotiate. The theme of this history has been that university teaching, once a marginal activity concerned with finishing the education of gentlemen, has become, largely during the present century, the key profession in modern society, in the sense of the profession which educates the other professions and of the principal agent in the process of selection for the key posts in industry, commerce, government and the other power-structures of modern society. It is in fact much more even than this. As we shall see, it is also the key profession in two further senses. First, it is the sole profession in an increasingly specialized world which still embraces the whole gamut of knowledge and professional skills, and the only one which can hope to retain the flexibility to influence the character and purposes of the rest either by providing a general, unifying background of common cultural education or by providing the means and opportunity of changing the scientific and technological bases of old professions and of supplying them for new ones, or both. And, secondly, it is the sole profession which has the time, the means and the skill not merely to make new discoveries, as distinct from applications of old ones, in learning, science and technology, but to do society's fundamental thinking for it, not least about the nature and purposes of society itself.

It can do all this because the academic profession, like the university itself, that brilliant medieval invention whose resurrection during the last century and a half was described in the first chapter, is a microcosm of society in its intellectual and professional aspects, and from its privileged position, at once detached from society and in close contact with it at its most vital points of activity, can objectively yet with inside knowledge advise and criticize society and its aims and values. Like the university, too, it is at once typical of the society to which it belongs and exceptional to it. It is as exceptional and necessary to modern society as the medieval borough was to feudal society, that island of freedom of tenure and contract in a sea of obligatory service, an island which feudalism was forced to create to ensure its supplies of craft-made goods and luxuries and its contacts with the outside world and its revitalizing ideas. Just so, the modern world, deprived by social progress and political reform of the leisured class which once, however inefficiently, supplied or supported its thinkers and discoverers, has been forced to create or adapt islands within itself called universities, to accommodate the professional thinkers and discoverers it must have and who can find no refuge in the sea of obligatory economic service and bondage to income-earning outside. In return for their enormous privilege of leisure for thought and discovery the professional thinkers and discoverers undertake to educate the young, or the ablest and most promising of them, not merely in independent thought and discovery – for the mere self-perpetuation of a privileged caste of intellectual mandarins would be indefensible – but for all those jobs throughout society which require a capacity for independent thought, objective judgement and rational decision-making.

These two functions, the professionalization of thought and discovery and the education of the abler young in independent thought and rational judgement, could in theory be segregated, in research institutes and colleges of higher education. Yet in practice government and industrial research institutes have proved to be fruitful only where the objectives have already been defined, that is, in the application and development of fundamental ideas discovered elsewhere, while their staffs are entirely recruited from the universities. Similarly, colleges of higher education staffed by teachers who are not themselves thinkers and discoverers, in a world which cannot afford to stand still in science and technology, can only be parasitic upon the universities, which alone can train the teachers for them and supply them with their ideas. In practice, of course, such college teachers who are worth their salt and who have gained anything worth having from their university training, are not content to be passive channels for other men's ideas but demand the time and facilities to search out and create their own. Conversely, the research institutes consider it wasteful not to pass on their expertise to postgraduate and post-doctoral students. In short, both research institutes and colleges of higher education, if they do their job properly, are forever transforming themselves into universities. We may, indeed, assert that if universities did not exist they would inevitably be replaced by other institutions performing the same functions.

To many people outside the universities, and above all to busy politicians and overworked civil servants jealous of a profession which is paid out of public funds to do what it likes in its own good time and, worse still, to criticize *them* and the way they run the State and society, this claim to the professionalization of thought and discovery is outrageous and provocative. Hence that perpetual sniping, that wilfully ignorant backlash, at the universities for their supposed idleness and inefficiency, their long 'holidays' and short teaching hours, and their reluctance to accept schemes of so-called productivity such as stretched staff–student ratios or 'Box and Cox' arrangements of the academic year. There are no doubt, as in all professions, academics who are idle, inefficient and only interested in time off and a quiet life in their few hours on the job. But they are likely to be fewer in an occupation in which people only do work which they themselves have chosen and, being self-driven, are highly motivated to perform, and in which self-respect and a desire for the regard of highly critical colleagues are reinforced day in, day out, by the criticism of the harshest of taskmasters, the intelligent and intellectually merciless young. Much play has been made by critics of the self-confessed working hours of academics, 40.5 hours a week during term compared with the 44·2 hours of the average manual worker in manufacturing industry.[1] Yet not

1 *Robbins Report, Appendix Three*, pp. 55–6.

only are these hours longer than the normal hours of other brain workers – now about 37½ hours a week for most office workers – but they are *actual hours worked*, deducting all times for tea breaks, casual conversation, going to the lavatory, etc., and not gross hours of attendance at a place of work.[1] Academics are here the victims of their own honesty: if other occupations returned their actual hours of work, deducting all stoppages for every purpose whatever, the results would be illuminating. As for holidays, I have yet to meet the academic who takes more than a month, and a fortnight is the most usual, during which the university teacher who resists the temptation to pick up a book or an article on his subject must be rare indeed.[2] Finally, productivity is as much a question of quality in the thing produced – research output and educated students – as of quantity, and in this field of production two half-baked ideas or two semi-educated students are *not* equal to one good one. There is undoubtedly room for improvement in the organizational efficiency of British universities, and a great deal more is being done in this direction than is known to the outside world, but in higher education as in any other service industry – who would attempt to measure a surgeon's productivity merely by the number of appendixes he cut out, a dentist's by the number of teeth he pulled, or even a hairdresser's by the number of heads of hair he cut, in an hour? – improvement in quantity may be purchased at a prohibitive cost in declining quality.

If the power of control over his own work, hours and standards makes the academic judge and jury in his own cause, this is no more than is claimed by any profession whose expertise is beyond the immediate judgement of the lay public. The doctor, the lawyer, the clergyman and a host of other protagonists of professional mysteries must insist that they really do know their own jobs better than their clients do and must be trusted to carry them out in the way they think best, subject to the client's right to take his patronage elsewhere if he can find a better practitioner, and to the public's right to question obviously restrictive practices. It is up to the profession in each case to

1 It occurs to me that I am writing these words on a Sunday, and that a large part of my 'own work' of research and writing is done at weekends.
2 Last year (1968) I took a total of ten days' holiday with my family, during which I read five reports in preparation for an international conference. No doubt many academics have similar holiday memories to relate.

The Academic Profession in Professional Society

persuade the client and the public that the service is valuable and worth paying for, and to persuade the State that recognition of the qualified service and exclusion of unqualified practitioners are necessary for the public good. In the case of a public service like university teaching and research the profession has also to persuade the State to provide the financial resources for it, a task which is not made easier by the academic's acute awareness of the enormous privilege which the State is being asked to confer upon him.

And yet both the State and the profession know that at bottom the service is indispensable and must be paid for. The enormous growth of university education in this century is not a fortuitous or arbitrary development, but the inevitable response to national needs and public demand. Student numbers have grown from about 17,000 in 1900 to about 212,000 today in response to the demands of young people and their parents for university education and of industry, commerce, government and the professions for trained men and women.[1] These figures represent a change in the order of magnitude and thus in the role of university graduates in society. In 1900 university students represented only one in 150 of the relevant age group (0·66 per cent). Today they represent about ten times that proportion, one in fifteen (about 6·5 per cent).[2] By 1980 they will be more than one in ten of the age group (the Robbins figure is 10 per cent, and the Robbins rate of expansion is already being exceeded). In 1900 only about a hundred thousand people in an occupied population of 16½ million could have been university graduates,[3] and with the exception of the administrative civil service, secondary school teaching, medicine and the Anglican clergy – the last three scarcely at the centre of power in late Victorian society – none of the leading occupations or professions, least of all politics and industrial management, was recruited necessarily or normally from amongst university graduates. Today there are nearly a

1 A. N. Little, in *Sociological Studies in British University Education: Sociological Review, Supplement No. 7* (Keele, 1963), pp. 186, 196; and information kindly supplied by the U.G.C. (211,750 full-time students, 1968–69).
2 *Robbins Report, Appendix One*, p. 151, gives 6·5 per cent for 1970 (all higher education, 12·8 per cent).
3 Annual output of graduates in last forty years of the 19th century rose from about 1,500 a year to about 5,000 a year in the late 1890's: average, allowing for demographic wastage, say, 2,500 a year; total about 100,000.

million university graduates in an occupied population of 25½ million,[1] and with the exception of the trade unions and popular entertainment (and only there on the performance not the production side) there is scarcely a profession or leading occupation offering incomes over, say, £3,000 a year which is not normally recruited from amongst university graduates. By 1980 there will be about 1½ million in an occupied population little larger than today's,[2] and it will be almost impossible to get a job with prospects of promotion to the top of any professional, managerial or administrative ladder without a degree of some kind, either from a university or a polytechnic. Whether society will be better run or happier because of that, or whether the new helots will already be rising against the tyranny of the meritocracy,[3] must remain an open question. This is not the place to argue that professional society can be what we make of it, and can be used to create a world in which, with the aid of automation, all the routine manual and non-manual work is professionalized and the working class itself becomes a professional, salaried class of controllers and supervisors of complex systems of machine production, transport, distribution, banking, insurance and similar services. Meanwhile, the fact of recruitment to most of the positions of power, influence and high income in society from amongst the highly educated is not in dispute. Whether we like it or not, modern society in all advanced countries and not only in Britain is dominated by trained experts and specialists, because only such trained experts and specialists can run the excessively complex organizations and services of which it is composed and on which it depends not merely for its high productivity and standard of living but for its very existence and survival.

It is because of this dependence on and domination by the professional expert that modern society deserves to be called professional society. This is not necessarily to say that a new class

1 In round terms there were about 150,000 graduates 1929–39, about 150,000 1946–50, about 250,000 1951–60, and about 350,000 1961–8; total, deducting for demographic wastage and adding for external and other part-time degrees, about 900,000.

2 As above, deducting 150,000 for 1929–39 (now mostly retired), and adding about 750,000 for 1969–80 (including C.N.A.A. graduates).

3 Cf. Michael Young, *The Rise of the Meritocracy, 1870–2033* (1958), in which the Populist rising takes place in 2034.

or professional élite has already – in the West, as distinct from the Eastern bloc, where the destruction of the old ruling and economically dominant classes has left the meritocracy a clear field[1] – replaced the capitalist class in the control of the private economic sector. The professional managers of industry, commerce and finance are not all new men, born in a vacuum and raised in an incubator. Like the rest of the professions they are recruited largely – though not exclusively – from existing middle and upper-middle-class families, who can buy professional education or the formal and informal preparation and prerequisites for it as readily as they can buy any other advantage. Upper middle-class boys, besides monopolizing the private, fee-charging sector of education, have a 60 per cent better chance of reaching the grammar school, and amongst those of high ability a 50 per cent better chance of staying at school after 15 to qualify for a university place, than the sons of the manual working class. At the university middle-class students, from about one-fifth of the nation's households, represent over three-fifths of the student population, while working-class students, from two-thirds of the nation's homes, represent only a quarter of the total. In 1960 16·8 per cent of boys from non-manual families went to university compared with 2·6 per cent from manual working-class homes; that is, the middle-class boy had 6½ times the chance of a working-class boy of getting to university.[2] Nevertheless, even in private enterprise the stage has been reached where, at least in the science and technology-based industries, hereditary succession to controlling positions can no longer be allowed to operate without some assistance from professional training and ability, except with diastrous consequences for the company. The fool of the family may still occasionally be allowed to sit on the board, but the real decisions will be taken by the experts. If the latter cannot be recruited from within the major shareholders' families, they have to be recruited elsewhere, and such is the shortage of managerial talent that where all else fails the take-over bid brusquely redresses the balance. Managerialism, in the narrower sense of the control of industry (as distinct from society as a whole) by

1 Cf. Milovan Djilas, *The New Class: An Analysis of the Communist System* (1957).
2 Derived from *Robbins Report, Appendix One*, pp. 49, 51, 54.

professional managers, does not necessarily mean the end of capitalism and the replacement of the capitalist by meritocrats who all start equal in the struggle for wealth and power. It merely means the adaptation of capitalism to the facts of modern technology and the need for the capitalist either to become a professional expert or to leave the actual management, with the risk but not the certainty which that entails of losing control, to other professional experts.

Outside the private sector the professional expert, albeit still recruited from a narrow social range, reigns supreme. In the public sector which now accounts for about a quarter of industrial production the non-capitalist manager has come into his own. In the civil service the university graduate has monopolized the administrative grade since 1870, the scientific civil service since its formation, and increasingly since the last War has infiltrated the executive grade. In the major professions the professional expert rules by definition, but whereas at the beginning of the century lack of a degree, outside medicine and university teaching, was no bar to advancement, now a university education is increasingly a prerequisite of ambition. There are still professions – accountancy, the 'junior' branch of the law, estate management, and several types of engineering, for example – in which graduates are still in a minority, and training is a mixture of apprenticeship and part-time preparation for the examinations of a professional body, but in all of these the unmistakable trend is towards full-time academic training in a university or a polytechnic. Indeed, much of the expansion of higher education is due less to the general demand for university places than to the particular demands of individual professions for the universities to take over the training of their recruits. The Vice-Chancellor of the University of London told the Home Universities Conference in 1946:

The truth is that all the professions are pressing us, as universities, to take on a greater part, if not the whole, of the requisite professional or technical training for their own professional subjects. I think I could mention at least five professions which have recently been in contact with the University of London with a view to our undertaking, or, at least, extending our present facilities for what is really technical or professional training. I refer to the accountancy profession, veterinary medicine, estate management, youth leadership, and journalism.[1]

1 *Home Universities Conference, 1946: Report of Proceedings.*

Since then accountancy and veterinary surgery have been expanded in several universities, youth leadership has acquired a postgraduate course at Manchester, the College of Estate Management has been incorporated with Reading University, and only journalism, except in so far as it is catered for in English and other arts and social studies departments, remains outside the university fold. Meanwhile, other specialized professional institutions such as the Royal Veterinary College have been absorbed into the university system, Wye College has become the Department of Agriculture and Horticulture of London University, and amongst the most rapidly growing subject areas elsewhere are the 'business technologies', in the new schools and departments of management, business studies, operational research, systems engineering, marketing, financial control, and the like, at London, Manchester, Lancaster, Warwick, Sussex and other universities. Some idea of the expanding provision for specialized training can be gained from the proliferation of subjects on which advanced students were engaged, which rose from 123 in 1928–29 to 448 in 1964–65, including an increase from seven to 26 kinds of engineering and from one to five branches of economics.[1] Even the trade unions and the police, the professions with the smallest proportions of graduates, are offered courses in industrial relations and criminology, which some of them take advantage of: George Woodcock, General Secretary of the T.U.C., took a mature student's degree at Oxford University, and the Lancashire Constabulary send officers on criminology courses at Manchester University and pay for three policemen a year to take full undergraduate courses at Lancaster University. Thus there is no major profession for which the universities do not provide specialized training, and none which does not seek to recruit from amongst university graduates. In part this is the natural consequence of the expansion of educational opportunity in this century, which increasingly, if still inefficiently, creams off the intelligent and ambitious children from every social class into higher education, so that business firms and other employers are forced to recruit potential managers and leaders from the products of that system. But still more is it the need of industry, government and every other increasingly complex and specialized occupation for highly trained professional recruits. For reasons

[1] U.G.C., *Report . . . 1928–29*, p. 6; *Returns . . . 1964–65*, pp. 29–32.

partly economic – the enormous and increasing cost of professional education and the inordinate fees which private institutions have to charge by comparison with State-supported universities and colleges – and partly educational – the narrowness of most private professional and managerial training in comparison with the broad intellectual foundations provided by the universities which are found to be more relevant to the complex problem-solving and decision-making of modern management and administration – professional bodies, public corporations and private companies increasingly prefer to hand over their educational functions to the universities and colleges. Training on the job still continues, necessarily, but it is both very specific to the immediate purpose and based on the assumption that the trainee's mind has already been educated to think and handle the requisite ideas and principles. And even here the universities are taking over part of the task in the comparatively recent development of post-experience courses in subjects ranging from operational research for managers to educational psychology for remedial school teachers. When to this increasing responsibility for professional education are added the growing demands of industry and government for research into any and every problem of science, technology, political administration and social pathology, it is clear that the universities have become the power-houses of modern society, to which the rest of society looks for most if not all of its sources of intellectual and economic regeneration.

Whether the academic profession is capable of meeting these vast and growing responsibilities may at this point very properly be questioned. Since the days when universities were mainly finishing schools for young gentlemen the profession has not only expanded *pari passu* with the increase in student numbers, from about 1,700 in 1900 to over 25,000 today; it has also changed considerably in its nature and composition. Some changes are very obvious: the old domination of the profession by the arts faculty, which still in the 1920's accounted for more than half the members and now accounts for no more than a quarter, and by Oxbridge dons, who still in the 1920's accounted for about a third and now for little more than a tenth, has gone. The typical university teacher, if that concept means anything, is a scientist in a large civic university: pure and applied scientists account for over 40 per cent and the larger civic universities for about a third of the profession.[1] Other changes are more esoteric, since very little research has been done on the social origins or even the qualifications of university teachers, and none of it until very recently. In an effort to plug this gap in our knowledge, however inadequately, a questionnaire was sent in April 1968 to 1,000 university teachers in 29 institutions selected so as to cover in the correct proportions every faculty except the medical sciences, each major category of university (Oxbridge, large and small civic, ex-C.A.T.s, Scottish, Welsh and New), each grade and both sexes. The institutions are listed and the questionnaire printed, together with the resultant statistical tables, in Appendix 3. 681 (68·1 per cent) were returned in time to be analysed by my research assistant, Mr. D. A. Chivers. The results of so small a sample must be treated with caution, and the historical comparisons between the cohorts who entered before 1945, between 1946 and 1959, and since 1960, with special care, since the earlier ones necessarily excluded considerable numbers who for age and other reasons have left the profession. For example, the much lower average age of recruitment of those who entered before 1945 is partially accounted for by the exclusion by retirement of those recruited at the higher ages.

The results, nevertheless, are convincing and illuminating. Academic qualifications, as measured by the attainment of a first-class honours degree, appear to have declined with expansion: three-quarters of those recruited before 1945 and two-thirds of those between 1946 and 1959 have firsts (perhaps slightly inflated by the possibly greater wastage of those without), compared with less than half of those recruited since 1960. On the other hand, the decline in quality has not been great, since there has been a compensating rise in the percentage with good second-class degrees, the proportion with firsts or II.1's declining from 83·1 and 83·4 per cent to 80·8 per cent; and we must also make allowance for the undoubted though inadequately documented rise in academic standards, both of university entrance and of the quality of first-class honours, especially in the arts, where the percentage of firsts awarded has been declining for several decades. In spite of the latter, the

---

1 U.G.C., *Report . . . 1928–29*; *Returns . . . 1964–65*, p. 36; and information kindly supplied by the U.G.C. (25,353 full-time staff, 1967–68).

percentage of firsts is still higher amongst teachers in the arts faculty (72 per cent) than in pure science (64·7 per cent), applied science (57·6 per cent) and social studies (39·7 per cent), mainly because university teaching is still the height of ambition for many graduates in arts whereas graduates in science, technology and social studies find more attractive openings in industry, commerce, government and the professions. Higher degrees also appear to be declining in number, from 82·3 per cent amongst those recruited before 1945 and 73·8 per cent amongst those in 1946–59 to 68·5 per cent amongst those since 1960; but this may be more apparent than real, since the immediate post-war cohort contains many who were recruited after war or peace-time national service with less time and incentive to begin higher degrees before being plunged into teaching duties, while the 1960's cohort contains many who are still in process of obtaining higher degrees. Certainly, as Table 9 in Appendix 3 indicates, it is now rare for scientists to be appointed without a higher degree, while anyone responsible for appointments in arts or social studies knows that a higher degree in possession or in prospect is now expected, whereas a generation ago it was not. One other change in academic qualifications is the sharp decline in the proportion of graduates of Oxford and Cambridge, especially since 1960, from 43·4 and 40·7 per cent in the first and second cohorts to 29·5 per cent in the third. This is partly due to the statistical decline in the proportion of Oxbridge graduates, and to the increased proportion of scientists and technologists, long recruited in large numbers from elsewhere, but it is also due to a much greater readiness in recent years even in arts and social studies to recruit from other universities, a much healthier sign for the future of the profession.

The social origins of the profession are also changing somewhat, whether measured by father's occupation or by type of school last attended. There has been a sharp decline in the proportion of ex-public and other boarding school pupils, from 22·3 per cent in the pre-1945 cohort to 15·5 per cent in the 1946–59 and to 9·2 per cent in that of the 1960's. At the same time there has been only a slight increase in the proportion educated at State secondary schools, from 54·5 per cent and 53·4 per cent to 56·9 per cent. Apart from an increase in those educated abroad, most of the compensating increase has come from the direct-grant schools, which supplied 17·8 per cent of those recruited before 1945 and 23·5 and 23·6 per cent since then. Since the direct-grant schools are increasingly selective and tend to cream off talented children from a wide area, this is consonant with a tendency towards meritocratic recruitment to the profession which one would expect. At the same time the advantage which we have already noticed the middle and upper-middle classes to possess in access even to the direct-grant and State grammar schools suggests that meritocratic selection would still favour their recruitment to the academic as to other major professions, and this is borne out by the returns of father's occupation. There has, it is true, been a sharp decline in the proportion coming from the higher professional and managerial class, from 40·7 per cent in the pre-1945 cohort to 25·9 per cent in the post-1945 and 21·5 per cent in that of the 1960's; but this has been partly offset by a rise in the proportion coming from the lesser managerial and other professional class, from 42·5 per cent in the first cohort and 36·7 per cent in the second to 44·2 per cent in the third, which again suggests that meritocratic selection is tending to favour that level of the middle class which generally cannot afford to send its children to fee-paying schools. On the other hand, the post-war cohorts show a considerable increase over that recruited before 1945 in the proportion of academics of lower middle-class (routine non-manual) and working-class origin, from 7·1 and 5·3 per cent in the earliest to 12·9 and 19·8 per cent in the immediate post-war and to 10·8 and 20·3 per cent in that of the 1960's. The higher proportion attained in all but the skilled manual class in 1946–59 than in the 1960's may have been due to the special atmosphere of the immediate post-war period and to the Further Education and Training Grants which enabled many ex-servicemen to take a degree who had never previously considered it; but the symptoms of an inegalitarian trend in the recruitment of the 1960's are nevertheless disturbing, and suggest that we may already be reaching the limits of the capacity of our present educational system to select by merit.

The influence of class and home background shows up in the choice of academic subject. Arts university teachers are still drawn from the upper-middle and middle class to a larger extent (70·2 per cent) than those in pure science (68·3 per cent), applied science (65·4 per cent) and social studies (61·7 per cent), and, if the differences are not perhaps large enough in so small a sample to be very significant, they confirm the accepted belief that working-class children take more readily to the newer and more socially 'neutral' subjects in which lack of a cultivated home background is no handicap. What is perhaps a still greater influence both in choice of subject and in ambition for higher education generally is the educational background of the parents, which may communicate itself to the child in the form of the availability and a love of books and of encouragement to academic effort. In the generation of motivation to school work the mother's attitude may be more important than the father's, but until very recent years this may not be closely correlated with the mother's schooling. Mainly to save the patience of the respondents and to ensure a large return the questionnaire asked for details only of the father's education, and the answers are analysed in Tables 13–18 of Appendix 3. These show, surprisingly, a declining trend in the age at which the fathers of the different cohorts terminated their formal education, which runs against the general trend in this century towards longer periods of schooling. A similar trend is visible in the type of school the fathers attended, fewer at public and other boarding schools, only slightly more at grammar schools, and twice as many fathers of the recruits of the 1960's as of the pre-war cohort at non-grammar State schools. Again, there is a sizeable increase after 1945 in the proportion of fathers who enjoyed no form of university or other higher education. Such fathers had, however, on average attained higher social status than their education suggested, and were therefore upwardly mobile.

All this suggests a rather surprising but nevertheless understandable conclusion, that university teaching is especially attractive to first-generation grammar and other secondary school pupils and to first-generation university students, the children of less educated but socially ambitious fathers, probably because it is, by the time they graduate, a familiar, secure profession which satisfies ambitions which have until then taken a mainly academic shape, and which requires no capital, family connections or parental income to bridge several years of lowly-paid pupillage. If this is so it is an even more meritocratic profession than it appears from the educational background of the recruits themselves, and may be fulfilling a social function as a stepping stone in the rise of families over three or more generations from lower social and educational status to the higher and more lucrative positions in society. For such a role it is ideally placed, at the gateway for the intelligent and ambitious young to most of the prestigious and profitable careers in society, and able to advise its own sons and daughters on where to aim next. It would be surprising if the first-generation academics did not take advantage of their opportunity and become the fathers of first-generation leaders in many of the 'interest pyramids' – public and private industry, public administration, banking, insurance and the major professions – which make up the power-structures of professional society. In yet one more way university teaching may be the key profession to social mobility and recruitment to positions of power and influence in society.

But this is mere speculation, and still does not answer the question whether the profession is capable of meeting its vast and growing responsibilities. Academics, as their roles as sons, fathers and social climbers remind us, are merely human beings, with individually as well as corporately selfish interests. If they are chosen for being cleverer than others in their own narrowly specialized subjects, this is no guarantee that they will be wiser or less selfish than others in dealing with the larger affairs of the world or even with the affairs of their own small university world. Their handling of the recent wave of student unrest has shown them to be as perplexed, divided and inept as the rest of the middle-aged and elderly in dealing with the younger generation. It is not the argument of this book that men and women who have great influence and responsibility thrust upon them are thereby endowed with the wisdom to deserve that influence or the willpower to carry that responsibility. It is a fact that university teachers have acquired a key role in the education and selection for most of the controlling and directing positions in our society. It is merely wishful thinking to suppose that a profession which has expanded more than tenfold in this century and absorbed practitioners from a wide range of professions either new in themselves or new to the universities should automatically perform that role with superior wisdom and good-will. That is a question which only time can answer. Meanwhile, we may gain some slight insight into the task and their hope of fulfilling it by looking briefly at what should be their attitude to the four major responsibilities which are always with them but which are certain to test them severely over the next few decades: their responsibility to higher education and its expansion; their responsibility to their students; their responsibility to their subjects, to learning and science generally, and to truth; and their responsibility to society at large.

Academics are inevitably divided and ambivalent about the expansion of higher education. On the one hand they stand to gain, like all professions, from an expanding demand for their services and from the prestige and self-respect which accompany the material assurance that society needs and values them. On the other, they are bound to be apprehensive about the possible deterioration of standards, of the students, of the conditions of work and facilities for research, and even of the profession itself, which may accompany massive expansion. The only objective survey of British university teachers' attitudes to expansion, that of A. H. Halsey and Martin Trow, concluded that they were 'a deeply conservative society' exhibiting an 'extraordinary wariness and resistance to large-scale expansion of the system of higher education'. Yet the same survey found that 27 per cent of the respondents favoured a doubling of the university system in the next decade, 40 per cent of them an increase of 50 per cent in student numbers, 28 per cent an increase of 25 per cent, and only 4 per cent no increase at all, and this in spite of the fact that a majority of every group except the first (and nearly half of those) feared some deterioration in standards as a result of expansion.[1] To fear the worst (from an academic's point of view) and yet to welcome expansion and face the risk of change is not perhaps the clearest proof of conservatism.

The most important question for the next few decades, however, is not whether or not to have a percentage increase in student numbers which will not materially affect the nature and purpose of universities as we know them, but whether to continue with our present, albeit expanding, system of higher education for a comparatively small and highly selective élite or to replace it by a system of mass higher education for all who can benefit by it. Existing academics are élitist by origin and conditioning and might be expected to oppose mass higher education with its

1 A. H. Halsey and M. Trow, *A Study of the British University Teachers* (Report for U.S. Office of Education, 1967), chap. iii, pp. 5, 15–16, 42.

threat not only to academic standards but also to the quality of life and work in the mass institutions it would require. If by mass education it meant something on American lines, catering for upwards of a third of the age group and providing degree courses in subjects with little or no intellectual content such as hairdressing or morticianry, then most British academics would oppose it. Halsey and Trow found that only 13 per cent of their respondants favoured the provision of higher education for more than 30 per cent of the age group. Yet a majority (52 per cent) favoured provision for more than 20 per cent, and all but one per cent for 10 per cent or more.[1] Moreover, this was in the context of higher education as they know it: there would probably be few academics who opposed a full-time provision for, say, the large numbers of students who now take part-time advanced courses, or indeed for the still larger numbers taking non-advanced courses, providing that they were catered for in non-advancced institutions. It is perfectly consistent for an élitist profession, which exists to provide a service of very high standard, to favour expansion of their own type of institution only so far as is compatible with the maintenance of the standard, and to favour the expansion of other kinds of higher education in institutions of another type. Whether or not those other institutions should offer degrees in any and every subject which they teach is another question to which, no doubt, most academics would give a prejudiced answer, but the cause of truth is not served by those educational journalists and spokesmen of the D.E.S. and N.U.T. who accuse university teachers of snobbery, jealousy and exclusiveness in wishing to preserve some academic meaning for the word degree. As has been made clear in Chapter V, the A.U.T. has never opposed the granting of degrees by new colleges as long as their staffs were qualified and had the time and facilities to teach them, but only the debasement of the currency and the fobbing off of students with something which has the name but not the quality of a degree. It may still be argued that higher education should be open-ended in the sense of admitting all who can profit by it and letting them proceed as far as they can go, without taking the further step of saying that all higher education should take place in institutions of equal status and standards and should everywhere lead to something

1 *Ibid.*, chap. iii, p. 7.

called a degree. The A.U.T., as the representative of the academic profession, need not feel ashamed to demand at one and the same time the expansion of higher education to the furthest limit which the country needs and can afford and the maintenance of the universities as centres of excellence within that system.

One of the severest tests of the academic profession in the next few years will be its attitude to and relations with its most immediate clients, the students. The causes of student unrest are more profound than most of the superficial debate and emotional discussion about the war between the generations and the question of student power. The malaise is due to the nature of professional society itself, and to the students' sense of being manipulated by it, of being selected, trained and shaped to fit its purposes, as square pegs for square holes. In this process of manipulation and moulding the university is the key institution, and it is by an unerring instinct that the activists, at the exact moment when they are still free from the commitments and pressures of a slot in the constraining power-structures of 'the system', select the university rather than the government or the other professional and managerial hierarchies as their main target. If they can capture or influence its administrative organs and procedures they can perhaps control the instrument which manipulates and moulds them, or at least mitigate the uncertainty and suspected arbitrariness of its processes of selection and classification of human beings into less or more saleable commodities on the professional labour market. No doubt the great majority of students are still content to be manipulated and to await the all-important stamp of graded professional quality with patience or at least resignation. But the activist few are speaking for the fears and apprehensions of them all in concentrating their attention on the disciplinary system (which, by sending a student down, can fine him the equivalent of £30,000, the difference between the career earnings of a graduate and a non-graduate), on examinations, which symbolize the whole process of selection and classification for life, and on representation on Senate, where the decisions which determine the whole process of manipulation and moulding are made.

On student participation in academic decision-making university teachers are again bound to be ambivalent. On the one hand they stand for the power of rationality and argument and for teaching students to think for themselves, and so can hardly deny them access to the rational arguments behind the decisions and the places where they are made. On the other, they have a higher responsibility in academic matters than that to their immediate students of one generation: to the subject they study, to the academic standards they profess, to their colleagues in the profession now and in the future, and to society which pays them to study and to teach the truth as they see it and to guarantee the qualifications of those whom they educate. It would obviously be intolerable in medicine or engineering if the apprentices were to certify themselves and treat patients or build bridges without further guarantee against professional incompetence. In other university-trained professions the results might be less lethal, but if professional competence is to mean anything its certification can hardly be left to the unqualified, least of all to that section of the unqualified which has a vested interest in low standards. The great strength and chief defence of professional society is that it provides for all its members expert services which are guaranteed by competent and qualified judges. No society would pay for incompetent services or for expensive training for self-certified 'experts'.

Thus the dilemma is a real one, and derived from the clash of two opposing rights, the right of society to properly qualified service and the right of the young not to be manipulated by their elders for the benefit of a system over which they have no control. Fortunately, if certain principles are admitted the two rights are not in fact diametrically opposed or mutually exclusive, and need not lead to a head-on collision. The first principle is the distinction between academic decision-making which, on the grounds that professional decisions must remain in qualified hands and that in natural justice persons cannot be judges in their own cause, must be controlled by bodies in which qualified academics are in a clear majority, and consultation which, on the ground that the wearer knows best where the shoe pinches, requires the admission of student representatives to the main decision-making bodies. The second is the acceptance by both sides of the chief academic aim of the university, which is not to manipulate and mould students for specific vocational slots in the power-structures of professional or any other society but to teach them to think for themselves within the context of a certain expertise so that they can question, criticize and help to shape the power-structures which they join instead of being passive victims of them. In this way their experience of sharing in the rational democracy of the university, which is in danger of preparing them merely for the disillusionment and frustrations of the autocratic professional and managerial hierarchies outside, may contribute to that democratization of large-scale organizations of which the modern world stands so much in need. The A.U.T.'s policy on staff-student relations should stand firmly on the principle of a community of scholars, older and younger, graduate and under-graduate, masters and apprentices, in which in social, including disciplinary, matters all are equal but in academic matters some are more equal than others. To welcome student participation is wisdom, but to yield on the question of the certification of academic competence would be to abdicate all professional responsibility, and to give up all claim to society's support.

To most university teachers the highest academic responsibility is neither to the students nor to society, important as they are, but to the subject itself, and in the final analysis to truth, or, if that is too absolute and abstract a concept in a relativistic age, to mankind's total stock of objective knowledge. We have seen that the academic stands above all for the professionalization of independent thought and discovery, and has inherited the independence and some of the time free from the slavery to income-earning of the now defunct gentleman-amateur. But that independence and free time for study are now under great pressure from politicians, civil servants, industrialists and others who want higher education, preferably of an immediately vocational kind, and research, preferably of immediately 'useful' application, on the cheap. This the academic profession and the A.U.T. must resist with all their might. Society has a right to ask university teachers to do its thinking and discovering for it, but it has not the right to fore-ordain what shall be thought or discovered. The academic has had thrust upon him the mantle of the Old Testament prophet: he has a higher duty than blind obedience to secular authority, and must speak the truth as he sees it, whether or not it is comfortable or acceptable to the powers that pay. At bottom, society has no choice: it must either pay for truly independent thought and discovery, and provide adequate time and resources for academics of integrity to do it, or it must do without, or make do with second-rate hacks and yes-men who will ensure the rapid decline of science, culture and higher education, and so the deterioration of society itself. An uncivilized society is a contradiction in terms, a body without a soul, a rotting corpse. It is not merely dying, it is dead already, killed by its own hand.

The academic profession's final responsibility, to society, therefore, is to stand no nonsense from it, but to tell it, firmly and fearlessly, what it costs to do those things which alone justify its existence, the endless improvement of our knowledge of ourselves and our world and the enrichment of the quality of life in it. In return the academic profession must not only do its job, of thinking and discovering and educating the young in independent thought, but must be seen to be doing it with honesty and integrity. It must open its affairs to the fullest public inspection and its accounts to the most searching public audit. Those who live by the search for truth and rational criticism of the obscure and indefensible have no need to fear the light of truth and reason. The universities came into existence as searchlights in a world of intellectual darkness and obscurantism. In a world in which the currently fashionable 'flight from reason' threatens to plunge us all once again into darkness and obscurantism the duty of the academic profession and of the Association of University Teachers is to make sure that the light of truth still burns in the next fifty years at least as fiercely as it has done in the last.

Appendix 1

Officers of the A.U.T., 1919–69

U r w i n

Appendix I

Session		Subject	University
1952–53	Dr. V. E. Cosslett	Physics	Cambridge
1953–54	Dr. G. R. Tudhope	Pharmacology	St. Andrews
1954–55	Prof. R. Niklaus	French	Exeter
1955–56	Prof. J. L. Montrose	Law	Belfast
1956–57	Dr. Constance M. Rigby	Mathematics	London (U.C.L.)
1957–58	Prof. R. G. D. Allen	Economics	London (L.S.E.)
1958–59	Dr. K. Urwin	French	Wales (Cardiff)
1959–60	Prof. T. N. George	Geology	Glasgow
1960–61	Dr. D. Chapman	Social Science	Liverpool
1961–62	Mr. D. W. Reece	Humanity (Classics)	Aberdeen
1962–63	Prof. W. W. Chambers	German	Glasgow
1963–64	Mr. A. L. Binns	English	Hull
1964–65	Dr. F. W. Chattaway	Physiology	Leeds
1965–66	Mr. M. Hookham	Politics	Leicester
1966–67	Prof. V. S. Griffiths	Chemical Physics	Surrey
1967–68	Prof. D. A. Bell	Electronic Engineering	Hull
1968–69	Mr. D. E. Varley	Economics	Nottingham

HONORARY GENERAL SECRETARIES

1919–20	Prof. F. Raleigh Batt (Secretary)	Law	Sheffield and Liverpool
1920–53	Prof. R. Douglas Laurie	Zoology	Wales (Aberystwyth)
1953–65	Lord Chorley	Law	London (L.S.E.)

GENERAL SECRETARY

1965–	Dr. K. Urwin (Executive Secretary, 1959–65)	Formerly French and Philology	Formerly Wales (Cardiff)

ASSISTANT GENERAL SECRETARY

1966–	Mr. Fred Garside	Mathematics	Formerly headmaster of St. Clements Dane's Grammar School

Appendix 1

HONORARY TREASURERS

1919–46	Asst. Prof. R. J. Tabor	Botany	London (Imperial)
1946–61	Prof. H. V. A. Briscoe	Chemistry	London (Imperial)
1961–	Dr. T. G. Halsall	Chemistry	Oxford

HONORARY EDITORS

1922–23	Prof. Frank Smith	Education	Leeds
1923–26	Prof. John Strong	Education	Leeds
1926–61	Mr. (Prof.) C. M. McInnes	History	Bristol
1962–66	Mr. A. L. Binns	English	Hull
1966–	Dr. P. H. Mann	Sociology	Sheffield

Appendix 2

1919–20	1,163	(1,319*)	1936–37	1,787	1952–53	4,523
1920–21	n.a.	(1,324*)	1937–38	1,850	1953–54	4,949
1921–22	n.a.	(1,286*)	1938–39	1,899	1954–55	5,415
1922–24	n.a.		1939–40	1,739	1955–56	5,468
1924–25	1,101		1940–41	1,598	1956–57	5,837
1925–26	1,035		1941–42	1,480	1957–58	6,157
1926–27	1,154		1942–43	1,514	1958–59	6,862
1927–28	1,272		1943–44	1,579	1959–60	7,368
1928–29	1,360		1944–45	1,677	1960–61	8,231
1929–30	1,430		1945–46	2,167	1961–62	9,942
1930–31	1,461		1946–47	2,470	1962–63	10,492
1931–32	1,426		1947–48	2,942	1963–64	11,409
1932–33	1,528		1948–49	3,293	1964–65	13,015
1933–34	1,626		1949–50	4,041	1965–66	14,222
1934–35	1,671		1950–51	4,087	1966–67	15,508
1935–36	1,738		1951–52	4,421	1967–68	16,550

Figures subject since the Second World War to the addition of a small and varying number of Life Members (mostly retired).

* Figures of 'Branch Membership' from *University Bulletin*, April 1923; all rest from Council Minutes, except 1967–8 supplied by Assistant General Secretary.

Appendix 3

Copies of the following Questionnaire were sent in April 1968 to a thousand university teachers, selected from University Prospectuses, etc., so as to provide a representative cross-section of the profession by faculty group (except the medical sciences, which have a long and changing history of part-time appointments), grade or status, sex, and type of institution. The Universities and Colleges sampled were: Aberdeen, Bath, Birmingham, Bradford, Bristol, Cambridge, (Downing, Emmanuel, St. John's and Trinity Colleges), Edinburgh, Exeter, Glasgow, Hull, London (King's, Queen Mary, University and Westfield Colleges), Manchester, Newcastle, Oxford (New, Queen's, St. Catherine's and Somerville Colleges), St. Andrews, Sheffield, Wales (Aberystwyth and Cardiff), and Warwick.

Appendix 3

SURVEY OF UNIVERSITY TEACHERS FOR THE
HISTORY OF THE A.U.T.

This questionnaire is STRICTLY CONFIDENTIAL, and no information capable of identifying individuals will be disclosed.

1 (a) Date of birth: .... (c) Sex (please tick)

   (b) Place of birth: .... M .... F ....

2 Present status (please tick): Professor............... Reader...............
Senior Lecturer............... Lecturer............... Assistant Lecturer...............
Other (please specify)...............

3 (a) Subject (please specify):...

   (b) U.G.C. Subject Group (please tick):
      Arts............... Medicine............... Social Studies............... Dentistry...............
      Pure Science............... Agriculture............... Applied Science...............
      Veterinary Science...............

4 (a) Secondary school last attended (please name): ....
....

   (b) Type of secondary school (please tick):
      Public boarding (Headmasters' Conference or Governing Bodies Association)............ Other boarding............ Day public or Direct Grant............

Maintained (by L.E.A.)	Grammar or High ....
	Technical or Art ....
	Comprehensive ....
	Secondary modern
	or senior elementary ....

      Educated abroad .... Otherwise educated (please specify):...............
....

5 (a) University of first degree (please name):...............
   (b) Class of first degree (please tick):
      Honours: I .... II.1 .... II.2 .... III .... IV ....
      Pass (or 'Ordinary') ....
      Other (please specify) ....
      No degree ....
   (c) If other equivalent qualification, please specify:...............
....

6 (a) Higher degrees, with dates attained (please specify):

Degree	*University*	*Year*
....	....	....
....	....	....
....	....	....

   (b) Other higher qualifications (e.g. fellowships of professional bodies) (please specify): ....

Appendix 3

7 (a) Dates and places of appointments and promotions:

	University	Year
Assistant Lecturer	....	....
Lecturer		
Senior Lecturer	....	....
Reader	....	
Professor	....	....

   (b) If substantial service in another occupation before or between university appointments, please specify, with approximate dates: ....

   ....

8 (a) Father's occupation at date of your admission as a university student (or at the age of 18). Please specify as fully as possible (if father was then dead, please tick here .... and give last occupation before his death):

   ....

   (b) Would you describe your father's occupation as belonging to one of the following categories? (please tick):
   Higher professional and managerial (e.g. doctor, lawyer, clergyman, university teacher, administrative civil servant, accountant, engineer, surveyor, company director, owner-manager of large firm, large employer, etc.) ....
   Lesser managerial or other professional (e.g. small employer, shop-keeper, owner-manager of small business, executive civil servant, bank manager, army or navy officer, school-teacher, etc.) ....
   Routine non-manual (e.g. clerk, clerical civil servant, shop assistant, policeman, N.C.O., etc.) ....
   Skilled manual, including foremen and supervisors (e.g. carpenter, bricklayer, mechanic, driver, printer, pattern-maker, etc.) ....
   Semi-skilled manual (e.g. process worker, machine operator, store-keeper, bus conductor, farm worker, etc.) ....
   Unskilled manual worker or labourer ....

9 (a) At what age did your father finish his formal education? .... years.

   (b) What type of secondary school did your father attend? (please tick):
   Public boarding (Headmasters' Conference) ....
   Other boarding .... Day public or Direct Grant ....

   Maintained (by L.E.A. or School Board) ⎰ Grammar or High................
   Technical or Art ....
   Senior elementary ....
   or Secondary modern ......

   Educated abroad .... Otherwise educated (please specify):................

   ....

   (c) If your father attended a University, please name it:................

   (d) If your father received any other higher education, please specify:................

   ....

THANK YOU VERY MUCH INDEED FOR YOUR KIND ASSISTANCE

H. J. Perkin
Professor of Social History,
University of Lancaster

April, 1968

681 completed Questionnaires were returned in time to be analysed by my research assistant, Mr. D. A. Chivers, now Research Officer to the Department of Educational Research, University of Lancaster, a rate of return of 68·1 per cent. A number continued to trickle in throughout the Summer vacation, but it was not considered worth while to process the sample again. Those analysed were divided by date of entry to the profession, subject group, grade or status, and sex, as follows:

Date of entry (age cohorts)	*No.*	*Percentage*
1. Up to 1945	113	16·6
2. 1946–59	317	46·5
3. Since 1960	251	36·9
Subject groups		
Arts	229	33·6
Social Studies	141	20·7
Pure Science	198	29·1
Applied Science	113	16·6
Status		
Professor	210	30·8
Reader	63	9·3
Senior Lecturer	145	21·3
Lecturer	215	31·6
Asst. Lecturer	48	7·0
Sex		
Male	613	90·0
Female	68	10·0

The processed results are given in Tables 1–18, and discussed in Chapter 6, pp. 237–41, above.

TABLE I

Average age of recruitment (by date of entry)

	years
1. Up to 1945	26·2
2. 1946–59	29·0
3. Since 1960	28·4
Total Average	28·3

Notes :
(a) Years of service in overseas universities not included.
(b) In (3) these holding positions in C.A.T.s when they became university institutions not included.

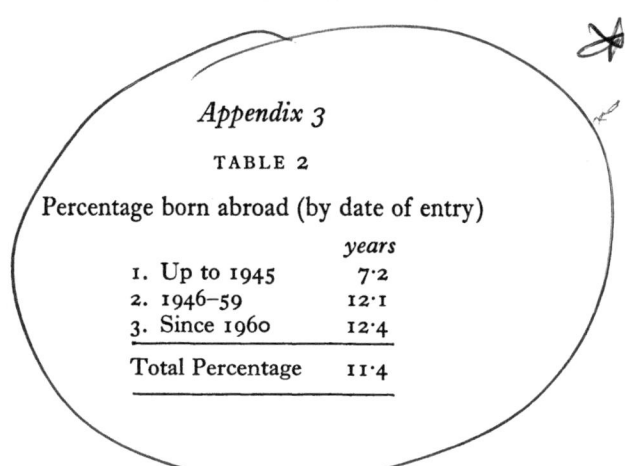

Appendix 3

TABLE 2

Percentage born abroad (by date of entry)

	years
1. Up to 1945	7·2
2. 1946–59	12·1
3. Since 1960	12·4
Total Percentage	11·4

TABLE 3

Type of school last attended (by date of entry): percentage

	up to 1945	1946–59	since 1960	Total
Public boarding	17·8	13·3	8·4	12·2
Other boarding	4·5	2·2	0·8	2·1
Day public or direct grant	17·8	23·5	23·6	22·5
Grammar or high	54·5	51·6	53·9	53·2
Technical or art	–	0·6	1·2	0·7
Comprehensive	–	0·6	1·2	0·7
Sec. modern or sen. elem.	–	0·6	1·6	0·9
Educated abroad	5·4	6·7	9·3	7·3
Otherwise educated	–	0·9	–	0·4

TABLE 4

Type of school last attended (by U.G.C. subject groups): percentage

	Arts	Social studies	Pure science	Applied science	Total
Public boarding	17·9	9·9	8·6	9·7	12·2
Other boarding	1·3	2·1	2·5	2·7	2·1
Day public or direct grant	24·9	17·7	24·7	19·5	22·5
Grammar or high	47·2	58·3	53·6	58·3	53·2
Technical or art	0·4	0·7	0·5	1·8	0·7
Comprehensive	–	1·4	0·5	1·8	0·7
Sec. modern or sen. elem.	1·3	0·7	–	1·8	0·9
Educated abroad	6·6	9·2	9·1	3·5	7·3
Otherwise educated	0·4	–	0·5	0·9	0·4

Appendix 3

TABLE 5

University of first degree (by date of entry): percentage

	up to 1945	1946–59	since 1960	Total
Oxford or Cambridge	43·4	40·7	29·5	37·9
Other British	52·2	53·6	63·3	55·8
Overseas	3·5	4·4	6·0	5·0
No degree	0·9	1·3	1·2	1·3

TABLE 6

Class of first degree (by date of entry): percentage

	up to 1945	1946–59	since 1960	Total
I	75·1	66·7	46·9	60·7
II.1	8·0	16·7	33·9	21·6
II.2	0·9	2·2	6·0	3·4
Undivided II	7·1	6·9	6·0	6·6
III	–	0·9	0·8	0·7
Pass or 'ordinary'	–	0·3	2·8	1·2
Unclassifiable	8·0	5·0	2·4	4·6
No degree	0·9	1·3	1·2	1·2

TABLE 7

Class of first degree (by U.G.C. subject groups): percentage

	Arts	Social studies	Pure science	Applied science	Total
I	72·0	39·7	64·7	57·6	60·7
II.1	9·6	35·5	22·7	26·5	21·6
II.2	0·4	5·0	5·6	3·5	3·4
Undivided II	9·2	10·6	4·5	–	6·6
III	0·9	0·7	0·5	0·9	0·7
Pass or 'ordinary'	0·9	2·1	–	2·7	1·2
Unclassifiable	6·6	5·0	2·0	4·4	4·6
No degree	0·4	1·4	–	4·4	1·2

Appendix 3

TABLE 8

Higher degrees (by date of entry): percentage

	up to 1945	1946–59	since 1960	Total
1. Doctorate	60·2	56·4	49·4	54·5
2. Other higher degree	22·1	17·4	19·1	18·8
3. No higher degree	17·7	26·2	31·5	26·7

Note:
Category 3 includes those who indicated they were in process of submitting a higher degree.

TABLE 9

Higher degrees (by U.G.C. subject groups): percentage

	Arts	Social studies	Pure science	Applied science	Total
1. Doctorate	38·9	30·5	86·9	59·3	54·5
2. Other higher degree	28·8	29·1	3·5	13·3	18·8
3. No higher degree	32·3	40·4	9·6	27·4	26·7

Note:
Category 3 includes those who indicated they were in process of submitting a higher degree.

TABLE 10

Average age of promotion to professorship (by U.G.C. subject groups)

	years
Arts	43·0
Social studies	42·8
Pure science	40·5
Applied science	42·3
Total average	42·1

261

Appendix 3

TABLE 11

Social class of fathers (by date of entry): percentage

	up to 1945	1946–59	since 1960	Total	heads of households, G.B., 1951
1. Higher professional and managerial	40·7	25·9	21·5	26·3	3·3
2. Lesser managerial and other professional	42·5	36·7	44·2	38·2	18·8
3. Routine non-manual	7·1	12·9	10·8	11·5	12·3
4. Skilled manual, including foremen and supervisors	3·5	12·3	15·5	13·4	38·6
5. Semi-skilled manual	1·8	5·0	3·2	4·2	11·2
6. Unskilled manual and labourers	–	2·5	1·6	2·2	15·8
Not known	4·4	4·7	3·2	4·2	–

Note:
Last column derived from Census, 1951, as rearranged by G. D. H. Cole, *Studies in Class Structure* (1955), p. 153; the categories must be regarded as only a rough approximation to those used in the A.U.T. questionnaire.

TABLE 12

Social class of fathers (by U.G.C. subject groups): percentage

	Arts	Social studies	Pure science	Applied science	Total
1. Higher professional and managerial	31·4	19·9	28·3	23·0	26·3
2. Lesser managerial and other professional	38·8	41·8	40·0	42·4	38·2
3. Routine non-manual	10·5	11·3	13·6	8·0	11·5
4. Skilled manual, including foremen and supervisors	9·2	15·6	12·1	13·3	13·4
5. Semi-skilled manual	3·5	4·3	3·0	5·3	4·2
6. Unskilled manual and labourers	3·1	1·4	0·5	1·8	2·2
Not known	3·5	5·7	2·5	6·2	4·2

TABLE 13

Age of fathers at termination of formal education (by date of entry): percentage

	up to 1945	1946–59	since 1960	Total
Up to 15	39·8	53·3	54·2	50·0
16–19	18·6	15·8	17·1	16·8
20 upwards	29·2	20·5	23·5	23·5
Not known	12·4	10·4	5·2	9·7

TABLE 14

Age of fathers at termination of formal education (by U.G.C. subject groups): percentage

	Arts	Social studies	Pure science	Applied science	Total
Up to 15	46·3	58·9	50·0	54·9	50·0
16–19	19·7	13·5	16·2	15·9	16·8
20 upwards	27·9	17·7	24·2	17·7	23·5
Not known	6·1	9·9	9·6	11·5	9·7

TABLE 15

Type of secondary school attended by fathers (by date of entry): percentage

	up to 1945	1946–59	since 1960	Total
Public boarding	7·1	6·0	2·8	5·8
Other boarding	2·7	2·2	2·0	2·5
Day public or direct grant	15·0	7·9	8·8	9.7
Grammar or high	17·7	18·9	21·5	18·3
Technical or art	–	1·9	2·8	3·2
Sen. elem. or sec. mod.	18·5	31·0	35·3	28·5
Educated abroad	6·2	6·6	10·0	7·9
Otherwise educated	5·3	2·2	3·6	4·1
None	13·3	9·1	6·8	9·5
Not known	14·2	14·2	6·4	10·5

Appendix 3

TABLE 16

Type of secondary school attended by fathers (by U.G.C. subject groups): percentage

	Arts	Social studies	Pure science	Applied science	Total
Public boarding	7·0	2·1	5·6	4·4	5·8
Other boarding	3·1	2·1	1·0	2·7	2·5
Day public or direct grant	10·9	9·9	9·1	6·2	9·7
Grammar or high	23·6	19·1	19·2	13·3	18·3
Technical or art	–	2·1	2·5	4·4	3·2
Sen. elem. or sec. mod.	25·7	32·2	30·7	36·2	28·5
Educated abroad	7·9	8·5	8·1	6·2	7·9
Otherwise educated	3·1	2 8	5·6	0·9	4·1
None	8·7	11·3	6·1	11·5	9·5
Not known	10·0	9·9	12·1	14·2	10·5

TABLE 17

Higher education of fathers (by date of entry): percentage

	up to 1945	1946–59	since 1960	Total
University	25·7	18·6	19·1	20·3
Other higher education	12·4	7·9	10·0	9·7
No higher education	54·8	67·5	67·7	64·4
Not known	7·1	6·0	3·2	5·6

TABLE 18

Higher education of fathers (by U.G.C. subject groups): percentage

	Arts	Social studies	Pure science	Applied science	Total
University	23·6	12·1	23·2	16·8	20·3
Other higher education	10·0	9·2	9·6	8·0	9·7
No higher education	63·8	72·3	63·2	65·5	64·4
Not known	2·6	6·4	4·0	9·7	5·6

INDEX

Index